PAKISTAN'S DEVELOPMENT

Social Goals and Private Incentives

Written under the auspices of
The Center for International Affairs
Harvard University

PAKISTAN'S DEVELOPMENT

Social Goals and Private Incentives

GUSTAV F. PAPANEK

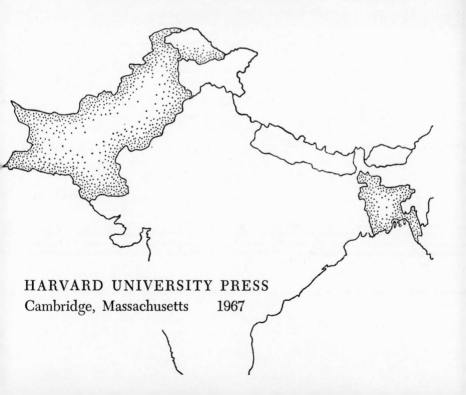

HARVARD UNIVERSITY PRESS
Cambridge, Massachusetts   1967

Distributed in Great Britain by Oxford University Press,
London

Library of Congress Catalog Number 67–22871

Printed in the United States of America

For
H, T, J

FOREWORD

EXPLANATIONS and theories of economic development have in recent years appeared to move backward toward "first principles" in an almost infinite regression. First it was technical assistance — placing at the disposal of the less developed world the expertise of the West — that was expected to do the trick. Then came the exponents of capital flows who talked of saving rates, foreign investment and foreign aid, capital-output ratios, and various kinds of "gaps" that needed to be filled. Behind them infiltrated the devotees of "human capital," who drew up tables of man-power requirements and advised on how to shape the educational system to meet these requirements. Then there appeared the serried ranks of sociologists, cultural anthropologists, and psychologists who talked of social values, motivations, aberrant communities, and need achievement. It has appeared at times that, unless one is privy to the ultimate relationship of nature to nurture, he had better eschew comments on the development process.

In this progression of development theories, Dr. Papanek represents something of a "cultural lag." He appears to believe that with such elementary concepts as economic incentives, capable administration, sensible economic policies affecting the private sector, effective planning of public investment, and an enlarged capacity to import, one can go far toward explaining Pakistan's rather remarkable growth record. And he could be right.

Pakistan *has* had a remarkable record, although it is much too soon to talk of "self-sustaining growth." It remains one of the poorest countries in the world; its savings rate, though doubled, is still relatively low; it remains heavily dependent on aid-financed imports in a period when aid flows are in jeopardy; and the still unsettled dispute over Kashmir saddles both India and Pakistan with levels of military expenditures that seriously inhibit economic development in both countries. Nevertheless, the period beginning approximately in 1958, and extending to date, has witnessed a change from almost hopeless stagnation to ebullient expansion that is rare in the annals of the less developed world. And, despite a serious worsening of some prospects, growth continues.

Expansion of manufactured output, it is true, was rapid even in the period before 1958. But the high percentage rate of growth was measured from an extremely low base; it was limited to a small number of consumer's goods; and it occurred behind an almost impregnable barrier to imports. So-called large-scale industrial output in the early years of Pakistan's existence amounted to not more than 1 to 2 percent of national income and, despite a 12–15 percent per annum growth of industrial output, the rate of growth of national income barely kept pace with population increase. What is so remarkable in the Pakistan experience is a continuation of a relatively high industrial growth rate from an enlarged base, together with industrialization in the area of intermediate and capital goods production; a significant expansion of agricultural output; and, in recent years, a remarkable increase in export earnings. The too frequent pattern of early development is that industrial growth is arrested after the easy substitution of domestic manufacture for imported consumer goods has taken place; agricultural output stagnates; and export earnings grow extremely slowly. To date Pakistan has succeeded in breaking away from this pattern.

Partly by accident and partly by design, according to Dr. Papanek, Pakistan has found a successful combination of private initiative and government intervention. Private initiative manifested itself first in response to the very lush profit opportunities in the domestic production of cotton textiles, footwear, cigarettes, and other consumer goods. In his perhaps too colorful language, the author describes these early entrepreneurs as robber barons, but the interesting thing is that they were attracted to industry from a group that had hitherto produced few businessmen. The Muslims of the subcontinent were traditionally soldiers and farmers, with a sprinkling of small craftsmen and traders. Profits were large and, again somewhat surprisingly, a large fraction of these profits were reinvested not only in an expansion of consumer goods production but later in metal working, building materials, and machinery.

Although some of the early industrial enterprises were initiated by the public sector, public investment in Pakistan has emphasized infrastructure, railways, roads, port facilities, power plants, and irrigation projects. Furthermore, a number of the early public sector plants have been sold to private interests. Industrialization in Pakistan has been mainly a private affair. Dr. Papanek unveils this industrialization process, and thereby contributes greatly to an understanding of its mechanism. The information generated from his comprehensive survey, firm by firm, covering 60 percent of the country's industrial output, provides a body of first-hand data rarely available in less developed countries.

Industrialization came first in Pakistan and, as usually happens, the high prices of domestic manufactured output worked hardship on consumers, particularly the farmers which made up three-quarters of the total population. By the end of the 1950's, competition had begun to bring these prices down. The terms of trade began to turn in favor of agriculture. This, plus a freeing of food grains from compulsory government procurement and price controls, and the provision of increased inputs — particularly of water and fertilizers — at subsidized prices, provided strong incentives for agricultural expansion. The development of irrigation via private tube wells in West Pakistan, and the Public Works Program in East Pakistan are two programs worthy of study by anyone interested in agricultural development.

Pakistan established a Planning Commission in 1953 and, after a few years of uncertainties and vicissitudes, this has grown into an effective advisory body. It has been concerned not only with the pattern of public investment but, unlike many other planning commissions, it has been actively consulted on matters of current economic policy. And whatever the predominant views in the Civil Service concerning the proper roles of the public and private sectors, the views of the Planning Commission and of the top decision-makers it has advised have been essentially pragmatic. It is this blend of private initiative and government action, plus generous assistance from abroad, that principally explains the economic advance made by Pakistan since 1958.

Dr. Papanek has been in a particularly fortunate position to observe this development. For four years he was an adviser to the Pakistan Planning Commission, and since then, as Deputy Director and Director of the Harvard Development Advisory Service, he has kept in close touch with events. This study grows out of a long experience and a deep understanding of the development process.

EDWARD S. MASON

PREFACE

AN analysis of the relationship between government and private enterprise may be regarded in some quarters as not quite scholarly. The subject has obvious ideological overtones, and an economist in his scholarly role is not supposed to deal with ideologies. Yet, the economist who is concerned with understanding the process of development can hardly ignore an important, though controversial, issue. This book, therefore, is concerned with a subject that engages the emotions, and engages those of some people rather deeply.

The book concentrates on activities that are not clearly allocated to either the private or public sector in most underdeveloped countries. In addition, it is concerned with activities critical to development, not with a complete economic history. Fortunately, the activities which were critical in Pakistan happened generally to be those most in dispute between advocates of the private versus the public sector — namely, modern manufacturing, crop production, government policies and investment. There is no specific discussion in this book, for either or both of the reasons suggested above, of transport, communications, trade, services, housing, handicrafts, or small-scale and cottage industry; the discussion of agriculture concentrates on crop production; and nonmonetary investment is given little attention.

The book grew out of my experience in Pakistan. I originally went there in 1954 for 16 months as advisor to the Planning Board, firmly committed to return thereafter to an American university. Instead I spent 5 years in Pakistan and studied its economy for a dozen years, largely out of respect, enthusiasm, and friendship for many Pakistanis. Some of my colleagues have implied that the resulting book is more a hymn of praise than a critical analysis, and I must confess to a strong bias in favor of the country and its people.

In working on this book I had more cooperation and assistance than an author has any right to expect. I owe a fundamental debt to the large number of Pakistani government officials, industrialists, and friends whom I interviewed, with whom I worked, and from whom I learned in innumerable ways. The staff of the Planning Commission contributed massively to my education. There are, I am sure, few government agencies in the world whose staff would be as open, as patient, and as cooperative with a group of foreigners who, well meaning though they might be, start out woefully ignorant about the country on whose problems they are to advise. Practically everyone among the 300 industrialists and government officials contacted was fully cooperative; there must be few academic surveys which are as fortunate in this respect. Their cooperation made it possible to avoid some of the traps that so often ensnare the foreign researcher, and helped me to recognize that some features of the system of which foreigners are prone to be critical were part of a generally creative and positive process.

On rereading the book, I realize that I have relied heavily on the generosity, balance, and good sense of my Pakistani friends and acquaintances. My choice of terms may strike some readers as less polite than normally considered desirable. My purpose, however, was to make a point unambiguously, to avoid pedantry. Still, some of the nomenclature may pique some readers. Industrialists certainly do not think of themselves as "robber barons"; few writers in this century speak of "peasants," only of cultivators or agriculturalists; and while being a "gentleman" is still deemed more or less a good thing, the suspicion may well arise that, in this book, the term is not meant to be wholly flattering. Even "underdeveloped" has lost favor recently in describing the poorer parts of the world. "Developing countries" is considered more desirable, although some poor countries are not developing and some rich countries are.

Most disconcerting, perhaps, is the implied criticism of *some* members of every important group in Pakistan. Unfortunately, it would be difficult to write a worthwhile book about the major forces in any economy without some critical remarks. I have been told that the critical remarks in the book, though they are outweighed by positive ones and reflect human shortcomings which are not limited to any group or nationality, inevitably will mean the loss of most Pakistani friends. This I do not expect.

In addition to a very large general debt, both personal and intellectual, to Pakistani friends, colleagues, and interviewees, I have the usual very specific debts of any author. A full acknowledgment would leave the impression that little in this book can be ascribed to its ostensible author. Even after vigorous pruning, the list of acknowledgments remains impressive.

The original inspiration for a study of government and private enterprise came from Edward S. Mason. He also initiated and in a real sense guided the Harvard group advising the Planning Commission (originally Planning Board) of the Government of Pakistan, which stimulated my interest in Pakistan's economic problem. Finally, he commented extensively on the manuscript. My debt to him is great.

The survey on which many conclusions in the book are based took about two years. It would have taken three times as long if the work had not been shared by a highly competent group of economists: the interviewing by Dr. A. Farouk (of the University of Dacca) and Dr. S. A. Abbas (of the University of the Panjab), the organization and coding by Dr. A. Rab and others at the Pakistan Institute of Development Economics. The Institute's facilities, generously made available, were particularly valuable for a large survey. Processing of the survey and general research on Pakistan would have taken additional years but for the highly professional work of Susan Schmidt, Susan Cowan Jakubiak, and especially Stephen Guisinger.

Many colleagues were generous in reading and commenting on the book. I am especially grateful for the extensive comments of Richard Gilbert, Eric Gustafson, Walter P. Falcon (on agriculture), and Hanna Papanek. Raymond Vernon devoted time and thought to a degree which went far beyond the requirements for a professional colleague and almost exceeded those for a friend.

Authors are required by convention to retain responsibility for errors. This seems too obvious to require restatement.

Ideas lose some of their excitement when their written expression is revised for the fifth time. How much more boring to type for the fifth time someone else's ideas, especially when they are expressed in atrocious handwriting. Sophia Magoulias managed this magnificently along with a host of other responsibilities, with a cheerfulness as admirable as it was sometimes incomprehensible.

A United States Department of State grant to the Center for International Affairs, Harvard University, financed some of the local expenses. Basic support came from a Ford Foundation grant for research on government and private enterprise, which financed all the dollar costs of the research.

CONTENTS

TABLES

PAKISTAN'S DEVELOPMENT

Social Goals and Private Incentives

CHAPTER I

CONFOUNDING THE PROPHETS

A Brief History of Economic Development

Pakistan [is] an economic˙wreck and serious social unrest [is] rising.

TIME, December 8, 1947

. . . for . . . Pakistan it is going to be a long tough road . . . the country is in a precarious economic situation.

DAVID E. BELL, TESTIMONY BEFORE SUBCOMMITTEE FOR REVIEW OF THE MUTUAL SECURITY PROGRAMS, HOUSE COMMITTEE ON FOREIGN AFFAIRS, January 21 and 22, 1959, p. 31

Pakistan may be on its way toward an economic milestone that so far has been reached by only one other populous country, the United States.

NEW YORK TIMES, January 18, 1965

The survival and development of Pakistan is one of the most remarkable examples of state and nation building in the post-war world.

THE TIMES (London), February 26, 1966

AT INDEPENDENCE, Pakistan — simultaneously created and disrupted by the partition of British India — was widely considered an economic monstrosity. The country was among the poorest in the world and had no industries to speak of, almost no industrial raw materials, no significant industrial or commercial groups. It was difficult to see how Pakistan's economy could grow more rapidly than its population. Economic chaos and political disintegration seemed more likely. The 1950's were a period of apparent stagnation and mounting economic problems, when early dire predictions seemed to be fulfilled.

Prophets of gloom and doom were disappointed by radical economic changes which began in the late 1950's. By the middle 1960's the rate of economic growth was more than double the rate of population growth; investment was approaching a healthy 20 percent, and savings exceeded 10 percent of domestic resources. Prices were stable, foreign exchange earnings were increasing at 7.5 percent per year, and foreign resources were being used with increasing effectiveness. Pakistan was widely regarded as one of the half dozen countries in the world with the greatest promise of steady development. In the face of its pitiful resource and capital endowment at independence, and in comparison with other countries, Pakistan's performance was outstanding.

Obviously the millennium has not arrived. Pakistan remains among the poorest countries in the world, its increase in income is small in absolute terms and, above all, its economy is still precariously based. Formidable problems remain; growth can be brought to a standstill by inappropriate economic policies, political upheaval, or by a sharp decline in foreign earnings or aid. Whatever may happen, however, the record so far is well worth examining for clues on how really poor countries can develop.

Pakistan's relative success raises a number of basic questions. How could a very poor country, traditionally an agricultural backwater, achieve a respectable rate of savings? Where did the investors come from? How could the output of peasant agriculture achieve a high rate of growth? What role did government and private initiative play in Pakistan's development?

INDEPENDENCE AND PARTITION

Any analysis of Pakistan's development must begin with its initial endowment and the effects of Partition. Compared to other underdeveloped countries, Pakistan had an able, though limited, civil service and an effective army. West Pakistan had a good transport network and a fine irrigation system. Aside from this, the country had very few assets. In 1947, Pakistan had almost no known natural resources, except agricultural land, practically no modern industry, or modern banking, or commercial establishments. Power production was negligible. Few technicians, professionals, or political leaders existed among Pakistan's 75 million people, because Muslims in the subcontinent were largely peasants, artisans, and soldiers. The partition of British India had serious effects for both successor countries, but was proportionately much more serious for Pakistan. Refugees, concentrated in a few areas of West Pakistan, made up about 10 percent of her total population; and a similar proportion of the population had left the country, with inevitable disruptive effects. Transportation, communications, and trade were interrupted, especially in East Pakistan. Cotton and jute producing areas were cut off from their customers, suppliers, and sometimes even from their ports. The distance between the two parts of Pakistan — with substantially different problems, different resources and without good transport or communications links — aggravates the problems.

In 1947 many knowledgeable observers doubted that Pakistan was viable. Its remarkable achievements have now dimmed the memory of that judgment. Progress since 1947 should be, but often is not, measured against the poor endowment and the partition problems which Pakistan faced.

Pakistan's assets and problems affected the relationship

between government and private enterprise. At Independence, the most important tasks could be performed only by the government, and these absorbed an unusual proportion of the resources, energy, and attention of the country — reestablishing law, order, and confidence; preventing epidemics; resettling refugees; and pulling together the fragments of government, transport, communications, and the irrigation system. To deal with the effects of Partition, the government had to exercise vast powers. Government meant the civil service, far better equipped by training, experience, and numbers to handle the problems than was the limited political leadership. Its role was increased also by the ineffectiveness of private business and industry. No significant centers of economic initiative other than the government existed.

It seemed certain that this situation would not change rapidly since there were no readily exploitable natural resources to attract private investors, and since the uncertain future of the state was bound to discourage businessmen. Muslims were thought to have little interest in, or aptitude for, commerce or industry; they were the "peasants and proletariat, while some of their landlords and all of their millowners (were) Hindus" (*164*, p. 196). The Muslims of Pakistan were considered by some outsiders to be fatalistic, feudal, and generally poorly equipped to operate a modern society. It was therefore only natural to expect that the government would have an overwhelming role in the economy of Pakistan.

GROWTH

The civil service dealt with the problems accompanying Partition with remarkable success. By the 1950's they could turn to the more difficult business of developing the economy. To describe and analyze what happened, one must use Pakistan's national accounts and other such available data, although the statistics are of doubtful accuracy. Unreliable data are unfortunately but inevitably endemic in underdeveloped countries. If inaccurate statistics were considered an insurmountable obstacle, the flood of material on these countries would long since have become a trickle. Thus, they are used, but such data need to be evaluated with caution; any spurious accuracy must be discounted, and only major changes can be accepted as genuine.

Given these caveats, it is likely that between 1947 and 1959 Pakistan's national income increased at an annual rate of less than 3 percent, barely exceeding population growth. This simple figure hides important structural changes. As in other countries, it was agriculture that stagnated. The rate of growth in the urban economy — in industry, power and related activities — was extremely high; modern manufacturing grew at a phenomenal rate. However, since the industrial-commercial base was negligible in 1947, even rapid growth could not result in a significant rise in per-capita income so long as agricultural production grew more slowly than population.

The government proved capable of repairing the damage to the infrastructure inflicted by Partition. It developed power, transport, communications, and urban facilities with sufficient rapidity to prevent insurmountable bottlenecks to rapid industrial growth. Government action also produced an environment in which there were strong incentives for private development of consumer-goods industries. But by the late 1950's the momentum of growth seemed to be coming to an end. Stagnation of agriculture meant inadequate production of food and of export crops; agricultural exports declined and the balance-of-payments problem worsened. Inadequate food production also meant rising prices and the threat of inflation, especially since savings had stagnated while consumption demands had increased. The strategy of replacing consumer-goods imports with domestic production had come close to the end of its potential. Frequent changes in government meant that long-run economic policies could neither be framed nor consistently carried out. Some economists once again saw a dim future for Pakistan.

With the change in government of 1958, the political environment changed radically. The new government was not particularly adept at framing economic policies. As a matter of fact, its initial policies would have proved disastrous. However, it was sure of a long lease on political life, and thus could learn from its mistakes and frame plans and policies for their long-run effect. The government also made economic policy a central concern, since it had justified its takeover largely in terms of economic mismanagement by previous governments. Finally, the new government was strong enough to carry out policies that offended particular groups and were unpopular in the short run. The year 1959, when the new regime abandoned some of the controls it adopted on assuming power, marks the beginning of a new economic environment.

Subsequently the over-all growth rate increased dramatically. The rate of increase in manufacturing remained among the highest in the world and, with a much larger base, its effect was greater. Construction shot up with a rapidly stepped-up public development program. Most important, Pakistan became one of the very few underdeveloped countries where the increase in agricultural production significantly exceeded the growth of population. By the middle 1960's, the economy was growing about twice as rapidly as population.

The rate of growth is the first economic puzzle one encounters in Pakistan. What caused the very high rate of industrialization, and who carried it out? Why did agri-

TABLE 1. GROSS DOMESTIC PRODUCT AND POPULATION.

SECTOR	ABSOLUTE AMOUNTS (crores of rupees[a] at 1959–1960 market prices)				ANNUAL RATES OF GROWTH (percent)		
	1949– 50[b]	*1954– 55*[b]	*1959– 60*[b]	*1964– 65*[b]	*1949–50 to 1954–55*	*1954–55 to 1959–60*	*1959–60 to 1964–65*
Agriculture[c]	1,439	1,536	1,639	2,000	1.3	1.3	4.1
Manufacturing[d]	30	110	192	382	29.6	11.8	14.7
Other	1,027	1,217	1,403	1,996	3.5	2.9	7.3
Total	2,496	2,863	3,234	4,378	2.7	2.5	6.2
Population (millions)	78.9	88.3	98.9	112.5	2.3	2.3	2.6
Per capita income (rupees)[e]	316	324	327	389	0.5	0.2	3.5

Sources and explanations: Appendix Table 1.

[a] One crore is ten million; one crore of rupees roughly equals $2 million since 1955.

[b] Most statistics in Pakistan are for a July 1 to June 30 year.

[c] N.B. For the contribution of major crops actual production was *not* used since this is heavily influenced by weather. Trend values were used instead.

[d] Manufacturing includes output of all units using power and employing more than 20 workers on any day of the year.

[e] One rupee equaled $0.30 before 1955, $0.21 after 1955, at the official rates.

cultural production stagnate for years and then increase quite rapidly? The changes that took place in investment, savings, and consumption provide the first clues.

INVESTMENT, SAVINGS, AND CONSUMPTION

Underdeveloped economies are supposed to be incapable of a rapid increase in investment. Elaborate theories for allocating foreign aid have been built on the assumption of a limited "absorptive capacity" of such countries;

that is, the assumption that they cannot rapidly increase their ability to use capital without unacceptable waste and inefficiency (*121*). In Pakistan, gross investment about doubled every 5 years in real terms. The increase since the early 1950's would have been even greater if more foreign exchange had been available to import required machinery, vehicles, and steel.

There is a rough correspondence between investment and the availability of foreign exchange. Investment shot up before 1953, when Pakistan drew on inherited reserves and benefited from Korean boom prices for her exports. Foreign aid became important in the middle 1950's and continued to increase for the next decade. However, the decline in export earnings with the end of the Korean boom outweighed the increase in aid. Inadequate foreign exchange therefore became a serious constraint during the 1950's. In the 1960's export earnings increased by about 7 percent per year. Foreign aid more than tripled and investment again increased rapidly. When greater imports could be purchased, private industry and transport and a number of government agencies seemed able to step up their rate of investment very quickly. Several questions are obvious. Did Pakistan's "absorptive capacity for capital" — that is, the ability to carry out investment with reasonable efficiency — really increase very rapidly? Did savings or foreign exchange impose the major limit on investment? What organizations carried out this rapid increase in investment, and how did they function?

Changes in savings and consumption are particularly interesting. Between 1947 and 1950, gross domestic savings were negligible; Pakistan's very modest investment was financed largely from foreign-exchange reserves. In the early 1950's large profits in foreign trade and industry were saved and reinvested, despite a decline in average per capita consumption. It is quite surprising that a very

TABLE 2. THE SHARE OF INVESTMENT, SAVING AND
CONSUMPTION IN RESOURCES.

Category	1949–50	1954–55	1959–60	1964–65
	(constant 1959–60 prices; crores of rupees)[a]			
1. Resources from:				
(a) Gross domestic product	2,496	2,863	3,234	4,378
(b) Import surplus	69	17	104	325
Total	2,565	2,880	3,338	4,703
2. Monetized investment	99	203	350	745
	(rupees)			
3. Per capita resources	325	326	338	418
(a) Monetized investment	13	23	35	67
(b) Consumption	313	303	302	351

| | *(current prices; percentages)* | | | | | | | |
	Res.	GDP	Res.	GDP	Res.	GDP	Res.	GDP
4. Percentages of resources and Gross Domestic Product								
(a) Monetized investment	3.6	3.7	7.4	7.5	10.5	10.8	16.2	17.3
(b) Nonmonetized investment	0.9	0.9	1.5	1.5	1.4	1.5	1.2	1.2
(c) Total investment	4.5	4.6	8.9	9.0	11.9	12.3	17.4	18.5
(d) Import surplus	1.7	1.7	0.4	0.4	3.1	3.2	6.3	6.7
(e) Saving (a minus d)	1.9	2.0	7.0	7.1	7.4	7.6	9.9	10.6
(f) Saving (c minus d)	2.8	2.9	8.9	9.0	8.8	9.1	11.1	11.8

Sources and explanations: Appendix Table 2.

[a] One crore is 10 million; each crore of rupees roughly $2 million.

poor society was able to increase savings despite the decline in per-capita consumption. After the middle 1950's, the rate of saving behaved more as expected — it stag-

nated, together with real per-capita income. There may
have been a limit to the austerity that could be imposed,
or the necessary complementary imports may not have
been available, or both. By the 1960's, when national income rose rapidly and foreign exchange became less of a
bottleneck, savings rose again.

The average consumer suffered in the 1950's as per-
capita consumption declined. During the investment boom
of the early 1950's, consumer-goods imports were cut off,
domestic production remained small, and the population
grew. Later in the decade consumers benefited from increased domestic production of manufacturers, although
the availability of food declined. The "average" consumer
found his lot improved only in the 1960's. These averages
are discouraging in themselves; worse, there are few average consumers. Inequality in incomes had probably increased in the 1950's. Groups that participated in the
rapidly growing industrial and urban sector did quite well
— civil servants; business, professional, and managerial
groups; and some peasants who became industrial workers. Losers included the bulk of the population — families
dependent on agriculture and, particularly, landless workers. They paid higher prices for manufactures, while agricultural prices remained relatively low. How it was possible for the consumption of the majority to decline while
savings rose is obviously another important question posed
by Pakistan's experience.

DEVELOPMENT STRATEGY

That agricultural production and rural incomes ceased
to grow in the 1950's, while industry expanded rapidly,
was no accident. Before Independence the area that became Pakistan was a supplier of agricultural products to
much of North India — rice and jute for the people and

mills of Calcutta, wheat and cotton for the people and mills of Ahmedabad and Bombay. Muslims often grew the crops which were financed and marketed by Hindus, and processed in industries owned by Hindus. In the area that became East Pakistan, many landlords were Hindus as well. Small wonder that the development of agriculture was given even less attention in Pakistan than in other underdeveloped countries. Independence provided an opportunity for Muslims to develop commerce, industry, and the professions. The assumption was that the country had, and would continue to have, a surplus of agricultural crops.

After Independence, development strategy necessarily emphasized the aftereffects of Partition. It was important to develop government buildings, power, transport, and communications which were no longer available in Pakistan. However, emphasis soon shifted to investment in industry; Pakistan concentrated on replacing imports of consumer goods by domestic production. Data are lacking for agriculture. On a net basis there was probably disinvestment. The population exchange during Partition resulted in the deterioration of wells, homes, irrigation and drainage ditches, protective levees, and coastal embankments.

A radical change in the stated development strategy, though not always in action, occurred in the mid-1950's. Agriculture was given higher priority, in part because of improved planning, but more because of an agricultural crisis. Population had been rising, especially in urban areas, and with it rose the demand for agricultural products. With agricultural production lagging behind population growth, the surplus available for towns declined. Inevitably there was a year of poor harvests (floods were a major factor) and the country faced sharply rising food prices and local shortages. The need to appeal to the

United States for emergency food assistance lent emphasis, as nothing else could, to the argument of the Planning Board that agriculture could not be neglected. Pakistan may have been fortunate in having a serious food crisis at an early stage; other countries with a better agricultural endowment, or fooled into complacency by several years of good weather, continued to neglect agriculture.

Plans and public statements after the middle 1950's emphasized the priority of agriculture. The first concrete result was a rapid increase of government investment in irrigation facilities. Despite "the highest priority" assigned to agriculture, however, resources devoted to it increased slowly. Agricultural production never increased as much as population in the 1950's. The performance in the 1960's is, then, all the more surprising. What factors were responsible is obviously a key question raised by Pakistan experience.

Fields other than agriculture and industry also experienced shifts in strategy designed to increase the efficiency of the development program. After 1955, plans increasingly stressed technical education and training rather than general education, preventive rather than curative health measures, and increased efficiency in small-scale industry. Plans called for a shift in emphasis from railways to road and water transport. As the most urgent requirements of the new country for government buildings and civil-service housing were met, there was a shift to more general urban development. The strategy which the Planning Board adopted in 1953 was to direct investment funds and human resources to areas and agencies that promised the highest returns, rather than to those which could exert greatest pressure or which started with the best staffs. As with agricultural strategy, deeds lagged far behind plans. During the 1950's railway investment continued to dominate transport development. High-cost private housing in-

TABLE 3. THE COMPOSITION OF GROSS MONETARY
INVESTMENT (CRORES OF RUPEES — CURRENT PRICES).

SECTOR	1949–50		1954–55		1959–60		1964–65	
	Public	Private	Public	Private	Public	Private	Public	Private
Agriculture	1.0	1.5	2.0	2.5	7.5	7.0	15.5	14.0
Irrigation, etc.[a]	7.0	0.5	15.0	1.0	44.0	2.5	51.0	8.0
Power	2.5	–	5.0	–	14.0	–	119.0	–
Manufacturing, mining, fuels	1.0	20.0	10.5	66.5	18.0	104.5	30.5	226.0
Transport and communications	(7.5)	(3.5)	(14.5)	(2.0)	(45.0)	(8.5)	(99.5)	(46.0)
Railways	5.0	–	7.5	–	25.5	–	37.0	–
Roads and road transport	1.0	3.5	2.5	2.0	9.0	8.0	36.0	37.0
Post, telephone, telegraph	0.5	0.5	2.5	0.5	4.5	–	13.5	–
Other (aviation, ports, shipping, broadcasting)	1.0	–	2.0	–	6.0	0.5	13.0	9.0
Housing and urban development	5.5	14.5	8.5	20.5	15.5	47.0	35.5	84.5
Education, health, other	–	–	3.5	–	5.5	–	29.5	–
Traders' stocks	–	11.0	–	10.0	–	30.0	–	53.0
Total	24.5	51.5	59.0	103.0	149.5	199.5	380.5	431.5

Sources and explanations: Appendix Table 3. (For a sectoral breakdown in
percentage terms see also Appendix, Table 3-B).
[a] Includes Indus Basin Replacement Works.

creased especially rapidly because it required less of scarce
imports than did private industrial development. Government investment in housing continued to be concentrated
on government buildings, on civil servants' housing, and
on the new capital cities. Gradually, however, the pressure
of plans and planners began to be felt. Planned strategy
and actual development showed increasing similarity, and
closely resembled each other by the middle 1960's.

In short, Pakistan adopted a conventional strategy followed by most of the larger underdeveloped countries, but the results were unexpected. The expansion of domestic production to replace consumer-goods imports is supposed to be limited by narrow domestic markets and by an inability to export the high-priced output of inefficient industries which were developed behind extreme protection. Several observers concluded that Pakistan had reached these limits in the late 1950's. What then explains the subsequent spurt in growth?

FOREIGN TRADE AND AID

A development strategy which stressed import substitution was natural for Pakistan. Since the end of the Korean boom Pakistan had faced a serious foreign-exchange problem. As in other developing countries, Pakistan's demand for imports increased more rapidly than its national income. The growing urban population, with a sharply increasing income, demanded manufactures, a large proportion of which had to be imported. The rapidly expanding development program added to import needs. At the same time, export earnings declined. Exports consisted almost wholly of agricultural products, with 80 to 90 percent of earnings contributed by jute and cotton. The production of these exports stagnated along with the rest of agriculture, while increasing domestic demand for such goods as cotton and tea reduced the proportion of output exported. The terms of trade for Pakistan deteriorated; about one-third more exports were required to buy the same imports after the middle 1950's as had been required before the Korean boom, and the situation continued to worsen until 1959–60. The overvalued currency encouraged the demand for imports and discouraged exports. The rapid growth of industry did reduce the need to

TABLE 4. PRICES OF IMPORTS AND EXPORTS.

YEAR	PRICE INDEX FOR IMPORTS		PRICE INDEX FOR EXPORTS		RATIO OF EXPORT PRICES TO IMPORT PRICES	
	Base 1948–49	*Base 1959–60*	*Base 1948–49*	*Base 1959–60*	*Base 1948–49*	*Base 1959–60*
1948–49	100	–	100	–	100	–
1950–51	85	–	106	–	125	–
1952–53	78	–	66	–	84	–
1955–56	121	–	81	–	67	–
1959–60	156	100	81	100	52	100
1962–63	159	108	95	112	59	104
1964–65	–	97	–	120	–	124

Source: (*16*), May, 1964, p. 965 for indices based on 1948–49, and (151, p. 171–2) for indices based on 1959–60.

Note: These indices of commodity terms of trade suffer from all the short-comings of their kind.

import consumer-goods to some extent. However, inevitably raw-material imports had to increase to meet the needs of new industries, especially since Pakistan had few natural resources. Machinery and spare parts imports increased as well. Though value added in manufacturing increased more than tenfold over a dozen years, industrial output remained small in absolute terms; modern manufacturing industry contributed about one percent of the national product in the late 1940's, and only 9 percent 15 years later.

By the middle 1950's, when the foreign-exchange reserves accumulated during the Korean boom had been depleted, the problem of rising import-demand and declining export-earnings had to be met. Imports were drastically curtailed. This is typical of underdeveloped countries, but Pakistan was forced to carry import austerity further than others. Import restrictions at first affected primarily consumer goods. The bald figures are rather staggering: over three years from 1951–52 imports of consumer goods and their raw materials were reduced to one-quarter. Two caveats need to be entered. First, reported imports in 1951–52 were unusually large because this was a year of stockpiling and of capital export; a year in which foreign exchange was illegally sent abroad in unusual amounts. For instance, importers claimed to be paying for dyes, but received colored water; the substantial difference in foreign exchange cost was banked abroad. Second, domestic production increased very rapidly and compensated to some extent for the reduction in imports. Value added in industry increased by Rs. 50 crores. However, imports for consumption declined by well over Rs. 100 crores and the population continued to grow. The availability of manufactured consumer goods was thus roughly halved on a per-capita basis. The degree of austerity imposed on the economy is still awe-inspiring.

To meet the foreign-exchange problem of the 1950's required more than a reduction in the import of consumer goods. Imports of raw materials were also kept substantially below requirements, resulting in idle capacity. Private investment, especially in industry, was also restricted, although in absolute amounts the import of capital goods and materials for their production continued to increase. The result was that machinery was imported to establish new capacity in some industries while existing capacity was idle for lack of imported raw materials.

Not even the drastic curtailment of imports, however, was adequate to meet the balance-of-payments problem in the 1950's. No government was willing to face the political dangers and administrative difficulties of further steps. Austerity had been carried far indeed, and further austerity was easier for the outsider to recommend than for either political or administrative leadership in Pakistan

TABLE 5. INTERNATIONAL TRANSACTIONS
(IN MILLIONS OF DOLLARS).[a]

TRANSACTIONS	1949–50	1951–52	1954–55	1959–60	1964–65
Exports of goods and services	287	716	399	439	632
Raw materials	263	641	345	257	335
Manufactures	–	6	12	111	167
Invisibles	24	70	42	71	130
Imports of goods and services	393	849	426	657	1,291
Consumer goods	136	299	70	90	125
Materials for consumer goods	54	133	39	52	128
U.S. surplus commodities (mostly food) — PL 480	–	–	–	79	169
Defense imports	36	57	48	42	42
Capital goods	51	136	139	195	464
Materials for capital goods	33	70	33	90	115
Invisibles	82	154	97	111	247
Financing items	106	133	27	220	659
Grants and loans (public)	–	–	51	241	657
Private investment	–	6	6	19	17
Debt servicing	–	–	−3	−8	−29
Changes in reserves (minus is increase)	212	142	−21	−27	59
Short-term changes	−106	−15	−6	−6	−44
Excludes estimated technical assistance of:	–	3	6	10	21

Sources and explanations: Appendix Table 4.

[a] Until the devaluation of August 1955, about 3.3 rupees equaled one dollar; after that 4.7 rupees equaled one dollar, both at the official exchange rate.

to carry out. In the longer run, an increase in agricultural production and a reduced dependence on imports for domestic production and investment could have helped. Although some steps to achieve both were taken, a drastic change in price incentives and priorities involved serious risks and was not carried out in the 1950's.

With declining export earnings and increasing demand for imports, and with exchange reserves used up, the economy continued to function and develop only because the inflow of foreign resources rose substantially. The inflow of private foreign investment was small. Pakistan had neither the readily exploitable raw materials nor the large internal market which is usually required to attract massive foreign private investment. Foreign resources, therefore, meant public resources. These increased from some $10 million a year in the early 1950's to $650 million a year in the mid-1960's. More than a third of gross investment was financed by foreign public funds.

In the early 1960's another significant change took place in Pakistan's foreign accounts. With rising agricultural production, exports of cotton, rice, and other agricultural products increased. On other products, the government raised by 30–50 percent the rupees received for foreign exchange, except for traditional exports. This stimulated both the export of manufactures and remittances by Pakistanis abroad. Total foreign-exchange earnings rose on an average of 7.5 percent per year. Pakistan's experience thus ran counter to yet another widely held view: that underdeveloped countries not endowed with valuable mineral resources cannot raise export earnings significantly by their own policies.

With increased export earnings and additional foreign resources, imports could also increase rapidly in the 1960's. Austerity in the import of consumer goods was relaxed somewhat; imports of raw materials and spare parts greatly reduced idle industrial capacity; imports needed for sharply increased investment could be made. Over the first half of the 1960's the availability to Pakistanis of manufactures that were imported, or based on imported materials, or that used exportable raw materials, increased by more than 50 percent. However, since restrictions on imports continued to be severe in absolute terms and exports had grown rapidly, the relative share of foreign loans and grants in financing imports began to decline.

REGIONAL DIFFERENCES[*]

Pakistan so far has been treated as a single economy. In many respects this is a gross oversimplification. Regional differences within a country are a widespread phenomenon in both the developed and underdeveloped world and have shown remarkable persistence over time. Pakistan's two Provinces are unusual in being geographically quite separate, with cultural and language differences, high transport costs and strong barriers to mobility. Labor migration on any scale is out of the question; physical and cultural distances are too great. Mobility of other resources is restricted by inadequate shipping space, and sometimes by government regulation. As a result, prices paid for identical goods in the two parts of the country can, and do, vary by much more than the cost of transport.

At Independence, East Pakistan had almost half of the tiny stock of investment in medium- and large-scale industry. Its potential for a rapid increase in agricultural output was great, because irrigation water for double and even triple cropping could be obtained without the need to build dams and extensive irrigation channels. East Pakistan had a higher literacy rate and better political organization than West Pakistan. Its refugee problem was insignificant compared to the other Province. Its land-tenure problem was largely solved by the exodus of Hindu landlords. However, its per-capita product was significantly less than that of West Pakistan and the Province lost most of its administrators, merchants, and professionals during partition.

[*] For a more extensive discussion, see (161).

The available figures indicate that the per-capita product of West Pakistan increased significantly over the first decade after Independence while East Pakistan's stagnated or declined. The over-all figures are shaky at best, but they are confirmed by obvious physical differences in the capital stock. By the late 1950's, West Pakistan had developed a good transport system, a substantial integrated power grid, and a sizable industrial sector, while

TABLE 6. REGIONAL GROSS DOMESTIC PRODUCT, POPULATION, AND RATES OF GROWTH.

SECTOR	1949–50		1954–55		1959–60		1964–65	
	East	West	East	West	East	West	East	West
	(Crores of rupees: 1959–60 prices)[a]							
Agriculture[a]	850	589	887	649	938	701	1,151	849
Manufacturing	12	18	31	79	50	142	80	302
Other	451	576	514	703	567	836	768	1,228
Total	1,313	1,183	1,432	1,431	1,555	1,679	1,999	2,379
Population (millions)	43.1	35.8	48.1	40.2	53.9	45.0	61.2	51.3
Per capita (rupees)	305	330	298	356	288	373	327	464

ANNUAL RATES OF GROWTH (PERCENT)

	1949–50 to 1954–55		1954–55 to 1959–60		1959–60 to 1964–65	
	East	West	East	West	East	West
Agriculture[a]	0.9	1.9	1.1	1.6	4.2	3.9
Manufacturing	21.0	34.0	10.0	12.4	9.9	16.3
Other	2.6	4.1	2.0	3.5	6.3	8.0
Total	1.7	3.9	1.7	3.2	5.2	7.2
Population	2.2	2.3	2.3	2.3	2.6	2.7
Per capita	−0.5	1.5	−0.6	0.9	2.6	4.4

Sources, explanations and more detailed per capita data: Appendix Table 5.
[a] Data for major crops included in "Agriculture" are not actuals, but trend values.

East Pakistan was still predominantly a rural community, with poor transport, a poor power supply, and little industry. It was not "a semi-organized swamp" nor "a great, big, beautiful garden," as suggested by two outsiders, but it had characteristics of both.

Per-capita value added by East Pakistan's agriculture in the 1940's was somewhat greater than West Pakistan's. The increase in agricultural production in the East lagged slightly behind the other Province during the 1950's. The original difference in per-capita product stems from the urban sector. In 1947 West Pakistan was better endowed with transport, housing, government facilities, defense installations, and commercial establishments. The widening disparity in the 1950's was also due to West Pakistan's greater urban development; above all, to its phenomenal industrial growth, but also to the more rapid expansion of construction, banking and commerce, urban facilities, and government services. By the late 1950's, efforts to redress the imbalance in growth were becoming effective and in the 1960's the growth rate in East Pakistan began to catch up with that in the West.

There were a number of reasons for the greater growth in West Pakistan. First, many of the traders and merchants who left India, especially those from the Bombay area, preferred to settle around Karachi. It was more congenial, closer in language and habits, and closer geographically to the area they had left. Many of these refugees became the businessmen, importers, and industrial entrepreneurs of the new nation. They naturally located their enterprise where they lived, if at all possible, and thus provided Karachi with a better supply of imports, a rapid development of commerce, and, above all, an initial spurt in industrial development.

Second, and perhaps most important, was the location of the powerful Central Government in Karachi. In an economy in which most scarce resources are controlled by the government, ease of access to that government is of great importance to entrepreneurs and managers. Personal contact is more effective than correspondence, especially in a society that puts great value on personal relations. To some extent government favors depended on influence, bribes, and pressure, and personal contact was essential — by mail it is hard to become socially intimate with government officials, or to bribe them by flattery or money. Businessmen and industrialists, therefore, preferred to invest in Karachi. Those who did found it easier to obtain the import licenses and permits they required for operation and expansion.

Equally important, a government is likely to perceive most clearly and to act most expeditiously on problems under its nose. In a country in which much of the investment is determined by the central government, the capital city is likely to have the best power supply, schools, roads, air connections, water supply, sewerage, housing, and even police. These facilities also attract private investment.

The tendency to concentrate government investment in the capital was reinforced by the fact that East Pakistan was substantially underrepresented in the civil service and practically unrepresented in its higher echelons. The civil service dominated the government, and West Pakistan dominated the civil service. It is inevitable that civil servants from a particular area are more concerned with its problems and are better able to deal with them. Evidence that this quite natural bias existed comes from the civil servants themselves. When questioned, nearly two-thirds of West Pakistan civil servants said that they believed regional considerations influenced the decisions of public servants (7, p. 112). It is impossible to appraise the importance of this factor, but it played some role where government initiative or participation was crucial — as in urban, power, and transport development.

Foreign-trade policy also favored West Pakistan's development. All importers and manufacturers could sell their goods above international prices in the protected market of Pakistan, but since the great majority of importers and manufacturers were in West Pakistan, the resulting profits accrued primarily to the West. At the same time, the overvaluation of the rupee, and export duties, meant that producers of exports received fewer rupees than they would have received in a free market. Because about 60 percent of all exports were produced in East Pakistan, that Province bore disproportionately the cost of exchange policies.

West Pakistan also received an overwhelming share of the technical manpower and financial resources that flowed in from India. It had a better port and transport system than East Pakistan. Foreign firms and embassies were located in Karachi, and they too tended to direct foreign resources to the area they knew best. Later, industrial development was spurred by the discovery of natural gas in West Pakistan. Investment in industry and in infrastructure, thus, was concentrated in West Pakistan, and especially in Karachi. It became increasingly desirable to locate new industries in the most developed area, where other industrialists, technicians, and professionals were located. Thus, spare-parts producers, supply and distribution channels developed around Karachi. The pressure for roads, power, railway connections, housing, water, and sewerage became so great that the government had to satisfy it, thus lending further encouragement to new industries to locate in the most rapidly developing areas.

Beginning in the mid-1950's, pressure mounted for government policies that would increase the rate of growth in East Pakistan. Improved prices for exports, and reduced prices and profits for manufactures, had a favorable effect in East Pakistan. The allocation of government funds and of foreign resources gradually became less biased. However, to achieve the political and constitutional commitment to equal per-capita incomes, despite West Pakistan's momentum and the advantages which accrue to any area with a substantial industrial base and infrastructure, will continue to be an important reason for government intervention in the economy.

GOVERNMENT AND PRIVATE ENTERPRISE

In terms of ownership and management, Pakistan clearly has a private-enterprise economy; government and semi-government agencies contribute less than 15 percent to the national product, a considerably lower percentage than in the United States or Western Europe. Private ownership prevails in agriculture, services, trade, and commerce. Most of industry, and residential and office buildings, are in private hands. Foreign private investment is encouraged.

The government or its agencies own and manage only a part of industry, but they control nearly all the infrastructure. They operate power generation, transport, and communications. Trucking and long-distance buses, on the other hand, are privately owned. Curiously, many municipal bus systems, publicly owned in most countries, are strongholds of private enterprise in Pakistan. Competition is fierce and inevitably takes the form of racing to the next bus stop to snag customers. It is customary for three buses to roar down the street side by side, occupying both lanes. This may bring joy to the confirmed private enterpriser as an example of the true competitive spirit, and to the confirmed advocate of government ownership as an example of capitalist waste, but most motorists and commuters do not take a joyful view of such procedures.

While private ownership is widespread, the major decisions in the economy are made by the government. About 40 percent of gross monetary investment has been public. Government agencies carry out any desired industrial investment for which no private interest exists — and some for which it does. Most private investment is closely controlled through the government's allocation of foreign exchange and other controls. Major investments require some imported capital goods or raw materials, and imports have been tightly controlled by the government. Since the demand for imported goods exceeds the supply, the government effectively determines which firm can be set up and which can operate profitably. Government policy, therefore, dominates all large-scale investment in industry, transport, and related fields. Government policy on export and import taxes, on export subsidies, and on guaranteed prices for agriculture substantially determines relative prices. Much of the irrigation system is government managed, and the power to give or withhold water is crucial in West Pakistan. Using the tools at its disposal, and especially its control of investment funds and of all foreign exchange, the government can influence and if necessary determine all significant economic decisions.

SUMMING-UP

Pakistan does not fit some of the stereotypes of economic development. Rapid development of industry is not unusual, but the process was especially dramatic in Pakistan. Its rate of industrial growth exceeded that of other underdeveloped countries despite the fact that it could not draw on prior industrial experience. The ability of Pakistan's government to step up its rate of investment, especially in developing the infrastructure, was unexpected. The successful increase in savings, despite the absolute poverty of the country and stagnation in average consumption, was even more surprising. The relatively rapid growth of Pakistan's exports and agriculture in the 1960's was probably the most unusual feature for a country with a peasant agriculture, no available land, and no readily exploitable raw-material resources.

How and why these developments took place makes a more dramatic tale than their description. At its center stands the private industrial entrepreneur, part hero and part villain.

CHAPTER II

ROBBER BARONS'
PROGRESS

The Development of
Industrial Entrepreneurs

If we wait for the mercantile community, Pakistan will never
be industrialized.

A LEADING PAKISTANI BUSINESSMAN AND INDUSTRIALIST

Even the traditions of Muslim society worked against industrial progress. Muslims had habitually invested in land and
trade, not industry or banking.

BOOK ON PAKISTAN (*177*, p. 94)

INDUSTRIAL development requires entrepreneurs —
economic innovators ready to abandon such traditional
activities as agriculture, trade, or the civil service in order
to develop industrial enterprises. Their decisions must be
rational in economic terms if industrialization is to be
efficient. An economy whose industrialists regularly divert
all of their profits to prestigious but non-productive activities is unlikely to grow very rapidly.

A substantial body of opinion holds that the development of private entrepreneurs is slow and unpredictable
and that the behavior of the few industrial enterprises
established in underdeveloped countries is often inefficient from society's point of view (*90*, Chaps, 3, 5, 9, 12;
96, pp. 36–38; *119*, Chaps. 7, 9; and *97*, pp. 60–66, 151–
156). The details of the argument vary, but the approach
is similar. It stresses the obvious fact that industrial enter-

prise is not traditional in underdeveloped countries. A substantial number of people will engage in this new activity only if the motives, values, or institutions of a society change fundamentally, or if a significant minority is prepared to act in a deviant fashion. This takes time and is difficult to predict or influence. Even in underdeveloped countries where some industry has been established, the influence of traditional behavior remains strong. Industrialists therefore do not sensibly pursue private gain. Seeking the prestige of landownership, they divert industrial income to land acquisition, and thus abort industrial development. They retain a trader's or gambler's mentality — unwilling to invest in profitable industries that require waiting for returns. They have learned from the landed aristocracy, foreigners, or political leaders the joys of conspicuous consumption, and they dissipate the returns from industry in riotous living. In short, the argument goes, the development of private industrial entrepreneurs is a slow and difficult process, because of a variety of social, psychological, and institutional factors which are subject to little influence, and which also lead to socially undesirable behavior on the part of any industrialists who do emerge.

These analyses are sometimes cited as conclusive evidence that the government alone can provide the initiative for industrial development. Centralized government decisions reduce the number of decision-makers required. Government-initiated industrialization need not rely on economic incentives and on indicators provided by the market. Once a country's political leadership has decided on industrial development, for political or military as well as for economic reasons, the government machinery can see that this decision is carried out. The government can undertake socially desirable but risky investments which are neglected by private businessmen with strong risk-avoiding preferences. It is quite irrelevant, the argument goes, whether industrial development in private hands would be desirable in the abstract; in fact it would be slow and uncertain.

Pakistan, like other countries in Africa and Asia, not only lacked industrial entrepreneurs; it seemed unlikely to develop them in the short run. Muslims in pre-Independence India played a very small role in commerce, banking, or the professions and were negligible in industry. The few Muslims who were in trade operated mostly on a small scale. It was widely assumed that they had a "trader's mentality," looking for short-term speculative profit. Since the future of Pakistan was uncertain this kind of trader's mentality made a good deal of economic sense. In 1947 Pakistan apparently was an excellent example of a country where industrial growth would be slow, and largely in government hands.

THE SPEED OF INDUSTRIAL DEVELOPMENT

In fact, industry grew rapidly indeed and was largely developed by private entrepreneurs. The speed of the process and its phasing give some indication of the causal factors.

The dynamic sector in Pakistan has been so-called "large-scale" industry. It is defined as including units that use power and employ more than 20 workers on any day in the year. In fact, it includes many small units. The remainder of industry — mainly handlooms, workshops, handicrafts, and village processing of agricultural products — has declined in relative importance. Little is really known about "small-scale" industry, especially since part of its output is exchanged on a barter basis. The subsequent discussion deals with "large-scale" industry only. Most of the data on entrepreneurs, and other data subsequently used without specific attribution, came from a sample survey (identified as "Survey") covering all "large-scale" industry. The 255 sample firms, which were interviewed in the early 1960's, included about 9 percent of all firms, but since the sample included more of the large firms, 58 percent of value added by Pakistan's modern manufacturing sector was covered. Details of the Survey are given elsewhere (*141*).

The Survey confirms that a truly phenomenal growth of industrial output and investment took place in Pakistan. Even after the middle 1950's, when Pakistan had a significant industrial sector, the rate of growth in Pakistan's industrial output continued to be as high as, or higher than, that of any other country of the world. (Japan's rate of industrial growth was similar.)

The rapidity of actual industrial development is not the whole story. The number of potential entrepreneurs and the volume of potential investment greatly exceeded the actuals. From 1955 on, when foreign-exchange reserves had been depleted and short-term foreign credits were tightly controlled, foreign exchange available for investment fell far short of the demand. Since all significant industrial investment required imported goods, a substantial number of entrepreneurs were unable to carry out projects for which they had the domestic capital. An analysis of applications for foreign exchange in the late 1950's showed that many of those denied were for new, technically complex industries or for areas with little industry; that is, they had a significant innovational component.

There is other evidence that potential industrial investment was greater than the actual investment. Stock issues were commonly oversubscribed. In 1953, for instance, shares in a large paper mill developed by a government corporation were offered at book value to the public. Though the mill was only beginning its operation, the offering was substantially oversubscribed and the shares

TABLE 7. GROSS VALUE ADDED AND INVESTMENT IN
"LARGE-SCALE" INDUSTRY OR "MANUFACTURING"
(CONSTANT 1959–60 PRICES).

| YEAR | VALUE ADDED | | INVESTMENT (crores of rupees)[a] |
	Crores of rupees[a]	Index	
1947–48	18	9	
1948–49	23	12	+18
1949–50	30	16	+24
1950–51	41	21	+30
1951–52	54	28	+44
1952–53	66	34	+47
1953–54	80	42	+72
1954–55	110	57	+96
1955–56	128	67	+65
1956–57	143	74	+50
1957–58	158	82	+59
1958–59	183	95	+63
1959–60	192	100	–
1960–61	223	116	–
1961–62	256	133	–
1962–63	288	150	–
1963–64	328	171	–
1964–65	382	199	–

Sources: For 1947–48 through 1959–60 see (*141*); 1959–60 through 1964–65 is adapted from (*28*). The two sources are spliced together at 1958–59 and 1959–60. Estimated capital stock in 1947–48 is 89 crores.

[a] A crore is ten million. Each crore of rupees equaled Rs. 10 million or approximately $2 million after 1955.

were unofficially quoted at nearly double their face value. Other evidence comes from the reserve funds accumulated by industrial firms. These were often rupees held until foreign exchange could be obtained, and in anticipation that it would be. Data are available on only a handful of large companies. Their reserve funds, partly held as bank balances or as government paper, and earning little or no return, were about Rs. 78 crores ($150 million) in 1958, over 15 percent of all industrial assets.

The clearest evidence that the capacity to invest exceeded the actual rate comes from investment which took place when more foreign exchange was available. In the four years between 1950–51 and 1954–55, when imports financed by Korean boom earnings entered the country, the rate of industrial investment tripled. In the late 1950's investment dropped quite sharply along with available foreign exchange. With an improvement in the foreign-exchange situation between 1959–60 and 1964–65, private industrial investment more than doubled on a much higher base (Table 3).

Regardless of the indicators used, there was clearly an extremely rapid development of private industry in Pakistan. This was carried out almost entirely by indigenous Muslim entrepreneurs, although there had been very few industrialists or even substantial businessmen among the Muslims before Independence. Although it is impossible to prove conclusively which particular factors were most important, there is good indirect evidence that economic incentives played a very significant role.

ECONOMIC INCENTIVES

The nature of these incentives varied over time. Between Independence and the beginning of the Korean boom, factories abandoned by Hindus were readily available. Some Muslims who had small industrial plants or medium-sized trading enterprises in India, Burma, or East Africa brought modest accumulations of capital and, occasionally, technical knowledge to Pakistan. There was a ready market for goods previously supplied by firms now in India, and a potential for processing raw materials previously shipped to Calcutta or Bombay. The government was prepared to provide capital and assistance. Despite political and economic uncertainty, former industrialists and some traders responded to this favorable environment by establishing some new industrial enterprises, most of them rather small, with the exception of a few cotton textile mills.

With the Korean boom, export earnings and imports rose rapidly. The resulting prosperity stimulated further modest industrial growth, some of it involving farsighted individuals who realized that unlimited imports could not last. The Korean boom also had important indirect effects on later industrialization. First, it resulted in the development of a large group of substantial traders. Muslims, who had dealt on a small scale in grains, spices, or cloth, found their opportunities greatly increased at Partition with the removal of Hindu and British competition. Now, with export earnings and imports expanding rapidly, the abler among them began to operate on a very large scale, to expand foreign contacts, and to establish large-scale bookkeeping, accounting, control, and other management procedures. Former petty traders became accustomed to high incomes, and thought in terms of large business enterprises. Finally, the Korean boom enabled Pakistani businessmen to accumulate large cash reserves out of high profits.

When the end of the boom brought a sharp decline in export earnings and, consequently, in imports, there emerged a strong incentive to discontinue foreign trade and to produce goods previously imported. The quantitative restrictions on imports created a highly protected market for consumer goods. Machinery and other capital goods were cheap to import, since Pakistan maintained an overvalued currency and imposed low tariffs on capital goods. With high prices for consumer goods and low prices for the capital goods needed to produce them, annual profits of 50–100 percent on investment were possible. Investors could reasonably expect such profits, despite high costs which are normally associated with the early stages of industrial development. The 1950's, then, were years of very rapid private industrial investment, heavily concentrated on consumer goods, using a relatively simple technology. Most firms paid little or no attention to efficiency, finding it more profitable to devote their energies to expanding investment and output.

The incentives for Pakistani Muslims to invest in industry were effective in part because foreign competition was largely absent, tax concessions were generous, and tax evasion widely and effectively practiced. Unlike other countries, Pakistan was not faced with the problem, and the benefits, of having a large group of foreign or ethnically different industrialists. British firms had been concentrated in the great port cities of the subcontinent which remained with India. Doubtful of Pakistan's future during its first few years, and with only small investments at stake, they had little interest either in expanding their commercial activity, or in new industrial investment. The well-established Hindu commercial enterprises, and the few industrial firms, in the area of Pakistan were more anxious to sell out than to expand. Both the British and the Hindus operated under a severe handicap in that economic activity was largely controlled by the government, which naturally encouraged Pakistanis and Muslims. Foreign companies were not favored for import licenses and so did not participate in the high import profits of the early 1950's. Potential foreign investors also faced an ambiguous government attitude, and difficulties in obtaining permits and in remitting profits. At first, economic efficiency suffered as a result of these restrictions, but there was an undiluted incentive for Pakistani Muslims to become importers and, later, industrialists.

High profits were strongly conducive to industrial investment, but perhaps even more important were the

strong disincentives to alternative activities. With the end
of the Korean boom, international trade, and especially
importing, suddenly became unattractive. Large profits
per unit were still possible but volume was sharply down.
Businessmen who remained importers had to accept a reduced income. Under the government licensing system,
they could not expand their historically determined share
of business. Export earnings declined as well, and even
internal trade suffered from the shortage of imported
goods. Land ownership still brought prestige, but returns
on investment were a fraction of those in industry and
there was some risk of land reform. Moreover, the traders,
who had ready capital and a strong inducement to change
their occupation, had not been landlords for generations
and were even less familiar with agriculture than with industry. The market for urban real estate was limited by
the small number of persons who could afford to spend
much for housing and by the scarcity of imported construction materials. With little industrial production and
a small urban population, distribution and service activities were not terribly promising.

Traders, and especially those with heavy reliance on imports, who were pushed out of their accustomed activity
by dramatically declining earnings, were therefore faced
with attractive investment opportunities in industry, but
with very limited possibilities in other fields. They did not
have to invest in Pakistan, of course, but could have taken
their capital out of the country or have spent it in riotous
living. Capital export undoubtedly took place to some extent; illegal foreign-exchange holdings worth some Rs. 8
crores ($16 million) were turned over to the government
after martial law was imposed in 1958; other holdings, of
course, were never declared. However, large-scale capital
export was difficult and expensive. Consumption was restricted by the basic thrift of some of the entrepreneurs,

the pressure for austerity in the country, and the absence of goods or services on which much money could be spent. High profits in industry also helped to restrict both capital flight and consumption. When a rate of return of 100 percent per year was possible in industry, the attractiveness of exporting funds at a loss or spending them was bound to be less, at least for some people.

Although there were strong incentives for Pakistanis, especially traders, to become industrialists, there were serious obstacles as well. In the first few years, Pakistan's political and economic future seemed uncertain. The infrastructure was rudimentary, foreign suppliers were sometimes unreliable, and technical knowledge and skills were absent. The government had no experience with industrialists and distrusted the commercial and industrial groups. These facts tend to be forgotten with the benefit of hindsight. Some of those who did not see the opportunities in industry in the early 1950's claim in the 1960's that industrial investment never involved any risk.

The combination of incentives and obstacles produced an environment in which success was likely only for the ruthless individual, possessing some foresight and considerable energy, and willing to accept some political risk. This environment, in turn, produced a remarkably able group of entrepreneurs, whose economic behavior was not too different from their robber-baron counterparts of nineteenth-century Western industrialization.

THE DECLINE IN ECONOMIC INCENTIVES

Entrepreneurs needed strong incentives to overcome both external obstacles and their own reluctance to make the major shift to industry. But the extraordinary profits in industry and lack of good alternatives to industrial investment could not last long. With sharply expanded domestic production and an easing of import restrictions, competition in some industries inevitably brought declining profit rates.

The evidence that profits declined is naturally circumstantial. As in other countries, Pakistani industrialists hide their profits by various devices, and for various reasons, such as to reduce taxes. They are unlikely to give an accurate answer in an interview. Survey data in this area are unreliable, incomplete, and grossly understated, but not necessarily useless. So long as the understatement is consistent, comparative figures are still useful. (The profit rates reported by industrialists are not comparable to the rates of 50 to 100 percent cited earlier. The latter involved no deliberate understatement but were an estimate by knowledgeable industrialists of the returns from manufacturing enterprises, excluding low-profit Hindu, foreign, and government firms.) The rate of return to factors other than labor, as ascertained from interviews and balance

TABLE 8. RATE OF RETURN AS A PERCENTAGE OF ASSETS (REPORTED BY LARGE FIRMS).[a]

YEARS	(1) Profit	(2) Interest	(3) Management fees	(4) Taxes on profit	(5) Depreciation	(6) Total returns (1) through (5)
1947–1957	5.8	0.9	1.2	6.7	5.7	20.3
1958	4.9	0.5	0.5	3.5	3.4	12.8

Source: Survey.

[a] Large firms are those with capital of Rs. 1 million ($200,000) or more. Other firms are not represented because only a few gave information on their rate of return in years other than 1958 and the sample may have been biased. Note that the data in the first row also includes 1959 because all years other than 1958 were amalgamated. However, inspection of interview schedules indicates that inclusion of 1959 does not significantly change the results for 1947–1957.

sheets of a limited number of larger firms, averaged almost two-thirds higher in the years before 1958 than in that year. Profits alone averaged about 30 percent higher in 1947–55 than in 1956–58. It is possible that returns in earlier years were more understated than in later years, when government administration improved and penalties for tax evasion became more severe. The decrease in returns may therefore be even more pronounced than suggested in the figures.

More important than the Survey results is evidence from price changes. By far the most important industry in Pakistan is cotton textiles, which contributed over one-third of all value added by industry in 1958. Until 1954, domestic production was completely inadequate to replace eliminated imports. Domestic producers charged what the traffic would bear, which was a good deal. When imports

TABLE 9. APPROXIMATE PERCENTAGE CHANGES IN CLOTH AND COTTON PRICES AND THE WHOLESALE PRICE INDEX.

	Prices and Index	1951 to 1954	1954 to 1956
1	Wholesale cloth prices	Up 20–30	Down 20–30
2	Wholesale price index	Down 30	Up 60
3	Raw cotton prices	Down 30	Up 20

Sources: 1 and 2 derived from data in (*104*); 3 from (*27*, p. 297).

were cut off in 1951, wholesale cloth prices rose by almost a third for some varieties, despite a sharp drop in the general wholesale-price index. Simultaneously raw cotton prices declined, so profits clearly rose sharply in the early 1950's. After 1954 domestic production began to exceed domestic demand and Pakistan became an exporter of some varieties of cloth. As a result cotton cloth prices fell by 20–30 percent, running counter to a dramatic increase in the general wholesale price index. Because cotton prices rose at the same time, the drop in cloth profits must have been very sharp.

The effect of competition was similar for other goods. The prices of cigarettes and matches dropped nearly one-third in the middle and late 1950's in the face of a rising wholesale-price index. Cotton textiles, cigarettes, and matches accounted for nearly half of all value added in industry in 1958. They had been among the most highly protected and therefore most profitable industrial products in the early 1950's. The sharp drop in their prices due to competition, when other prices were rising, implied much lower average rates of profit for the consumer-goods industries.

Informed opinion is unequivocal that profit rates declined between the early and late 1950's. By the end of the decade businessmen were complaining that "incentives were disappearing." They reported that for some industries annual returns had dropped from 50–100 percent to 20–50 percent. The same phenomenon was also reported by government officials, economists, and others, although with less regret than glee. A very careful study of the terms of trade between industry and agriculture clearly indicates that the relative prices received by industry dropped sharply by the late 1950's (*116*).

Despite the sharp decline in the rate of industrial profits, investment continued to be high in the 1960's. The rate in 1964–65 was more than twice that in 1959–60 (Table 3). The probable reasons are complex. Obviously, some industrial investments were still very profitable. Though profits had declined, they did so from astronomical levels. Administrative obstacles facing the potential entrepreneur were less forbidding than earlier, institutions serving the industrial sector were better developed, and experience and competence in industry were more common. Economic incentives therefore remained strong, and economic obstacles were less formidable than in the 1950's. Since the status of industrialists had improved, the potential industrialist faced a more congenial social environment. Finally, an industrial investor in the late 1950's followed a rather well-trodden path, so industrial activity was not limited to the pioneer. It may also be, though this is speculation at present, that participation in industry changed the values and motives of the industrialists. That changed behavior can lead to changed values is at least consistent with the theories and evidence of some investigators in the United States. Now that industrialists had taken the plunge, they had become used to their new role and seemed prepared to continue to invest, although the rates of profit were lower than the rates required to induce an initial decision to enter a completely new field of activity.

ENTREPRENEURS AND THE TRADING COMMUNITIES[*]

Pakistani Muslims clearly were subject to strong economic incentives to become industrial entrepreneurs. The background of those who responded should throw light on the causal factors in Pakistan's industrial development. The overwhelming majority of industrial entrepreneurs have one characteristic in common, which sets them apart from most of Pakistani society. Two-thirds of private industrial investment owned by Muslims is controlled by individuals or families who had been traders previously, the great majority of whom belong to a few "communities," who had traditionally engaged in trade.

The "communities" or quasi-castes which played a disproportionate role in Pakistan's industry vary in their characteristics. The most important community was that of the Memons. In 1959 members of this group controlled

---

[*] For more extensive discussion see (143).

TABLE 10. PRIOR OCCUPATIONS OF MUSLIMS[a] WHO WERE
PRIVATE INDUSTRIALISTS IN 1959
(PERCENT).

ANTECEDENT CHARACTERISTICS	PREVIOUS PRIMARY OCCUPATION[b]		PREVIOUS SECONDARY OCCUPATION[b]		FATHER'S OCCUPATION
	Industrialists	*Industrial investment*[c]	*Industrialists*	*Industrial investment*[c]	*Industrial investment*[c]
1 Industrialist before 1947	17	16	4	30	6
2 Small industry, handicrafts	18	6	23	7	16
3 Traders — import, export	17	41	30	25	11
4 Traders — internal, government contractors	28	22	39	24	36
5 Employees — professional, other	18	10	4	12	20
6 Agriculture	3	6	negligible	1	11
	101	101	100	99	100

Source: Survey. Totals differ from 100 percent because of rounding.

[a] Excludes those who immigrated from the Near East in the last century.

[b] Primary and secondary are determined according to proportion of income received.

[c] Proportion of total industrial investment controlled by each category.

one-quarter of investment in privately owned Muslim firms. The community is defined mainly by its origin in a few small towns in the poor area of Kathiawar (between Karachi and Bombay). The second most important group, the Chiniotis, comes from a single small town in the Pakistani Punjab, though seemingly undistinguishable from other towns in the same area. Both of these groups belong to the majority in Islam, the Sunnis. Three other important communities (Bohra, Khoja Isnashari, Khoja Ismaili) are members of the minority (Shia) group and belong to distinct religious sects within this larger group.

Most of their members originated in Gujarat and Kathiawar.

TABLE 11. APPROXIMATE PERCENTAGE OF INDUSTRIAL
ASSETS BY "COMMUNITY" — 1959.

Community	Private Muslim firms only	All firms	Population[a]
Private Muslim enterprises	100	67.0	88.0
Halai Memon	26.5	18	0.16
Chinioti	9	6	0.03
Dawoodi Bohra	5	3.5	0.02
Khoja Isnashari	5.5	4	0.02
Khoja Ismaili	5	3.5	0.06
Other Muslim trading communities (including Chakwali, other Bohra, Delhi Saudagar)	5.5	4	0.08
Syed and Sheikh[b]	18.0	12	
Pathan	8	5.5	7
Bengali Muslim	3.5	2.5	43
Other Muslim (including unknown)	14	8.5	37.5
Private Hindu and foreign enterprises		21.5	12.5
Bengali Hindu		8.5	10
Marwari		2	–
Other Hindu and Sikh		1.5	2.5
Parsi		1	0.01
British		7.5	–
American, other foreigners		1	–
Public enterprises		12.0	
Pakistan Industrial Development Corporation		7	
Government		5	
Total		100.5	100.5

Source: Survey. Note that accuracy of data for any particular community
is limited because the total sample was small.

[a] Rounded and approximate percentages. Community membership data
from (144).

[b] Most Sheikhs, and some respondents classifying themselves as Syeds,
belong to traditional trading groups.

All of these communities, as well as other groups that contribute a disproportionate number of industrial entrepreneurs, shared a traditional occupation. For several generations members had by preference been petty traders rather than peasants, landlords, artisans, soldiers, or administrators. On the other hand, groups such as the Bengali Muslims, which included few traders, produced few industrial entrepreneurs.

It is not really surprising that traders, especially members of the few Muslim trading communities, took advantage of the changed economic environment after 1947. They were used to responding to market incentives, all of which pointed to industry. Traders also had the resources to respond. Market incentives did not affect the great majority of peasants, artisans, and others who were only indirectly and tenuously in touch with the market, and lacked the capital and knowledge required to take advantage of the economic opportunities. Elite groups — landlords, civil servants, professionals, and the military — had the resources but lacked the incentives of the traders. Elimination of the British and Hindus greatly increased the opportunities in traditional elite occupations. The strong economic disincentives which operated against the traders did not exist for the elite, who were doing well and had no strong incentive to take risks or accept lower status involved in becoming traders or industrialists. Landlords did not earn the high returns of industrialists, but their traditional occupation had prestige and provided a steady income. The landlords' incomes were not sharply reduced after Independence, unlike those of many traders.

Many traders had a further advantage in their access to a distribution system. When a cloth merchant set up a textile mill, he had a ready-made sales organization. Competitors with backgrounds other than trading had difficulties — in the absence of a well-developed, general distribution system — in distributing their output. A captive sales organization was also useful in evading price-control and taxes, since illegal income could be hidden in transfers between producing and sales units. Former importers, in addition, were in touch with foreign firms that could assist in buying machinery and imported raw materials and in arranging for foreign technicians.

Because trade was dominated by the "trading communities," it is hardly surprising that the incentives and ability which induced traders to become industrial entrepreneurs resulted in the domination of private industry by the same communities. In addition, the very fact of membership in a trading community had significant advantages for would-be industrialists. Community members tended to trust each other, especially since most communities imposed sanctions against violators of their code of behavior. Community membership therefore facilitated raising capital. Above all, the confidence among community members widened the pool from which accountants, managers, technicians, and partners could be drawn. Most businessmen drew on family members for these posts. No one else was trusted to act in a firm's interest in a situation fraught with uncertainty, with few institutional or professional standards, and with no traditional code of ethics in industry. Most successful industrialists found the need for deception, bribery, and semilegal activity almost inescapable and were therefore especially dependent on the loyalty of employees. Entrepreneurs from a trading community could often trust other members and could therefore draw talented personnel from a much wider group than their competitors.

A few communities played no significant role in industry. The differences between those who became industrialists and those who did not require further investigation, but chance and foresight may have played a role.

If a number of relatives or community members had decided to enter industry in the early 1950's they could still
obtain imported equipment and earn very high profits
from their investment. They were then in a good position
to expand their investment and to assist relatives. Fellow
community-members would be the first to know about a
successful venture and would feel easier about taking the
plunge into industry. Those who missed the crucial period
often had to be satisfied with lower profits. More important, latecomers were severely handicapped in the increasingly sharp competition for foreign exchange. They
did not have capital, experience, or past success to convince government officials that they were good risks. They
also had fewer means for bribery and less influence, unless
they had special channels to government. An industrialist
whose community had missed its opportunity complained
that: "In other families or communities, the members in
industry help each other. I get no such help. In addition,
I am constantly under pressure to employ and help community members who have no other place to go."

In short, in the 1950's, many traders were forced out of
their historical occupation, while those in other occupations usually gained in status and income. Traders were
directly exposed to the incentives for industrial activity
because they knew more about the opportunity in industry and were more accustomed to taking economic
risks. Traders had the ability to act in response to both
push and pull because they possessed liquid capital and
some relevant knowledge. Finally, members of trading
communities could draw on information and a wider circle
of trusted collaborators than could other traders. Trading
communities were the natural source for industrial entrepreneurs during early development.

In increasing numbers, others entered industry after the
middle 1950's. Many of the industrialists with back-

grounds in agriculture, or as employees or professionals, entered industry in the middle or late 1950's. (See Table 10; 21 percent of industrialists came from these backgrounds.) The rewards had become widely known, while the attraction of other occupations had decreased. When land reform became a threat, some landlords became industrialists. Some civil servants and professionals took the same step as the pay and prestige of their occupations suffered, or when they were removed from their government jobs during the martial-law regime. This was an extreme case of the disincentive to remain in one's accustomed occupation which, in a milder form, played a large part in pushing importers into industry.

By the late 1950's membership in a business community, with its situation of special trust, was less of an asset. Institutions to provide capital developed, as did the professional standards for managers, accountants, lawyers, and others. The need and opportunity for semilegal or illegal activities had declined. It was obviously both profitable and respectable to be an industrialist. Small industrialists, traders, civil servants, and others became eager to invest in industry or to expand their industrial investment. However, unless they had special connections with the government, they faced all the disadvantages of latecomers.

CAUSAL FACTORS IN THE DEVELOPMENT OF ENTREPRENEURSHIP

Clearly there were strong economic incentives in Pakistan for industrial entrepreneurship, and good economic reasons for the few traders in the country — largely members of trading communities — to respond to such incentives. The development of entrepreneurs, however, cannot be explained in economic terms alone.

To say that these developments were the result of mul-

tiple causes is not very original. It is standard operating
procedure in books on economic development to point to
multiple causation. It has become equally popular to point
out that the motivations, values, and institutions of a society are at least as important as economic factors in determining the nature and speed of development in general,
and entrepreneurs specifically. Acceptance of both points,
however, does not give much guidance to the policy-maker
concerned with influencing the development process. He
may be interested in basic causes, but he is even more
concerned with causal factors which he can influence, regardless of their relative importance. At the present time,
there is little agreement on the most important causal
factors in entrepreneurship, and there has been practically
no discussion of policies to influence the process. Much of
the writing in this field has dealt with the historical development of entrepreneurs under conditions that were
quite different from those existing at present in underdeveloped countries. Neither development in Western Europe, when industrial technology was in its infancy, nor
the experience of "traditional," stagnant societies may
have much relevance for a country such as Pakistan, ex-
periencing rapid change, able to draw on well-developed
technology, and with the attributes of what has been
called a "transitional" economy.

Without a good deal of further work, one cannot point
with assurance to the factors which ultimately caused the
development of Pakistan's entrepreneurs. Fortunately, the
proximate causes are of more relevance for policy. One
can draw some tentative conclusions from the Survey,
from general impressions, and from other studies, about
the relationship between economic and other factors in
the development of Pakistan's industrial entrepreneurs.

It is sometimes assumed that the emergence of a group
of industrial entrepreneurs is strongly affected by an edu-

cation or by the development of a "modern" (for which
usually read "Western") outlook (51, pp. 38–44; 97, pp.
59–60). Industrial entrepreneurs are assumed to be innovators, promoting change not only in the economic sphere
but also in other areas. The evidence from Pakistan lends
little support to these notions. Many of the industrial entrepreneurs had no significant formal education. The great
majority were not innovators in noneconomic fields; they
were often conservative and non-Western in religion,
dress, and social behavior. Interestingly, while the entrepreneurs were much more traditional than other groups,
such as civil servants, professionals, and intellectuals, the
best educated, most Westernized minority, the Parsis,
played no significant role in Pakistan's industry.

Another explanation is that Partition uprooted potential
entrepreneurs from their traditional environment and induced them to look for new activities. This seems irrelevant, because most industrialists had left their native town
or village much earlier to trade in cities or other towns.

Since the time of Max Weber, it has been argued that
industrial entrepreneurs are drawn from groups which
differ from the majority of a society and from its traditional elite, that they are outsiders or marginal to society.
A particular variant of this theory, advanced by Everett
Hagen, is that economic innovators develop from a previously prestigious group which has lost status (90). Over
several generations their personality therefore changes, so
that they are able to recover their lost position by economic innovation.

Industrial entrepreneurs in Pakistan did differ from
other groups in the society, as one would logically expect.
Almost by definition, any group which pioneers in a particular field can be differentiated from the majority of society, whether the field is a new religion or ideology,
lunar exploration, or industrial development. Nor is it sur-

prising that the economic innovators were drawn from outside the traditional elite. Members of the elite were in a rewarding, prestigious, and usually satisfactory situation, unlikely to pioneer in a new activity, with uncertain rewards and considerable risk.

However, the business communities of Pakistan were not true minorities or suppressed groups. They were not religious dissenters (at least not the two most important groups), racial or linguistic minorities, or groups that were prevented from entering activities other than commerce or industry. There had been no change in their religion to set them apart from other groups, although like the overwhelming majority of Muslims in India they were converted from Hinduism some generations ago. There is no evidence that they had lost a former prestige. So far as members of trading communities know, they had been traders for generations and, in the Indian subcontinent, commercial classes were looked down upon by the real elite through all of recorded history.

The role of members of different communities in modern, large-scale industry, as distinct from industry as a whole, throws some interesting light on the relationship between social behavior, minority status, and entrepreneurial activity. Members of the two communities that most closely resemble the majority of Pakistan in religion, education, and attitude to social innovation, the Memons and Chiniotis, are especially prominent in larger firms and in nontraditional industry. Dawoodi Bohras, members of a conservative sect, control about the same proportion of modern industry as all industry. The Khoja Isnasharis, who play an insignificant role in modern industry, are also conservative but are less rigorously organized as a religious group than the Bohras. The most educated, Westernized group among the major business communities, the Khoja Ismailis, is a clearly defined sect, with a strong

community organization and community pressure for industrial activity and modernization, who like the Bohras
control about the same proportion of modern industry as
of industry as a whole. Among industrialists owning modern, large firms, but not members of a trading community,
the Syeds and Pathans (especially the Yusufzai Pathans)
are prominent. The Syeds claim descent from the
Prophet and have high prestige. The Pathans of the
Northwest Frontier are renowned primarily for their fight-
ing ability, their independence, and their traditional tribal
organization. One might expect groups that are especially
well educated, or modern, or outside the main stream to
be particularly prominent in industries which require a
great deal of innovation. Yet there simply is no discernible
relationship between a group's role in modern large-scale
industry and the degree to which it is marginal in society,
or the degree to which its members are innovators in the
social sphere.

Two groups in particular behaved contrary to a script
written in terms of minority groups or "modern" behavior
— the Yusufzai Pathans and the Parsis. The former, a
highly traditional group, belong to the religious, ethnic,
and political majority of their area, yet are prominent in
industry and in modern industry. The latter are the minority par excellence and the most "modern" group in
Pakistan, yet they play an insignificant role in industry.
Differing economic circumstances chiefly explain the behavior of both groups. The Yusufzai industrialists had been
wealthy landowners and therefore had access to capital.
Living on the main trade route to Afghanistan, they were
involved in trade and transport before they became industrialists. Their large cash crops also linked them to the
market. Just as cloth merchants became textile-mill
owners, Yusufzai sugar cane growers became sugar-mill
owners. By contrast, the Parsis were well established at

Independence in profitable, nonindustrial activities —
stevedoring, real estate, shipping, and the professions.
They were not under the same pressure to move out of
their usual activity as were groups prominent in international trade. At Partition, as a non-Muslim minority, they
faced a greater objective risk than the Muslim traders if
they tied up cash in industry.

The explanations of entrepreneurial development so far
examined have focused on the education, motivation or
"modernity" of individuals and groups of potential entrepreneurs. Another set of explanations focuses on political
and social changes in society as a whole. In Pakistan the
political environment shortly after 1947 was hardly more
favorable than before Independence. The survival of the
state and its future political makeup were widely considered uncertain. The government administration was
stretched much too thin and was therefore inefficient and
corrupt to a degree. However, the government was able
to protect life and property, and to develop the infrastructure required by industry, although there were frequent
delays. Corruption was never so widespread, capricious,
or extortionate that it siphoned off substantial resources or
created great uncertainty. Given these minimum conditions, economic incentives were strong enough to overcome the effects of an inauspicious political environment.
When the expected rate of return on investment ap-
proached 50 percent, even the reasonably prudent investor
did not need long-term political security — he could re-
coup his investment with profit so long as there was no
drastic political change for a few years. Bribes, and losses
due to inadequate government services, could also be absorbed by this high rate of return.

For a variety of reasons the social environment was
similarly unpropitious to industrial entrepreneurs. Traders
and industrialists were accorded none of the prestige

given to government officials and landlords. Some Western writers have mentioned that the Islamic religion is not conducive to economic innovation, as the Protestant ethic was supposed to be. Patriotism and nationalism, as well as religion, were strong forces in Pakistan, but they focused on political and social, rather than on economic issues. While the social environment thus seemed unfavorable, it was not actively hostile to industrial development. There was a good deal of flexibility in Pakistani society as a result of Partition and Independence, and this greatly diminished effective pressure for conformity. The successful trader or industrialist could not find a place in literature or the power structure, but neither would he be ostracized in the fluid, confused life of Karachi. Within his own group the successful businessman had high prestige and, if he belonged to an organized community, his business success was likely to bring with it a position of community leadership.

Without further investigation, one cannot say whether substantial psychological changes had evolved over a long period of time, which affected the behavior of the business communities. Nor can one be categorical about changes in values, motivations, or institutions in the society as a whole. There must have been prior change to produce the situation just discussed — some tolerance for economic innovation, some measure of political stability and administrative competence, and some groups in touch with the market who were neither completely traditional in behavior nor completely satisfied with their position in society. Yet if those are the only changes required as preconditions for industrial entrepreneurship, one would be hard-pressed to find many countries which do not possess them today.

Whatever the previous fundamental changes, the developments after Independence are clear enough. There was little industrial activity by Muslims before 1947. In 1947, the social, political, and institutional framework was not particularly propitious for industrial development, but a radical change soon took place in the economic situation. Following this change there occurred such a rapid growth of industry that it seems unlikely that basic social or psychological changes took place concurrently. There was hardly time.

Further support for the thesis that economic incentives were important in Pakistan's industrialization comes from the speed and sensitivity with which changes in the economic situation resulted in changes in industrialists' behavior. The switch from trade to industry was closely attuned to changes in the relative profitability of the two occupations. A shift — from the cotton textile and similar industries to chemicals and other complex industries discussed in the next chapter — followed quickly on a changed economic outlook. Similarly, the move from concern with investment to concern with efficiency, also discussed later, showed responsiveness to economic incentives, though the evidence in this case is much poorer.

The final bit of evidence comes from the entrepreneurs themselves, who overwhelmingly indicated pecuniary motives when asked why they entered industry. Nearly half of those controlling larger firms specifically volunteered that poor prospects in trade were the primary reasons. They were not so much attracted by good profit possibilities in industry as pushed out of importing into the best possible alternative occupation. This kind of ex post facto explanation is not very reliable, because a brief interview question cannot generally elicit motives for past actions. However, since the natural inclination would be to give patriotic and other altruistic motives rather than strictly economic ones, any bias in the answers is likely to be in favor of patriotism or altruism. The negligible number of entrepreneurs, especially those with larger enterprises, who gave noneconomic reasons for entering industry should be of some significance.

TABLE 12. PRIMARY REASONS GIVEN BY MUSLIMS FOR ENTERING INDUSTRY (PERCENT).

Reason	All firms	Larger firms[a]
Family or individual in industry before	23	15
Poor prospects for trade	25	47
Expected profits	29	14
Incidental to his activity in trade (e.g., jute baling)	5	3
Industry superior, or patriotism	9	4
Government policy favoring industry, or chance, or other	9	16
	100	99

Source: Survey.
[a] Capital, $200,000 equivalent and over.

There cannot be conclusive proof of the relative importance of different factors in the genesis and later development of entrepreneurship. The hypothesis advanced here, for which some evidence has been provided, is *not* that economic factors are paramount. It is that in Pakistan strong economic incentives were sufficient to develop a number of industrial entrepreneurs, given, first, a social and political environment that was not excessively hostile, though it was not favorable, and, second, some groups or individuals in touch with the market and therefore affected by economic incentives. It is argued also that once industrial development was well under way, weaker economic incentives were sufficient to maintain its momentum.

Finally, it is suggested that industrial entrepreneurs were overwhelmingly drawn from the groups which were pushed most strongly out of their current occupation, which were exposed most directly to the incentives mak-

ing for entrepreneurial activity, and which had the ability
to exploit the opportunities in industry. The push factor
operated most directly on those in foreign trade, especially importers. They felt that they had little to lose by
shifting to another occupation. Others who might be considered potential entrepreneurs were doing well in their
current occupations. Traders, especially importers, were
also directly exposed to the pull factors, to the possibilities
in industry. They could perceive the profitable opportunities and appraise the risks, and could gain in status by
the shift. Other potential entrepreneurs knew less about
profit opportunities in industry and might lose in status by
becoming industrialists. Finally, some traders were in a
particularly good position to exploit industrial opportunities; they had liquid capital, they were acquainted with
foreign suppliers of machinery, they had a marketing network, and they were familiar with the government import
licensing machinery. Small industrialists, landlords, and
those in handicrafts usually did not possess all these assets.

During Pakistan's early period of industrial development, the disincentives to remaining in one's current occupation, the incentives to entrepreneurial activity in industry, and the capacity to respond to both particularly
affected the traders and importers. In other circumstances,
other groups might have provided the industrial entrepreneurs.

CHAPTER III

CAPITALISTS AT WORK

Efficiency and Concentration in Private Industry

Wealth is concentrated in the hands of a group which is greedy, anti-social, uneducated, and crude. Private industry has exploited the consumer. Its efficiency is a myth — it has never been exposed to international competition.

SENIOR PAKISTANI CIVIL SERVANT

THE MOST striking aspect of private industrial development in Pakistan was its speed, as though a movie taken at 16 frames per second were projected at 64 frames. But was this rapid process socially efficient? The robber barons, with a background in trade, were not trained in industrial technology. Such newly minted industrialists, ignorant of technology and with a trader's mentality, might be expected to neglect industries that were technically complex and had a slow payoff. Since the industrialists were drawn from a limited group, control of industry could be highly concentrated, with dangers for economic efficiency.

Rapid industrialization took place with investment largely in private hands, although Pakistan began with practically no industrial entrepreneurs. Did this capitalist development lead only to the creation of inefficient consumer-goods industries with simple technology and under concentrated control? This question, raised in Pakistan, is not a rhetorical one; the answer is obviously important since the efficiency, as well as the speed, of private development is relevant in appraising the role of private initiative.

THE SOURCES OF TECHNOLOGY

Most traders clearly lacked the technical competence to be successful industrialists. This lack has been cited as another serious obstacle to private industrial development, especially since traders in underdeveloped countries are supposedly unwilling to "get their hands dirty" on grubby technical matters (97, pp. 151–153).

Pakistani entrepreneurs met this problem in typically pragmatic fashion. They did not hesitate to use foreign technicians in considerable number, but only as long as foreigners were essential. Pakistani owners were anxious to get rid of them as soon as possible, both because they were foreigners and because they were costly. Foreign technicians did not linger as they might have in a foreign-owned company whose distant home office might not trust natives or wanted to put some of its people out to pasture. When factories were operating reasonably smoothly and Pakistani technicians had been trained, the more costly foreigners left. Something over 10 percent of all firms obtained their technical knowledge from foreign technicians. However, these were primarily large firms in more complex industries. If one excludes small firms and traditional industries, 60 percent of all investment was in firms that used foreign technicians. Even this very high figure is an understatement since most firms reported their situation at the time of the Survey (1960–61) when a large number had already dismissed their foreigners.

Many of the foreign technicians were included in purchases of imported machinery, to set up the factory and to operate it for some time. As a result, technicians in cotton

textiles were usually Japanese; in jute, British; in metals,
German. This diversity gave Pakistan better technicians
and technology than if it had relied on one country, and
it reduced any fear of foreign domination.

TABLE 13. PRIMARY SOURCES OF TECHNICAL INFORMATION
FOR FIRMS IN NONTRADITIONAL INDUSTRIES WITH CAPITAL
OF RS. 1 MILLION OR ABOVE.

Source	Capital assets (crores of rupees)
Mainly foreigners	109
Partly foreigners, partly nonfamily Pakistanis	75
Partly foreigners, partly family members	3
Mainly family members	11
Mainly nonfamily Pakistanis	113
Total	311

Source: Survey.

Pakistani technicians drawn from outside the controlling family became increasingly important. By 1959 family
members played a small role in supplying technical information to the larger firms. Increasingly engineers, plant
managers, accountants, sales managers, and other senior
officials were professionals. If the family had some members with the required ability and training they naturally
received preference. However, firms in a competitive industry found that they could not afford incompetent
family members in key positions, so they were relegated
to posts in which technical competence was not important. ("One of my brothers takes care of our contacts with
government officials, charitable organizations, and interviewers. Unfortunately he is away and cannot see you today.") Some of the brightest young family members were
sent abroad for training, and well-trained technicians from
outside the family were hired for responsible positions.

THE COMPOSITION OF INVESTMENT

Concentration on industries with a simple technology eased the shortage of technicians and skilled workers during early development. Entrepreneurs in underdeveloped countries are often criticized for concentrating on the simple processing of raw materials into consumer goods. Any other development, however, would have been very foolish in the early stages of industrialization, and Pakistan's entrepreneurs were anything but foolish. Industries such as textiles required few expensive foreign technicians and little of the scarce skilled labor. Since these industries were highly protected, they involved a minimum of risk and earned a maximum rate of profit. Given political uncertainty and the difficulty of raising capital during the first decade of industrialization, entrepreneurs naturally invested in technologically simple industries that promised a quick return. In addition they preferred industries that produced for domestic consumption, with low capital requirements and a short period between investment decision and production.

However, as circumstances changed so did entrepreneurial behavior, and in a remarkably brief period of time. Investment shifted to new industries when competition threatened to reduce profits in the industries developed first. It was relatively easy to make this shift because industrialists had become more knowledgeable, and capital and technicians were more readily available. Entrepreneurs began to develop such industries as cement, chemicals, paper, and metal working, in which technology is complex, capital per unit of output is high, and the period between investment and production is long. Of investment sanctioned by the government in manufacturing between 1960 and 1962, almost one-third was in chemicals alone and one-half was in all complex industries.* Of that sanctioned in 1963–64, over one-seventh was in the engineering industries and one-quarter in engineering, chemicals, electrical, and similar industries (*81*). The growth in output of different industries clearly shows the shift in investment from consumer goods to intermediate and capital goods. One study (*114*, pp. 94–140) showed that between 1954–55 and 1963–64 consumer-goods production grew at a much slower rate than the other two categories. The output of capital goods actually grew twice as fast as consumer goods, though admittedly from a small base.

From the Survey it is clear that the great gains in the textile, simple processing, and import-substituting industries occurred before 1955. The complex industries, machinery and chemicals, grew more rapidly after the middle 1950's. Even more striking is the shift in the stated investment plans of industrialists, since it indicates investments they wanted to undertake, not those forced on them by government policy. For the period after 1960 (less than 10 years after the rapid development of simple industry began in Pakistan), over one-third of the investment which industrialists were prepared to undertake in the next few years was in the more sophisticated industries. That industrialists were willing and able to shift to more complex industries was obviously important in maintaining the momentum of Pakistan's industrial development.

Many industrialists showed considerable foresight. They very quickly got the message implied in government pronouncements. In the early 1960's industrialists who based their decisions on past experience tended to invest in cotton textiles, the industry with a history of high returns; industrialists with more foresight realized, from govern-

---

* Compiled from government records.

ment statements, that protection for metals and chemicals was likely to improve, and were anxious to invest in these new industries.

TABLE 14. GROWTH IN ASSETS BY MAJOR INDUSTRY GROUPS.

INDUSTRY GROUP	1947	1955		1959		PLANNED — 1964	
	Crores	Crores	Percent increase over 1947	Crores	Percent increase over 1955	Crores	Percent increase over 1959
Simple processing of agricultural products	21	77	267	74	−4	105	42
Textiles and more complex processing	21	152	624	227	49	372	64
Jute	0	22	–	39	85	56	44
Processing of imported materials							
Traditional	2	27	1,250	36	33	48	33
Nontraditional	1	18	1,700	29	61	89	207
Machinery, chemicals, paper, cement	12	55	358	98	78	303	209
Total	58	351	505	503	43	973	93

Source: Survey. For details and definitions see Appendix B.

EFFICIENCY

Along with the shift to complex industries, there was an increase in attention to efficiency. It is often charged that private industry in underdeveloped countries is very inefficient, that only a highly protected internal market enables it to survive, and that it is therefore very costly to the economy. This was certainly true in Pakistan. Foreign technicians were costly, and serious shortages of skilled labor, clerical, and medium-level professional personnel made for inefficient operation. Since plants were new, in any one year a large proportion of all factories were going through a shakedown period, and this would involve inefficiency in any country. Overhead and auxiliary facilities were completely inadequate; the power supply was unreliable; supplies of imported spare parts, raw materials, and fuels were insufficient and uncertain; and transport equipment was in short supply. Some plants were too small for optimum operation.

The entrepreneurs devoted very little attention to the problem of technical inefficiency. Although technicians might deplore this neglect, it was sensible economics. First, there was little the individual industrialist could do about some of the factors that made for inefficiency. It would be expensive and time-consuming for him to improve the supply of power, skilled labor, transport, and service facilities. More important, the increased return from greater efficiency would be only a fraction of the return that could be obtained by devoting energy to new investment. For many industrialists the only significant obstacle to investment was the lack of a government permit to import the required machinery. Once this was obtained, the rate of return on invested funds could be 100 percent a year. It was thus wise to devote energy to obtaining government permits rather than to increasing efficiency in established plants.

This situation began to change in the late 1950's. When profit rates in some industries fell, it became more attractive to improve operations of past investment. There had been a marked improvement in the supply of services, especially those provided by the government (power and transport). Government policies that had imposed lower efficiency were changed. For instance, regulations which limited the number of shifts and the size of plants were modified. A steadier supply of imported spare parts and raw materials made it possible to use capital more effectively. There is some evidence that, as a result, a number of industrialists shifted attention to some extent from investment in new plants to improving the efficiency of existing ones. A few firms seemed to be achieving an efficiency of operation which was quite up to international standards.

Efficiency is notoriously difficult to measure. There is only indirect (and not wholly convincing) evidence for Pakistan. For instance, jute, cotton textile, and a few other industries have competed with increasing success in a very difficult international market. They were helped in the 1960's by a measure to compensate exporters for the overvaluation of the Pakistani rupee. In addition, Pakistan's ability to compete internationally depended in part on lower wages than those paid by some, but by no means all of its competitors. One can say only that, given its cheaper but less experienced and less productive labor, the quantity and quality of capital empoyed, and the whole organization of society, some of Pakistan's industries have become sufficiently efficient to increase quite rapidly the value of goods they sell in international competition (see also Table 5).

Somewhat better evidence on efficiency comes directly from the physical operation of plants. A study of the jute industry by the Food and Agriculture Organization (49), shows that output (in weight) of cloth per loom in Pakistan more than doubled between 1954 and 1959. By 1959 Pakistan's physical output was twice that in India, more than twice the output in Europe, and four times the output in Japan. In small part the difference results from a higher proportion of automatic looms and of new machinery in Pakistan. More important, other countries produce higher quality specialty goods which are more difficult to manufacture but have a higher value per unit weight. The major reason for the difference is more intensive machinery use in Pakistan, which averages over two shifts, while in other countries a single shift is typical. Even if these reasons are taken into account and a large margin of error is assumed, the FAO figures are interesting. First, they suggest that there has been a substantial improvement in Pakistan's efficiency over 5 years. Second, the firms have taken advantage of lower labor costs and have compensated for capital scarcity by working several shifts, even though this is considered a nuisance by Pakistani management and labor. Finally, the per-shift figures suggest that by 1959, after an average of only 5 years of operation, Pakistan's physical efficiency in using scarce capital was not too different from other countries. The same FAO study shows that labor costs per ton in Pakistan are two-thirds of those in India and one-third of those in the U.K., while the gross margin in Pakistan is about twice that in the other two countries. Although one must take account of the lower value per ton of product in Pakistan, and of its advantage in buying raw materials, these figures nevertheless indicate indirectly the efficiency of Pakistani plants.

Another study of the jute industry shows that value added per unit of investment doubled between 1956–58 and 1960–62 (1). The figures somewhat overstate the change in physical efficiency, since capital costs increased only slightly over this period while the prices received by the producers increased about 20 percent. In addition, a large part of the explanation lies in the increased number of hours during which the machinery was operated, but more intensive machinery use also reflects improved management and maintenance.

In the production of cotton yarn, Pakistan's physical efficiency has also improved substantially over time, though it remained low in 1959. Improvement was most marked in the low-quality yarn, in which production the industry had the longest experience. The improvement in the processes which began more recently is yet to come.

TABLE 15. OUTPUT OF YARN PER COTTON SPINDLE
(OUNCES PER SPINDLE PER SHIFT).

Quality of yarn	India 1948	Pakistan 1952	Pakistan 1959
10's	7.74	–	10.78
20's	5.20	4.50	5.35
30's	2.80	2.80	3.00
40's	2.20	1.80	1.95
80's	0.90	–	0.89

Source: (125).

A 1959 International Labor Organization report on the textile industry concluded that "the best mills in the country will stand comparison with any in Europe, while the worst are very inefficient" (105).

Finally, Survey interviews produced three bits of evidence regarding efficiency. Until the middle 1950's many textile mills operated one shift in weaving and two shifts in spinning. Prices were high and demand strong, but many firms considered it too much trouble to organize and supervise multiple-shift operation. (Some owners used the transparent rationalization that the "machines need rest too.") By 1958 two-thirds of all investment in this industry was being operated on an 800-shift per year basis or better, and nearly all the remainder operated 700 shifts. A significant proportion of plants operated as many as 950 shifts. The managers complained about the nuisance of supervising the night shifts, but felt they had little choice if they were to compete.

There was also visible evidence of good management in some factories. In 1960, a number of textile mills had recently added equipment to control humidity and temperature, had opened testing laboratories, were training workers, and were providing incentive plans and specialized maintenance engineers.

Most impressive were changes in the attitude and behavior of the families that controlled many of the larger enterprises. Often the original founder was indeed a textbook example of the modern robber baron. Ruthless, shrewd, he had little education and no technical knowledge, and only a rudimentary contact with the paraphernalia of modern business. The air-conditioned office seemed as strange to him as the suggestion that business had social responsibilities. He was an industrial promoter, in business to make quick and large profits, using methods that law and polite society frowned on at best. He invested and reinvested and had little concern with plant operation. Often he had spent his life in trade, turning to industry late in his career, and living in semiretirement by the 1960's. The sons of these men were quite different. The grandsons, just joining the family business, or hired managers, often resembled more the organization men of current American business than the robber-baron founders of American and Pakistani enterprises. This is not surprising since the grandsons might well be recent graduates of the Harvard Business School or of a textile-engineering program in North Carolina. Like their counterparts elsewhere, a small but increasing number of the new men are horrified at the cruder acts of their forebears. They would have been ineffective in the early days of Pakistan's industry, but now they are the men who can improve its efficiency, as well as its image. The development described here has taken place elsewhere, but the change, which took several decades in other countries, in Pakistan seems to be well underway after only a dozen years.

The change which has actually taken place should not be exaggerated. After all, the average age of Pakistan's

industry was less than a decade in the middle 1960's, and
it had begun to feel the pressure of competition only a few
years earlier. In this short time the shift of emphasis from
the establishment of new firms to the efficient operation of
existing plants had just begun. Most firms were still very
inefficient by international standards and were the despair
of foreign productivity teams. Progress was evident only
in relative terms. Still, there was a rapid response to changing economic circumstances. Most descriptions of industrialists in underdeveloped countries give the impression
that even the limited changes described above could not
take place in less than several decades.

CONCENTRATION AND COMBINATION

One cannot be as sanguine about another aspect of Pakistan's industrial development — it inevitably resulted in
a high degree of concentration. Those starting at the right
time with a medium-sized enterprise earned large profits
which provided capital for reinvestment. They also had
the experience and the funds to convince government officials that they were good risks and should be given permission to expand. They could employ technicians to prepare the impressive documentation required by government, and to set up and operate effective enterprises.

While there were over 3,000 individual firms in Pakistan
in 1959, only 7 individuals, families, or foreign corporations controlled one-quarter of all private industrial assets
and one-fifth of all industrial assets. Twenty-four units
controlled nearly half of all private industrial assets. The
resources, experience, and contacts of the leading private
families made them strong contenders when a semigovernment corporation sold some of its plants — over two-thirds
of the assets thus sold are estimated to have been bought
by the leading families. Government action in this instance

strengthened their hold on manufacturing. The largest 7 units controlled in addition Rs. 46 crores of other assets — in banks, insurance companies, or trade. It is also reported that approximately 15 families owned about three-quarters of all the shares in banks and insurance companies. This control of large pools of capital gave the leading families a clear advantage in financing new industrial ventures.

TABLE 16. DISTRIBUTION OF CONTROL
IN PRIVATE INDUSTRY, 1959.

UNITS[a]				NONINDUSTRIAL[c] —	
Industrial assets controlled per unit[b]	Number	Total industrial assets[b]	Total industrial sales[b]	Assets[b]	Sales[b]
1–1.9	23	34	40	3	25
2–2.9	13	31	21	9	8
3–4.9	8	34	35	1	5
5–9.9	9	61	51	11	61
10 and over	7	108	82	46	12
Total	60	268	229	70	111
All private industry	2,500–2,900[d]	442	526	–	–
All industry	2,600–3,000[d]	503	551	–	–

Source: Survey.

[a] Major decisions for each unit are made centrally, by an individual, a family, or the management of a corporation. A unit may have several plants.

[b] In crores of rupees.

[c] Controlled by same families.

[d] Estimates only.

Data for industry as a whole are a poor measure of concentration. In Pakistan they understate the potential for collusion. Concentration naturally was greater in the production of some goods than for industry as a whole. In addition, many of the dominant families were from the same community and had close personal ties. Finally, a

TABLE 17. DISTRIBUTION OF CONTROL IN PARTICULAR INDUSTRIES, 1959.

INDUSTRY	Assets[a] (all firms)	LARGEST PRIVATE UNITS		NUMBER OF UNITS BY COMMUNITY (largest units only)			ASSETS[a] BY COMMUNITY (largest units only)		
		Number of units	Total assets[a]	Memon	Chinioti	Other[b]	Memon	Chinioti	Other
Cotton textiles	151	14	79	4	4	6	23	20	36
Jute	39	5	33	2	–	3	18	–	15
Edible oils	15	4	3	–	2	–	–	1.5	–
Sugar	27	4	15	–	–	4	–	–	15

Source: Survey. Note, where only one firm is owned by a member of a community, it is not included in the table to avoid identifying the assets of a particular firm.

[a] In crores of rupees.

[b] The "other" communities vary by industry. (Sugar: three firms controlled by Yusufzhai Pathans with assets of Rs. 12 crores; other industries: scattered.)

few industries were dominated by a single private firm (tobacco, paper, machinery) or by the government or one of its agencies (shipbuilding, fertilizer, railroad equipment).

The very small number of private Muslim entrepreneurs who carried out the rapid industrialization of Pakistan is quite startling. The industrial firms controlled by some 30 Muslim families contributed something like 3 percent to total gross domestic product in 1959. The high degree of concentration meant that only a few effective entrepreneurs were required to carry out the rapid industrial development of Pakistan. On the other hand, concentration involved some potentially serious problems.

First, a good part of industry undoubtedly exacted monopoly profits from the consumers, traditionally and accurately called "hapless" under the circumstances. In most industries it required only price leadership by a single dominant firm, or a gentleman's agreement among less than a half dozen owners, to determine prices. Businessmen would have to be more saintly than shrewd to ignore such opportunities, and the rate of returns in Pakistan suggests that they preferred to be shrewd. Monopoly elements reduced the pressure for efficiency and for maximum output from a given investment.

Second, concentration of income and wealth is almost universally considered morally undesirable. These feelings were strengthened in Pakistan by the near-universal poverty, the emphasis on egalitarianism in Islam, and the fact that the dominant industrialists belonged to a few clearly identifiable groups and that many were presumed to have obtained their fortunes in part by circumventing the law.

Finally, concentration gave to a small group tremendous economic power, translatable into political influence. One way in which this influence was bound to be exerted was to prevent "cutthroat" or "unfair" competition or "unnecessary" investment. This meant that those who had arrived wanted to retain high protection against imports, prevent any new investment in their industry, and thus retain their monopoly position and high profits.

Concentration was not unmitigated. In several of the most important industries monopoly pricing had become difficult, if not impossible, by the late 1950's. In cotton textiles, for instance, there were well over 50 independent enterprises, each with more than 10,000 spindles. While two communities and less than a dozen firms had a large share of the assets, too many interests were involved for effective collusion. Other industries, notably jute, produced primarily for the world market and had little influence on prices. Some industries, for instance drugs and machinery, were given very limited protection and had to compete with imports. Finally, some industries included government or foreign firms, which made collusion much more difficult.

The potential existed for a rapid increase in the number of industrialists and consequently for lessening the dominance of a few families. It was obvious in the late 1950's that factory ownership was highly profitable and had become reasonably prestigious. With the rapid economic growth of the 1960's, the desire to enter industry or to expand industrial holdings had become widespread. Landlords, professionals, traders who missed the boat originally, civil servants, and even military officers increasingly clamored for permits that would let them in on an obviously good thing. This is confirmed by applications to government institutions and by discussions with would-be industrial investors.

The relative degree of concentration in Pakistan was probably not unusual compared to developed countries.

In the United States, for instance, something like one-half of 1 percent of all firms account for nearly 50 percent of all assets in manufacturing (2). In Germany, 50 companies were reported by the government to produce 23 percent of total industrial turnover (*128*). Obviously, however, the absolute number of units involved in Pakistan was so much smaller than in developed countries that the chance of monopoly or collusion was much greater. If a more appropriate index of concentration could be used (e.g., the share of assets in each industry controlled by the 4 largest units), the degree of concentration in Pakistan would be very much higher than in the developed world. That underdeveloped countries can, in many industries, support only a few units large enough to be efficient is a well known fact and problem. Equally obvious is the statement that, as Pakistan's economy continues to expand, the possibilities for competition can rapidly increase. Whether these possibilities are realized will depend to a considerable extent on whether government policy encourages new entrants or the expansion of existing firms.

SOME CONCLUSIONS

In Pakistan, the development of effective private industrial entrepreneurs was not a slow, haphazard process uninfluenced by government policies. It took place rapidly in response to economic stimuli, given the existence of groups in touch with the market and toleration by society of new activities. The behavior of the new industrialists was also significantly influenced by economic stimuli. At first very strong stimuli seemed necessary. Once initial resistances were overcome, weaker ones were sufficient to induce continued investment in established industry; to induce an expanded rate of investment in new, more complex industries; and to create additional entrepreneurs, many from groups that had previously shunned this activity. As a result of their quick response to changes in the economic situation, the rapid industrial development which has taken place in Pakistan could be and was largely in private hands.

Even if this analysis is accepted, it does not follow that future industrial development should be left largely to private enterprise. It does follow that it can be. It is possible in Pakistan to state with considerable confidence that entrepreneurs respond to economic incentives in deciding what investments to make, what to produce, and how to produce. In Pakistan, as in developed countries, there are at least some individuals who act largely as economic men in their business dealings.

Other issues that need to be taken into account in deciding on the role of the private sector in industrial development have not been touched on so far. The economic incentives that may be required to elicit the desired response from private enterprise can have serious disadvantages for economic, as well as political and moral, reasons. Concentration of wealth, and the distortion in economic decisions that may result, have been discussed but an analysis of their importance and of policies to deal with them has been postponed.

The two preceding chapters then had one major purpose: to examine whether economic incentives were instrumental in Pakistan in the development of a sufficient number of private entrepreneurs to carry out a large industrialization effort, and whether economic incentives can be used to affect the behavior of industrialists. This is a rather modest purpose, but there has been so much emphasis on the complex, ultimate, noneconomic factors in the genesis of entrepreneurship that an elaborate examination of evidence on this point is essential before discussing the role that private enterprise should play. Before doing this, however, the role of government, the development of agriculture and the sources of savings need to be examined.

CHAPTER IV

GENTLEMEN AT WORK

Planning and the
Government Development Program

A successful speculator, or a "merchant prince" may force his way into good society in England . . . but in India he must remain forever outside the sacred barrier which keeps the non-official world from the high society of service.

A LETTER (1857) (55, p. 247)

We do not think it to be a right policy for the State to offer such salaries to its servants as to attract the best available material. The correct place for our men of genius is in private enterprise and not in the humdrum career of public service where character and a desire to serve honestly for a living is more essential than outstanding intellect.

PAKISTAN PAY COMMISSION (1949) (55, p. 248)

Government must step in and establish industries. Without it development would not be one-third of what it is today.

A LEADING PAKISTANI BUSINESSMAN AND INDUSTRIALIST

PAKISTAN's rapid industrial development was obviously not the result of private initiative alone. Even the most rabid advocate of unbridled private enterprise would acknowledge the need for government to maintain law and order and to enforce some rules of the game. Like other governments, the government of Pakistan performed additional functions. It developed the infrastructure, provided credit, framed plans and policies, and carried out some industrial investment. Unlike private businessmen in some other countries, those of Pakistan joined the civil service, the political leadership, and intellectuals in assuming that government needed to play a decisive role in Pakistan's development.

THE GENTLEMEN OF THE CIVIL SERVICE

Without some understanding of Pakistan's civil service it is difficult to examine government economic policies and their effectiveness. The government in Pakistan was dominated by the civil service. Until 1958, the political leadership changed frequently; even when leaders had the capacity, they had little opportunity to become familiar with government operation. Civil servants participated frequently in the Cabinet. After 1958 the civil service and the military were dominant even at the political level of government. Traditionally power, prestige, and competence lay with the civil service, not with the political leadership (*142*).*

The Pakistan civil service was shaped in the pre-Independence period. Its most prominent component was and is a very small group of general administrators who held practically all senior positions — an elite in the true sense of the word. In the late 1950's some 400 of them administered a country of 100 million. Members of the administrative elite were selected in their early twenties, largely on the basis of a competitive examination. The ideal was a well-adjusted, intelligent, all-around individual. Participation in sports, an ability to write and talk well and to respond quickly on a wide range of subjects were more important for selection than a deep understanding of a few fields or an outstanding or unconventional intellect. By his middle twenties, one of these officials could be the administrator of, and the most powerful person in, an area

* For a more general discussion of the civil service, see (7); (55); (31); (11); and (54).

with a million people. His pay and benefits were 50 percent higher than those of his college classmates who joined the government but not the elite services. From then on he advanced regularly in the hierarchy, typically shifting between the administration of an area and the Provincial or Central governments. One year he was concerned with personnel policy, the next with agricultural development, and a few years later with price controls. His rank, influence, and specific function depended primarily on seniority, though actual performance and special aptitudes were also taken into account.

The result of this process of selection, training, experience, and promotion was the generalist par excellence, an educated gentleman, who made a remarkably fine civil servant. His greatest strength was in fields requiring a minimum of technical knowledge and a maximum of administrative ability. Protected in his career, well paid, and with high prestige, he maintained on the whole high standards of honesty and impartiality. Great responsibilities at an early age made for self-confidence, decisiveness, and an ability to work hard — of great importance when a tiny group administers the affairs of a large and complex country.

The weaknesses and limits of the group stemmed from the same set of circumstances. The generalists occupying all important positions had to make decisions which increasingly required technical knowledge they could not possess. Self-confidence and prestige often shaded into conceit and contempt for the technical staffs. The selection and promotion process was poorly adapted to deal with extremes in ability — it did not really penalize the incompetent, nor did it rapidly advance the brilliant individual. The most serious consequence was inflexibility. The outstanding civil servant who had not been accepted into the elite corps in his youth had little chance to reach a top position. Some men of ability were therefore wasted. The bulk of the civil service was less effective and more corrupt knowing that, almost regardless of performance, they were unlikely to be appointed to senior positions. The second main problem was that the civil service was out of touch with people's aspirations and not very effective in mobilizing widespread support. This was the result of the elite's self-contained, self-confident characteristics, its contempt of politics and politicians, and its isolation from the political process in a country where political organizations were in any case rather ineffective.

The bulk of the civil service, outside the elite groups, varied widely in quality. Activities that had been important in colonial times (and in which a significant number of Muslims had participated) had experienced people, prestige, and pay quite close to the elite groups; in this category were civil engineering, the railways, the army medical service, and the police. On the other hand, activities which had been of little importance in colonial days were often poorly staffed. These included most occupations having to do with agriculture and industry, modern education, and the formulation of economic policies.

In 1958 the newly installed military government brought changes in the civil service, as elsewhere. Some officers were assigned to civilian tasks, though most returned to military functions after a year or two. Much more important was the government's new strength vis-à-vis the civil service. Unlike previous governments, it fired a few officials accused of dishonesty or inefficiency. Occasionally, it ignored seniority to put outstanding individuals in charge of important programs. It reorganized the administration and changed policies, even if the changes were opposed by the civil service. Not all innovations were beneficial, but on the whole the civil service became more effective.

Civil service leadership came largely from families with a tradition of government service. Unlike the governing elites of other countries their antecedents were generally not landlords or businessmen. Their primary loyalty was to the nation, the government, their service, their family, or themselves, not to one of the major pressure groups seeking to influence government decisions.

TABLE 18. FAMILY BACKGROUNDS OF SOME
CIVIL SERVANTS (PERCENT).[a]

Background	All officials[b]	Elite group[c]
Government employees	64	64
Officials	33	58
Military	3	–
Clerical, etc.	28	6
Landowners	15	13
Large	6	10
Small	9	3
Businessmen	11	6
Professionals	6	13
Others	3	3

Source: (7, p. 53).

[a] Data refer to the profession of fathers of officials in the West Pakistan government stationed at Lahore, the Provincial capital.

[b] All "gazetted officers," that is, those officials sufficiently senior to be listed in the government gazette.

[c] The small elite service, the Civil Service of Pakistan (CSP).

The size and nature of the civil-service establishment meant first, that the government had an instrument for the effective execution of policies and programs; second, that government effectiveness was extremely variable, since the civil service was much stronger in some fields; third, that the really able and experienced civil servants were a tiny group, one of the scarcest resources in Pakistan.

THE GOVERNMENT INVESTMENT PROGRAM

A major function of the government and civil service was to carry out a large investment program, particularly for the development of the infrastructure. A theme that recurs in writings on development is the limited capacity of governments to carry out such programs and the slow increase in their capacity. Elaborate theories for allocating foreign aid have been built on this notion (*121*). If the "executing capacity" of governments is limited and increases only slowly, then there is a definite limit to the aid which countries can absorb effectively. This argument makes sense only in terms of a minimum acceptable rate of return, for the executing capacity of any government would be very great indeed if it was only required to spend money, regardless of return. If a rate-of-return criterion is adopted it means that executing capacity is not limited by the point at which *some* waste, or inefficiency, or corruption occurs, but only by the point at which the resulting losses become so great that the rate of return falls to an unacceptable level. If the criterion was the absence of *any* waste or inefficiency or corruption, no government or private firm anywhere would have a significant executing capacity. (In discussions of foreign aid one often gets the impression that American standards of expected efficiency and probity are higher for underdeveloped countries than for some government or private agencies in the United States itself.)

In the early 1950's the size of the government investment program and the efficiency of its execution were inadequate to prevent bottlenecks. The result was considerable waste in the private sector. Inadequate public power meant that individual industrial firms had to install their own costly power-generating equipment; shortages of equipment meant they had to wait weeks for railway wagons. The arrival of irrigation water at the wrong time or in the wrong amount reduced its benefits. Roads deteriorated for lack of adequate maintenance, even as new roads were built at great expense.

The total size of the investment program increased quickly as the government recovered from the initial disorganization following Independence and Partition. From 1949–50 to 1964–65 gross government investment more than doubled every 5 years in real terms (see Table 2). Government investment could have been stepped up further in some fields if foreign exchange had been available.

With this rapid increase in the size of the government investment program, efficiency might be expected to decline. There is no conclusive evidence, and very little that is even convincing, on what happened to the efficiency of, or to the return from, government investment over time. One can find the usual horror stories, inevitable in any large organization — whether public or private — of bribery and pilferage, and of investment not used to capacity, not properly maintained, or not fully suited to the task. One has only to read the remarkably frank reports written in the 1960's on the development program (by the Progressing Wing, President's Secretariat) to find projects for which "the progress is very slow," that "could not make any headway," whose "delay is upsetting the land development programme," with "cost of construction turning out in excess of estimates." A 1961 survey of the railways, a comparatively well run organization, found overstaffing, poor organizational arrangements, inadequate collection of fares, and low staff morale (130; 131).

Yet one can cite other stories to show that the efficiency of the government increased, despite — or with — a rapid increase in the investment program. The ton-miles of freight carried per railway wagon in West Pakistan in-

creased from 115,000 in 1955–56 to 137,000 in 1960–61
(138). The files for government development projects began to show a greatly reduced time lag between original
submission for approval and final decision. Also an increasing number of projects were approved at a lower level in
the hierarchy. The expertise with which the investment
budget was prepared improved. Of the industrial firms
interviewed in 1960 for the Survey, only 5 percent mentioned that the government's failure to provide facilities
was the most serious difficulty they faced, though about
one-quarter mentioned this as one of the difficulties. Only
a negligible number of firms gave lack of facilities as a
reason for below-capacity operations. An inadequate supply of power, transport, and water was a problem, but does
not seem to have been crucial.

Neither individual horror stories nor individual suc-
cesses are conclusive in assessing the results of the government investment program, and no suitable over-all
quantitative measures are available. The rate of industrial
growth is the best evidence that government agencies
were able to develop the infrastructure required by industry with sufficient speed and efficiency. The lack of power,
transport, or urban facilities never seriously slowed down
industrial production. One very crude index of industrial
efficiency, the relationship between the cost of investment
and the value of output, showed a rapid improvement in
the first few years after Partition, but then remained remarkably stable despite a sharp increase in the rate of
investment (141, p. 474). Also, many foreigners and Pakistanis close to the development program agree that,
compared with the middle 1950's, government projects in
the 1960's were better prepared, that their relative priority
was more carefully determined, that they were executed
with less waste, and managed more efficiently on completion (176; 178). The capacity of the government to carry

out investment programs increased very rapidly, probably even more rapidly than the size of the programs themselves, which more than doubled every 5 years.

There were a number of reasons for this. First, several government organizations were quite well staffed and organized from the beginning. As they recovered from the initial disorganization following Independence and Partition, they learned to use increasing amounts of capital effectively. The railways were a prime example. Second, there were a number of investments which required little technical knowledge, administration, or suitable institutions. A good example was the construction of a power station with imported machinery, which required only a handful of technicians and presented no complex organizational problems. Third, executing capacity was expanded rapidly in some fields by the use of foreign technicians. The Pakistan government was willing to use foreigners to a considerable extent, especially in the 1960's; such specialized and unique investments as the laying of a pipeline were entrusted entirely to foreigners. In the field of water and power development there were in 1964 about 1,000 foreign technicians in West Pakistan alone, working together with and under Pakistani technicians. Fourth, the effect of a rising rate of investment on executing capacity was an important point that is often overlooked. In the very short run, the higher the rate of investment, the more strain there is on existing manpower and organization, and therefore the less is the direct economic efficiency of investment. At the same time, however, there is no education so rapid and practical as the responsibility for carrying through an investment project. For a variety of political and economic reasons, the investment program was always somewhat bigger than the government could carry out comfortably. As a result, there was continuous pressure for more and better people from agencies that were already short-handed; from foreign sources of funds for the better use of aid; from the political leadership for better organization in order to carry out a program to which they were committed. These and other pressures resulted in a considerable decentralization of responsibility, the establishment of semiautonomous government agencies with greater flexibility on personnel and other policies, and considerable departure from seniority in order to place the abler civil servants in positions where they could do the most good. This process was accelerated in the 1960's by firm leadership. Government organization is far from perfect, but definitely much improved as a result of the pressure exerted by a rapidly rising rate of investment.*

PLANNING†

The government's management of the economy as a whole also improved gradually. Until the mid-1950's Pakistan had no machinery systematically to examine alternative programs and policies, to consider the full range of facts relevant to a decision, or to bring the alternatives to a political authority for decision. Nevertheless, many sensible decisions were made, and some turned out to be positively brilliant. For instance, it would have been difficult to devise a better set of policies than those actually followed in the early 1950's for rapid development of industry and for creating industrial entrepreneurs. But these policies were in part the result of accident and in part ad hoc decisions to deal with particular problems. They were not adopted as an integrated program to achieve a particular goal. Inevitably, many other policies and pro-

---

* For further discussion of both achievement and shortcomings see (100).

† For a further discussion of planning, see (91, 176, and 178).

grams suffered from inadequate staff work and economic competence.

Some investments made by government agencies were poorly planned. As a result dams were completed before irrigation channels to use their water were begun. Tax policies sometimes sacrificed export earnings to revenues because there was a strong agency concerned with revenues but no agency responsible for exports. Priorities for government attention were distorted, as strong agencies pushed through low-priority investment projects while weak sponsors let high-priority ones go by default. Dealings with the private sector were mainly administrative in character and involved direct, specific controls by government, in part because there was little knowledge about alternative indirect techniques. Excess capacity was permitted or encouraged in some industries because no systematic attempt had been made to forecast demand or the availability of raw materials.

Over a decade, however, a sophisticated machinery for framing economic policies and programs was developed. Separate planning agencies for the Central and the two Provincial governments were created. They became extremely influential, probably more so than any other central planning or economic staff in the underdeveloped world. By the middle 1960's they were usually consulted on all important economic decisions.

The planning agencies could be influential on all matters in the economic field, first, because they acted only as staff agencies with no significant executive responsibility. A second determinant of their importance has been the backing they have received, at least intermittently, from the highest political authorities. Planning bodies are rarely loved or admired by others in government. As coordinating agencies concerned with the allocation of resources, they inevitably come into conflict with agencies that do not want to be coordinated, that do not want economic criteria to supersede technical criteria, or that feel ill-treated in the allocation of resources. Without executive or political power in their own right, coordinating agencies can survive only if their judgment is backed frequently by someone who can implement their recommendations. In Pakistan this backing has come at various times from a powerful Finance Minister, a Prime Minister, or the President. A third ingredient in the role of Pakistan's planning agencies has been their professional competence. Such staff agencies will not long survive the hostility they inevitably generate if their professional work is not obviously useful. One highly valued function of the planning agencies was to prepare the professional documentation required by various foreign and international agencies. The use of foreign technicians helped greatly in establishing the agencies' professional competence.

Progress in establishing machinery to frame economic policies and plans was not limited to the planning agencies. Special bodies were established to systematically consider foreign exchange policies and allocate foreign exchange, to examine proposals by foreign private investors, to screen government projects, and to relate annual budgets and proposed private investment to the Five-Year Plans.

The development of a well-articulated machinery for framing economic policies and programs was a continuing process. Despite frequent changes at the political level, a great deal of progress was made between 1954 and 1958. The planning agencies and related bodies were so obviously useful that successive governments maintained them for staff work on economic problems. It was not until 1959, however, that a government made economic development a central plank in its political program. Therefore, it particularly needed staff agencies with economic competence. The new government also had the power to carry out acceptable economic advice, and expected to be in office long enough to weather the short-run costs of its policies. The new government thus gave the professional planning and policy machinery more backing than it had earlier received. During the 1960's the planning agencies came into their own.

Pakistanis produced professional staff work dealing competently with sophisticated economic policies and programs. There was a machinery for systematically considering the staff work and reaching a decision. Of course, staff work was not always of high quality, appropriate decision-making machinery was not always used, and decisions were sometimes based on personal or irrational considerations or, more frequently, on political rather than economic criteria. But then, there are no governments about which such statements could not be made. By 1965 Pakistan had the machinery to rationally examine and execute quite sophisticated economic policies. If it wanted to engage in considerable planning, it had the means to do so without making many more mistakes than would be inherent in the task or inevitable in most governments run by men.

CREDIT FOR INDUSTRY

Besides providing much of the infrastructure and doing the over-all planning which affected the economy as a whole, the government also carried out two activities specifically concerned with industrial development. It was instrumental in setting up institutions to provide credit to private investors, and it invested directly in industry. Government credit was extended on an ad hoc basis almost from the beginning of Pakistan. After Independence industrial investment was considered very risky, private credit for such investment was practically nonexistent, and most potential entrepreneurs had little capital. The government offer to provide capital was influential at that stage in convincing a private entrepreneur to start the first large cotton textile mill. The instance was isolated, though important. Subsequently formal credit institutions were set up. One agency, the Pakistan Industrial Finance Corporation (PIFCO), was started in 1949 to provide mortgage funds to existing companies. It was converted into the Industrial Development Bank of Pakistan (IDBP) in 1961, its scope widened to include new firms, and narrowed to medium-sized units. The Pakistan Industrial Credit and Investment Corporation (PICIC) was established in 1957 to make loans and equity investment for the expansion of existing or the establishment of new enterprises. It was to act not only as financier but to undertake promotional activities as well.

Neither credit agency played much of a role in Pakistan's early industrial development. As credit agencies, their control over the use of the funds they provided was limited. They therefore had to be cautious about their borrowers. For PIFCO, caution was reinforced by its conception and management as a banking institution, especially since it followed the tradition of British rather than Continental banks. Caution was also indicated for PICIC by its semiprivate character; private investors naturally were interested in a reasonably safe return. The understandable tendency of both agencies was to support the larger, established enterprise with good security and a known high rate of profit. It was estimated that PICIC provided nearly half of all its loans to a tiny group of leading industrialists, while IDBP distributed its small loans more widely. As late as the early 1960's, both preferred to concentrate in West Pakistan and on textile, food products (sugar), and other industries which were well established.

Both agencies also found that large firms had more capital than they needed. Lending to small firms was risky. The reasonably safe, medium-sized investment, for which PIFCO and PICIC were willing to lend, could often be financed by the entrepreneur himself, using profits from trade or from his existing industrial enterprises. Their total contribution to capital requirements therefore remained limited. The disbursed loans outstanding in 1961 were Rs. 8.5 crores for PICIC and Rs. 7.5 crores for IDBP — both small amounts when measured against total industrial assets of around Rs. 600 crores.

Both institutions became somewhat more venturesome as they gained confidence and reserves, as industrial development reached new areas and groups, and as pressures for investment in East Pakistan increased. In 1963 they were providing more loans than earlier to East Pakistan, to medium-sized firms, and to relative newcomers. The emphasis on consumer goods industries, however, continued and the credit agencies' contribution to total industrial assets remained small.

In the 1960's both agencies became useful in allocating foreign exchange to private investors. A large proportion of borrowers came to PICIC and IDBP not because they needed credit, but to obtain foreign exchange. Some of the local currency loans in fact were tie-in sales: borrowers were required to take a rupee loan and pay interest on it in order to obtain foreign exchange. These semi-independent credit agencies had some advantages over government departments in allocating foreign exchange. They were less subject to political influence since foreign and Pakistani investors, concerned about the rate of return on their funds, were associated with the allocation process. (On the other hand, neither group was anxious for the credit

TABLE 19. LOANS PROVIDED TO PRIVATE INDUSTRY BY
PICIC AND IDBP (PIFCO), BY CHARACTERISTICS
OF CREDIT (PERCENT OF TOTAL).

	PICIC		IDBP	
Characteristics	1961–62	1963	1961–62	1963
By currency				
Foreign exchange	87	92	79	67
Domestic	13	8	21	33
By size of loan				
Rs. 1 million or above	71	78	–	64
Below Rs. 1 million	29	22	–	36
By region				
West Pakistan	67	61	67	42
East Pakistan	33	39	33	58
By industry group				
Textiles	31	39	61	62
Processing of agricultural products	27	22	19	14
Machinery and chemicals	21	20	12	11
Other	21	19	8	13

Sources: PICIC (135; 136); IDBP (101; 102; 103).

agencies to follow a particularly venturesome policy with
respect to newcomers.) PICIC and IDBP also had more
flexibility in procedures and personnel practices than a
government department. Their exposure to economic pressure made it less likely that they would support uneconomic investments requiring continuing subsidies. Finally,
foreign suppliers of funds preferred dealing with a semiprivate credit agency rather than a government department. Allocation of foreign exchange was a useful function
for the two credit agencies, though hardly the purpose for
which they had been set up.

In addition, both agencies made other contributions to
later industrial development. PICIC helped bring together
some foreign and Pakistani investors. By providing tech-

nical assistance to Pakistani entrepreneurs, and by developing rather rigorous procedures for loan applicants, it forced borrowers to examine potential investments carefully, to improve their operation, and to deal more honestly with the tax collector.

Both industrial credit agencies were faced with the dilemma of semigovernmental enterprises. To innovate, to enter new fields or areas of the country, involved substantial risks. Losses could subject the agencies to attack for wasting government and foreign funds. A less innovating policy was less risky, but resulted in a negligible contribution to early industrial development. PICIC and IDBP (PIFCO) became really active only a decade after Independence. By that time Pakistan had developed entrepreneurs with sufficient capital and know-how to undertake all but the most risky investments or those with extremely high capital requirements. However, by the middle 1960's, PICIC and IDBP were beginning to support newcomers. Their function then was not so much to step up the rate of industrial growth as to reduce the concentration of control. They were the agencies not of Pakistan's impetuous youth, but of its industrial middle age.

THE PAKISTAN INDUSTRIAL DEVELOPMENT CORPORATION

More controversial and important than the credit agencies was the semiautonomous government company which developed and operated industrial enterprises, the Pakistan Industrial Development Corporation (PIDC). Although it made an important contribution, the PIDC was neither the initiator nor the primary agent of Pakistan's industrial development. It was not established until 1950, its Board was not constituted until 1952, and its first substantial investment did not take place until 1952–53. By then private industrial investment was well under way.

By 1953–54 PIDC's cumulative expenditures were only Rs. 17 crores, or about 7 percent of total industrial assets (*137*). (PIDC expenditures on nonindustrial projects have been subtracted. Subsequent PIDC data, unless other sources are cited, are from the same report.) It was not until 1956–57, almost a decade after the beginning of Pakistan's industrial growth, that PIDC investment exceeded 10 percent of total industrial assets. In industries with substantial profit incentives, private entrepreneurship preceded PIDC activity and did not depend on it.

The PIDC, however, pioneered in industries and areas which were neglected by private investors during the early period of industrialization. There were a number of reasons for such neglect. First, some investments exceeded the capital available to any individual, family, or group. Given the rudimentary nature of the organized capital market, and the unwillingness of entrepreneurs to pool their interests with other families, projects were limited by the capital available to one family. Private entrepreneurs were reluctant to borrow from the government since this would involve government control and supervision. At the same time, the government did not seem to have considered the alternative of lending to private entrepreneurs during the period of early industrial development. The first reason for PIDC, then, was the existence of investments acknowledged by private businessmen to be beyond their capital capacity.

Second, many of the investments needing a large amount of capital also required management of a high order, unavailable to all but a handful of private entrepreneurs. The PIDC hired a complete management staff from abroad for some of its projects. Private entrepreneurs were willing to use foreign technicians, but to turn over management to someone outside the family seemed strange and dangerous.

Third, there were complex projects requiring a long period between initial investment and profitable operation. For many PIDC projects, the construction period and the breaking-in time was 4 to 5 years (or even longer), though private investment in textiles often produced substantial profits 2 to 3 years after initial investment. There were risks involved in postponing returns — the risk that significant political changes would occur meanwhile, that import competition would be greater by the time the factory came into production, that taxes would change, or that reinvestment of earnings would become more difficult. The real time discount with which private Pakistani entrepreneurs were operating might be 50 percent per year. No wonder they were reluctant to invest in projects with long deferred and uncertain returns. A government corporation with access to government funds was not under much pressure to make profits. It could also afford not to worry about possible changes in taxes or government import policy.

Finally, some locations were unattractive to private investors because facilities were lacking, or political problems existed. A government corporation was in a better position to concentrate investment in a particular town, providing its own facilities for a number of projects and thus reducing their individual cost. In other words, it was better able to carry out investments with substantial external economies. It would also get more government cooperation in dealing with political problems and in developing facilities in backward regions.

In the case of some investments, several of the factors listed above occurred simultaneously. The very large Karnafuli paper mill in East Pakistan is an excellent example. The Karnafuli mill needed an investment of Rs. 12 crores (compared to Rs. 3 crores for a textile mill). It required a large "foreign" management staff, which was originally recruited from South Indian refugees, several of whom were killed in a riot — not the sort of situation private industrialists dote on. The plant was located in an inaccessible, primitive area of East Pakistan. There were political problems in dealing with a tribal Buddhist minority. It was decided to undertake this project in 1949–50; production began in 1954; and capacity was not reached until about 1956, a period of over 6 years. The paper mill was part of a complex investment program calling for an expensive access road, a very large dam to provide power and permit water transport for raw materials for the mill, and housing and communications facilities. This was a natural project for the PIDC and one which private entrepreneurs would not have undertaken on their own until at least half a dozen years later.

The PIDC concentrated on pioneering enterprises, but part of its investment arose from its preferred treatment by the government. It was favored over private enterprise in obtaining land, power, transport facilities, and above all, permission to import. Since it was one of the most powerful government bodies, it could approach other government agencies as an equal, rather than as a supplicant, the usual role of private entrepreneurs. As a result, some private entrepreneurs were delighted to have the PIDC join them in a venture because this assured safe passage through the bureaucratic jungles. The PIDC was also particularly suitable as a vehicle for government subsidies. A subsidy to a private firm was obvious and might raise awkward questions about its desirability. It could also result in strong pressures from other private firms for more and larger subsidies. A PIDC project could be subsidized discreetly and indirectly as the government absorbed the interest charges and any losses.

The PIDC was able to perform its functions only because it made maximum use of scarce entrepreneurship.

It is often argued that the major drawback of government enterprise is the inevitable close control exercised by political authorities and the regular civil service (50, Chap. 8). Such control is said to discourage risk-taking and innovation, and to cause delays in decision, all of which are worse for a modern industrial unit than are wrong decisions. This was not so in Pakistan.

Like Enrico Mattei in Italy, Robert Moses in New York, or Abol Hassan Ebtehaj in Iran, Ghulam Faruque, the first head of the PIDC, was a strong-willed, powerful individual who made rapid decisions, saw them carried out, and worried about government rules, procedures, or approval only afterwards, if at all. He was prepared to take substantial risks, smothered opposition by a combination of ability and ruthlessness, and thought constantly in terms of growth and expansion. As did some of his counterparts, he effectively used his control over huge investment funds, contracts, jobs, and advertising expenditures to develop a position of power. Very few political leaders or civil servants were prepared for the fight required to exercise much control over PIDC policies.

The PIDC used foreign technicians and managers wherever desirable, as did private entrepreneurs; but it could go further since it had fewer problems finding the necessary foreign exchange and no relatives who had to be given jobs. Its charter as a semi-independent corporation allowed it flexibility in salaries and personnel policies, so it could attract a good professional staff. Some especially able people considered it patriotic to work for PIDC and saw more possibility of advancement there since they did not have to compete with brothers, cousins, and nephews in a family enterprise. PIDC managers came from a background quite different from that of private entrepreneurs. Typically from the Punjab (not Bombay), they were well educated and had experience in other industry or management activities. The PIDC relied heavily on specialists — accountants, engineers, salesmen, and advertising men — and it operated in the manner of large, modern firms throughout the world. The entrepreneur at its head delegated authority for operation to his Pakistani or foreign managers, and concentrated on pushing through new projects.

Unhampered by excessive government control or supervision, the PIDC was able to move rapidly and effectively. By 1959, only 6 years from the time it started to invest on a significant scale, PIDC held an interest in completed industrial enterprises with assets of Rs. 85 crores ($170 million) and had itself invested over Rs. 60 crores ($120 million) (13). It thus had an interest in about one-sixth of total industrial assets. It was asked to take over coal mines and a textile mill from government departments because the PIDC operated more effectively than the regular governmental units.

The very effectiveness of the PIDC as an entrepreneurial unit, however, caused some problems. The PIDC had to have strong leadership and considerable freedom of action; in both respects it resembled a private firm. But a private firm that makes too many mistakes finds expansion difficult and may face bankruptcy; the PIDC was not exposed to such economic pressures. It could invest in and operate uneconomic enterprises on government funds. Its performance was not measured against any specific criteria. The length of time for which it could incur losses, or the rate of profit it needed to show eventually, were not defined.

Many of the PIDC's decisions were good; inevitably some were bad. The most serious error probably was in pressing ahead with some lower priority investments at the expense of higher priority ones. The PIDC in the 1950's spent 20 percent of its funds on shipyards and engi-

neering works and devoted a great deal of effort to a
steel-mill project, while neglecting the chemicals, especially cement and fertilizer. (It is odd how universal these
prejudices are, probably because of the importance of
metals in the development of the West, and especially the
U.S.S.R., and a lack of appreciation for the change in technology in the last decade or two.) Pakistan had neither
the raw-material base for the metal-working industry nor
the technicians and skilled labor required for its complex
technology. In the 1950's, investment in metal working was
probably premature. It proved unprofitable and made only
a very limited contribution to foreign-exchange savings.
Similarly, the development of sugar growing and refining
under PIDC auspices (15 percent of its total investment),
turned out to be a costly operation. Sugar demanded large
quantities of scarce water which, if used on cotton, might
have given a higher rate of return to the economy, especially in terms of scarce foreign exchange (127). Private
firms would not have pushed vigorously for a large expansion in these two fields. The PIDC could and did.

Foreign exchange required for low-priority PIDC projects meant that less was available for other PIDC investments or for imported raw materials and spare parts. The
PIDC's influence on government allocation of foreign exchange meant that it carried out some investment at the
expense of idle capacity in the private sector.

The PIDC also had less incentive than private firms to
reduce investment costs and to increase efficiency in established plants. The evidence on this is not at all conclusive because little comparable data exist for private
firms. It is hard to determine whether the PIDC's high
costs resulted from circumstances universal in Pakistan or
confined to the PIDC. The limited evidence which is available is cited below since the efficiency of government enterprise is an important issue.

A 1958 study analyzing 14 PIDC projects showed that
for many projects the actual completion dates were one
to three years later than the estimated completion dates;
that the actual investment cost was about two-thirds
higher than the estimated cost; that production averaged
50 percent or less of rated capacity; and that there were
a number of cases where actual production costs exceeded
estimated costs by 25 to 50 percent, or more. This clearly
indicates that PIDC estimates were erroneous, but their
optimism was probably intentional, in order to assure government approval of projects. Undoubtedly private investors also found that they had underestimated their
difficulties and costs.

By 1959, the rate of return on investment for the PIDC
was substantially less than one-half of the rate reported by
private firms, and the difference would have been even
greater if the real rates of return to private investment
were available. It should be noted, however, that the
PIDC's low returns came in part from industries which
the government wanted developed and which private investors were avoiding precisely because expected returns
were low. PIDC showed almost no return on investment
in jute, substantial losses on shipyards and engineering
works, and smaller losses on sugar mills.

A comparison of plants in industries having both PIDC
and private firms (jute, cement, sugar, and cotton textiles)
is of only limited use. The prices received by sugar mills
were fixed separately for each firm, based on assumed cost
of production. Since the private sugar mills in East Pakistan were Indian-owned, their prices were undoubtedly
fixed to assure that their profits were not too high. Cement
plants in West Pakistan were also Indian-owned, and cotton textile mills in East Pakistan were largely Hindu-
owned. While the government did not fix the prices for
individual firms in the cement or cotton textile industries,

it undoubtedly treated these private firms less favorably than the PIDC with respect to import licenses and facilities. The more favorable rate of return of the PIDC firms in these 3 industries is therefore not strong evidence. In the one industry where a direct comparison between private Muslim firms and the PIDC is possible (jute), the private firms reported a higher rate of return. Though the reported difference was not great, the real difference undoubtedly was.

TABLE 20. RETURNS OF PIDC AND PRIVATE FIRMS, 1958.[a]

Industry	Location	RETURNS[b] (percent of assets)		NUMBER OF FIRMS	
		PIDC	Private	PIDC	Private
Cotton textiles	East Pakistan	18	12	1	42
Sugar	East Pakistan	20	4	1	8
Cement	West Pakistan	17	15	1	4
Jute goods	East Pakistan	4	6	1	9

Source: Survey.

[a] Of course these are reported figures which, especially for the private sector, are undoubtedly grossly understated. Jute profits increased greatly after 1958 with the introduction of "bonus vouchers."

[b] Returns are the sum of profits, depreciation, interest and managing agency fees.

Another bit of evidence about the efficiency of the PIDC comes from the returns of PIDC public-limited companies in West Pakistan in the 1960's. Most of these companies had been in operation for 5 to 6 years, so the period of severe teething troubles should have been behind them. They were located in West Pakistan, where private profits had been very high. They included one of the most successful (Zeal-Pak cement) and one of the least successful (Karachi Shipyard and Engineering) of the large PIDC firms. For these 8 manufacturing enterprises, the gross rate of return for 1960–61 to 1962–63 averaged 6 percent. The rate of profit is only about one-quarter, and the rate of return only about one-half, the rates reported by large private firms in the low-profit year of 1958.

The problems faced by a semigovernmental agency such as the PIDC in maintaining efficiency in the absence of very strong leadership are shown by its fertilizer-plant project in West Pakistan. The project costs were nearly one-third over estimates. Failure to carry out a soil survey resulted in additional expenditures. The contract with a foreign firm related its fee directly to investment costs, thus giving the foreign firm an incentive to increase costs. The factory operated far below capacity for some time and was considered technically inadequate. This example occurred 10 years after the PIDC started operating, when errors of this kind should have been avoidable, and seems to have been the result of PIDC's inability to resist government pressures.

The PIDC's difficulties stemmed in part from frequent changes in top management and were compounded by the inexperience of most appointees. Civil servants (or military men) with no experience in business or industry dominated the PIDC Board. Some of them had little interest or aptitude for industrial management, and treated their Board membership like a regular government posting. Others, who were deeply interested and showed a real flair for industrial management, were often transferred to other posts by the time they had added experience to interest. Turnover among plant managers was less frequent, but was still more frequent than in private firms. This aspect of personnel policy was bound to reduce efficiency.

The discussion so far does not lead to any clear-cut conclusion on the relative efficiency of PIDC management, either in investment or in operation. Some evidence has been provided to support the judgment of one of the most experienced and able of the PIDC directors that ". . . it would probably be true to say that while the PIDC enjoyed an advantage over private parties in planning, financing, and erecting its factories, it was at a disadvantage in the operation of the industries established" (13). What this means, in effect, is that the PIDC was an effective entrepreneur. Like private firms, it paid little attention at first to the cost of its investment, or to the efficiency of its operation. Some private firms, under the pressure of competition, changed their attitudes, but the PIDC, able to draw on government funds, seems to have been less responsive to pressure for reducing costs.

So much for the PIDC's role as entrepreneur and manager. In addition to its pioneering role in some industries, it was also expected to invest in areas neglected by private enterprise. It did pay particular attention to backward areas within the Provinces. But, at least in the first crucial years, it further accentuated the tendency for industry to be concentrated in West Pakistan. At the end of 1958, almost two-thirds of net government investment through the PIDC was in West Pakistan, including Karachi, and only a little over one-third in East Pakistan. (Including foreign loans channeled through government and subtracting refunds to government, the figures were: West, 62 percent, East, 38 percent.) One can only speculate on the reasons. Part of the answer lies in development by PIDC of natural gas in West Pakistan and the better infrastructure there. More important was the PIDC's success in selling most of its interest in the large paper mill and in some jute mills in East Pakistan to private investors, thus reducing its net investment. The belief in East Pakistan that the disparity reflected bias hastened the establishment of separate PIDC's for the Provinces.

The general usefulness of the PIDC as an entrepreneur

declined in the late 1950's. By then, private entrepreneurs were able to make almost any potentially profitable investment. There were 13 industrial families, each with ready access to at least Rs. 3 crores ($6 million) for investment, and a few families had, or could obtain, Rs. 10–20 crores ($20–40 million). By 1960 there was no shortage of would-be entrepreneurs in general, and there were industrialists prepared to invest in complex enterprises such as a paper mill or in chemicals. Monopoly elements had become less important in most consumer-goods industries. Export industries were compensated for the overvaluation of the rupee.

Though the PIDC was less important in unprofitable export industries, or in projects beyond the capital or management capacity of private firms, there were two exceptions. First, emphasis in the 1960's shifted to intermediate and capital-goods industries where investment was more "lumpy" — an efficient factory is large — than for consumer goods. In some industries a single efficient factory in each Province was adequate to supply the market. The PIDC's function as a developer of monopoly industries therefore continued to be important. Second, industrial development in East Pakistan was likely to require a large role for its PIDC. The third Five-Year Plan called for a massive increase in industrial investment in the Province. There was no shortage of private entrepreneurs to carry out this program, but most of them were not considered "indigenous" to the Province. Continued domination of industrial development in East Pakistan by "outsiders" was not considered politically acceptable. The proposed investment seemed beyond the capacity of existing "indigenous," that is Muslim Bengali, industrialists. Not until the 1960's had this group acquired the experience and capital achieved by non-Bengalis a decade earlier.

The PIDC, as an arm of the "indigenous" East Pakistan government, therefore had a large role to play in that Province.

In the 1960's the two Provincial PIDCs were expected to continue heavy investment, at least in monopoly industries and in East Pakistan. They acquired complex management problems as the number of their plants grew. There was danger that they might use their influence with government to increase the level of protection or subsidy they enjoyed. Under pressure to show profits, the PIDCs were undoubtedly tempted to use their special position to preempt some profitable investment opportunities. Two rather obvious policy changes therefore seemed indicated. First, the PIDCs could sell their well-established enterprises in order to reduce the complexity of their management task, reduce their responsibility for operations where their weaknesses were greatest, and free their hands for investment where their strength lay. Second, they could concentrate on the few new industries and areas where private interest was still weak. Both policies were adopted to some extent.

However, like all government operations, the PIDCs faced a real difficulty in disposing of their assets. They could sell the profitable plants without difficulty, but part of their portfolio consisted of unprofitable units. The management was reluctant to sell its ailing ventures below book value, since this might reflect on the PIDC's judgment in making the investment originally. To sell only the profitable units would leave the PIDCs open to criticism because they would be left with a disproportionate number of losers. Any sales also reduced the scope and power of the organization and the prestige of its officers. They were naturally reluctant to carry this process very far. By 1959, the PIDC therefore had transferred only Rs. 9.5

crores, or a bit over 10 percent of its total investment in completed industrial plants.* While this was a significant amount, investment continued to exceed the proceeds realized from the sale of plants. Thus PIDC's total holdings continued to increase and, with them, the complexity of its management problems.

One can doubt that the PIDC will be able to execute the planned program in East Pakistan without great difficulty. The East Pakistan PIDC was investing about Rs. 20 crores a year in 1964–65. In the 5 years of the Third Plan it is supposed to invest about Rs. 225 crores, or about Rs. 45 crores a year (37). Thus by 1970 the two PIDCs should be managing an industrial empire roughly equal to the total of Pakistan's industrial assets in 1959. The latter was managed by at least 100 large-scale private Pakistani, foreign, and government units, and another 2,000 small private units. Maybe the PIDC will succeed; in any case its chances will be improved if there is an acceleration in sales to private firms and further delegation of authority for management.

The available evidence suggests that in the 1950's the PIDC fulfilled an extremely useful function in supplementing private enterprise. The PIDC gave to one, able entrepreneur command over the resources required for investments involving too much capital, or too complex a technology, or too much risk, for private investors. It had sufficient independence from political and administrative controls to carry out a large investment program rapidly and, on the whole, efficiently. However, independence, plus financial backing from the government, also insulated the PIDC from economic pressures and allowed it to carry out low-priority investments and to incur high investment

---

* PIDC investment from (13); sales to private investors from an unpublished memo in the Industries Section of the Planning Board and from the Survey.

and operating costs. As private firms became able to undertake most of the potentially profitable investments, the PIDC's effectiveness as an entrepreneur became less important in West Pakistan, while its drawbacks as a manager were more apparent. Its entrepreneurial function will increase in East Pakistan as long as "indigenous" entrepreneurship is inadequate and domination of investment by others is unacceptable. The PIDCs' role will also be increased by the shift away from consumer-goods industries. To play the entrepreneurial role creditably will require a substantial acceleration in the sale of established enterprises and further delegation of managerial responsibilities.

CHAPTER V

THE RISE AND DECLINE OF CONTROLS

In dealing with industrialists exhortation and threats produce no results.

A PAKISTANI GOVERNMENT OFFICIAL

Price and profit controls . . . sprung from the belief that (the) free market invariably tries to "exploit." . . . These medieval ideas of a "just" price naturally led to several absurdities.

A GOVERNMENT ECONOMIST (92)

THE PAKISTAN Industrial Development Corporation played an important, though limited, role in developing the economy. The contribution of industrial credit agencies was marginal. The government's important functions were the development of the infrastructure, and the execution of policies which controlled or guided private actions. Effective government action in these respects, largely creditable to the gentlemen of the civil service, made rapid private investment possible.

PROTECTION

Government control over foreign transactions was a necessary condition for industrial development. The need for infant-industry protection is widely accepted — and few countries had industries as young as those of Pakistan. It is sometimes argued that this kind of protection is required primarily until industry has a market sufficiently large to permit capacity operation of optimum-sized plants.

For most of Pakistan's industry, however, inadequate plant size was not the problem. Firms in such industries as cotton textiles, jute, cement, and simple metal-working could reach the optimum scale within the Pakistan market. This problem may be more relevant for future development; some petrochemical processes, for instance, involve substantial economies of scale, and optimum-sized plants may be too large for domestic demand.

Two more important reasons for protection existed in Pakistan. First, service, supply, and marketing facilities were inadequate for many years because industry had not developed to a scale which would justify some specialized services. Even in 1964, the textile industry, by far the most developed in Pakistan, was too small to warrant the establishment of training facilities for textile engineers and technicians, or an extensive marketing organization outside Pakistan. Earlier, this industry had to import packaging materials, dyes, and chemicals because the internal demand was inadequate to support even one efficient supplier. The absence of external economies affected even more the costs of industries other than textiles.

Second, most Pakistan industries had teething troubles, more elegantly called "the learning curve," and not always recognized in the discussion of infant industries. A new plant always operates inefficiently until management, technicians, and supervisors learn to work together, until schedules of materials' arrival and dispatch are worked out, until workers know their way around. A rapidly developing industry has a high proportion of new plants going through their running-in period. In Pakistan most industries were new in the country. To develop a skilled labor force and experienced management, and to create specialized supplying, servicing, and marketing operations, was costly and time-consuming, even where the scale of the industry was adequate to support both train-

ing and auxiliary services. Finally, there were teething
problems for industry as a whole. The supply of power,
transport, and other facilities lagged behind industrial
growth. The availability of manpower lagged behind the
need for a stable labor force. Because industry in Pakistan
as a whole grew very rapidly, these universal problems
of adjustment, of lag, of friction were greatly aggravated.

Until 1954–55 the annual investment in manufacturing
averaged 20 percent of total capital stock. New plants represented, therefore, a substantial proportion of all plants.
Shortages of skilled labor continued to be a problem. Even
in 1958 industrialists reported that over 5 percent of total
investment operated at less than capacity because they
were short of skilled workers. More important, a number
of firms, representing one-quarter of total industrial assets,
reported difficulties because government-provided services (power, water, transport) were inadequate. Delays
in obtaining railway wagons were frequent. (In Chittagong alone, as late as 1961, customers waited more than
a week for 1,000 wagons [130].) Power shortages occurred
periodically. While inadequacy of government services
was not serious enough to stop industrial investment or
operation, it did raise the cost.

Industry in Pakistan depended on some protection from
import competition to compensate for these inevitably
higher costs. In addition, effective control over imports
was necessary to discourage consumption. The virtual
elimination of luxury imports, and drastic restrictions on
the import of other consumer goods, encouraged savings,
especially by higher income groups.

The government of Pakistan, unlike governments in
some other countries, was able to impose and enforce
drastic import restrictions. Though consumers resisted
curtailment of imports, their political strength was inadequate to force a substantial relaxation. Smuggling was

risky and expensive and was therefore confined largely to goods with a very high profit per unit weight, such as gold. The high-cost domestic producer — of cloth and most other goods — faced little competition from smuggled, low-cost imports.

THE IMPORTANCE OF OTHER CONTROLS

The government also had to enforce effective controls on the export of capital in order to keep high profit and other incomes at home. Capital controls were more difficult to impose than import controls; significant sums went abroad. Rs. 8 crores ($16 million) were surrendered after the martial-law regime exempted owners from punishment (65), although this was only part of the funds held abroad. Another indication of the importance of capital export is given by "repatriation" of capital. Rs. 12 crores ($25 million) are reported to have come in over a few years, part of it repatriation of capital previously illegally exported. However, these indications for capital export are not particularly frightening when put in perspective. They are only four to six percent of reinvested industrial profits before 1960, or of annual export earnings. The risks and costs of capital flight were made sufficiently great by the civil service, and the rewards of keeping capital in Pakistan were sufficiently attractive, to keep capital flight within reasonable bounds.

Fiscal policy was the government's next most important instrument to affect development. Again, the effectiveness of the government machinery was limited. Tax evasion was widespread; many industrialists kept three sets of books — one for the tax collector, one for partners or relatives, and one for themselves. (One person claimed that sometimes there is a fourth set — to show the tax collector when he comes the second time insisting that he be shown the "real" books.) Others bribed excise-tax inspectors to report less production and therefore lower taxes. When the martial-law government exempted income-tax violators from prosecution if they paid their taxes plus a penalty, Rs. 135 crores ($270 million) of previously hidden income was reported. This sizable sum undoubtedly represented only part of the unreported funds, but fear of penalties under martial law produced a remarkable temporary honesty.

The rates of direct taxes were high and highly progressive, but were not really enforced or enforceable. In fact, it was the consensus of all industrialists, of most professional observers, and of some civil servants that effective tax enforcement in the 1950's would have aborted Pakistan's industrial development. It was only by widespread evasion of direct taxes that industrialists could earn the large profits which provided the spur and capital for industrial entrepreneurship.

In comparison with a perfect tax-collection system, Pakistan's left much to be desired. However, it was superior to that in most countries of Asia, Latin America or Southern Europe. Evasion of commodity taxes was limited. Since sufficient taxes were collected to finance the government's current expenditures, Pakistan did not have to create money for government operations, thus adding to inflationary pressures. Between 1949–50 and 1964–65, revenues quadrupled — a noticeable achievement. The tax system was also reasonably equitable. Because the rich succeeded in evading taxes more successfully than the poor, the sharp theoretical progression in the tax structure was in practice not effective. By and large, however, the rich paid proportionately more than the poor, large landowners more than the small, luxury-good consumers more than the consumers of necessities.

That taxes could be collected, and that some progression in tax structure could be enforced, had important consequences. Politically it made inequality in income more acceptable. It allowed the government to function without excessive money creation. Above all, it made possible the use of taxes to implement a variety of policies. Commodity taxes played an important role in discouraging consumption and encouraging savings. Differentials in taxes also affected the rate of savings and the pattern of investment.

Although there were other government policies which affected private decisions, one can draw three conclusions without further examples: First, for development to take place, a great and difficult task had to be performed by the government machinery in enforcing various policies, particularly those concerned with foreign trade, capital export, and fiscal measures; second, in Pakistan this function was performed with sufficient effectiveness to achieve in large measure the aims of various policies; third, there remained serious flaws as a result of which government could not adequately control the illegal export of funds and evasion of taxes.

THE EXTENT AND REASONS
FOR EXTENSIVE DIRECT CONTROLS

Some government measures to influence or control private decisions were essential. However, for a variety of reasons, the government went beyond such measures in the 1950's to develop an elaborate system of direct controls over private decisions.

The basic reason for government intervention in the economy was scarcity. The country's resources were inadequate to do all it wanted to do, especially after the end of the Korean boom. Pakistan could not achieve simultaneously the rate of growth and the degree of equity considered essential. Foreign-exchange earnings could not pay for all the imported consumer goods people demanded and the machinery required for development. Voluntary savings were inadequate to finance the desired development program. Growth in some areas was insufficient to satisfy political demands that were considered important.

Government intervention could have taken the form of indirect means to influence private decisions. By taxes, subsidies, interest rate, and foreign-exchange policies, the government could have influenced key prices, leaving detailed allocation to the market. Pakistan instead adopted a wide variety of specific controls to determine directly the allocation of resources. The reasons for this course were varied, composed of economic, political and psychological exigencies, some explicit, some implicit, some vigorously denied.

First of all, faith in the effectiveness of controls was strong. Direct controls over imports and investment were certain to keep consumption down and encourage investment, to favor the import and domestic production of necessities over luxuries, and to prevent concentration of economic power. There were serious doubts that indirect measures would be effective in promoting growth and protecting the poor. Many civil servants and political leaders saw the choice as between a free-enterprise economy — with low growth and inequitable distribution — and direct controls with higher growth and more equity.

It was assumed that the economy would function more efficiently if some decisions were taken by the government — that is, by civil servants — rather than by private businessmen. Civil servants were presumed to be better educated, less tradition bound, more experienced and farsighted, than the petty traders who became the businessmen and industrialists of Pakistan. Not only would private businessmen act for selfish personal gain, but it was thought that they would fail to pursue even that goal effectively because of ignorance, tradition, and lack of experience.

Then there was history. Pakistan inherited an elaborate, reasonably well-functioning control system from the British. As with all such institutional arrangements, sheer inertia would tend to preserve it and to lead to elaborating rather than scrapping it.

A difference existed in the competence with which the government could have managed indirect as against direct controls. Indirect controls required less administration, fewer administrators, but much more sophistication in economics, better data and more economists, none of which was in adequate supply.

Self-interest played a role. It is not surprising that economists at a planning agency are often firm advocates of their brand of planning. It is equally plausible that administrators see merit in direct controls which require administrators. An elaborate direct-control apparatus gives prestige and power to all administrators, and illegal income to some. It also works well for them. Price control and allocation for automobiles might not be universally effective, but they were likely to work for the automobile bought by the civil servant.

For some businessmen, self-interest also dictated support for direct controls. The established firm, especially if small and inefficient, was glad to be protected from competition. Political support for this form of protection was widespread. A small businessman or industrialist was considered to have a right to a reasonable living in his traditional occupation. Direct controls introduced monopoly elements that helped assure him that right. That this was at the cost of the consumer was not widely recognized. Nor was it recognized that the small importer, guaranteed a high profit on his inefficient, costly, protected business, was benefiting from a monopoly position. Monopoly was conceived as involving the large, rapidly growing firm against whom the small men needed to be protected.

Ideology was more directly involved. The rejection of the private-enterprise model was accompanied in Pakistan as elsewhere by a rejection of the market's allocating function, even within carefully circumscribed limits. In part, this was because in colonial times foreigners had a disproportionate share of commerce and industry, and private enterprise was therefore thought to be tainted by colonialism. More important was a sympathy for socialism and a mistaken notion that socialism meant direct controls. Until recently, European socialist writing did stress massive, direct government intervention in the economy. This was only natural, since the unsophisticated governments of the late nineteenth and early twentieth centuries, using the primitive economic tools then available, could not have achieved equity and growth in any other way. With time, a blurring has occurred between ends and means so that, in some countries, socialism has become identified with direct control over private enterprise. Although present-day governments are often powerful and possess highly effective indirect economic tools, direct controls are still demanded in the name of socialism. Ideology played a role in Pakistan, though it was less important than in most other underdeveloped countries.

All of these factors made for the use of direct rather than indirect controls to implement government policies. The heavy government involvement in the economy resulted from the severity of economic problems and the scarcity of resources. Additional intervention took place for historical and ideological reasons. Since some controls required further controls to be effective, there was a snowballing effect as well. The result was the development of a vast apparatus of direct physical controls over all aspects of the economy.

In 1958, when controls were at their peak, most significant economic decisions were made largely by the government, and nearly all were substantially influenced by it. Most important was control over foreign exchange, since imported goods were required for any investment of significance and for the operation of industrial firms, transport companies, and even some commercial enterprises. The government controlled imports in detail. It issued licenses for each import order and thus determined what specific commodities could be imported, by whom, from what currency area, and at what time. Because the demand for imports substantially exceeded the supply, the government's decisions largely determined what investment and what production would take place, where, and by whom (173). Producers were subject also to profit controls, substantial labor legislation, and an elaborate system of reporting to several Provincial and Central Government agencies.

Wartime price controls were continued to cover essential commodities, which at one time were defined to include nearly all important goods — foodstuffs, cloth and yarn, cigarettes, kerosene, drugs and medicines, matches, bicycles, timber, chemicals, and so on. Every sale of 5 rupees or more (equivalent roughly to $1) was supposed to be confirmed by a receipt. Price control naturally required price determination for different qualities, and elaborate record keeping and checking. Rationing was in force for some foods in urban areas. Distribution margins were controlled for a period.

Potential investors also had to obtain permission from separate government agencies to set up a plant; to make investments above a low limit; to issue stocks; and to obtain a building permit, land, a telephone, water, and sewage, power, or railway connections. Still other agencies gave special tax concessions or permission to locate a plant in some areas. Separate authorization was required if foreign investment, profit remittance, or foreign travel were involved.

Special industries, or particular decisions, were subject to further regulation. For instance, quotas were set on the tea that could be exported and the yarn that could be turned into cloth. To enforce price controls on foodgrains, surplus areas were physically prevented from exporting and were required to sell to the government, for resale in deficit areas. Individual prices were set for sugar mills, based on costs of production. The total acreage that could be planted in jute was fixed, and was allocated to growers; excess plantings were to be destroyed. Some goods were allocated by the government — notably cement, and iron and steel.

One could continue with the list of controls. It should be clear, however, that they were so far-reaching that even decisions not ordinarily subject to specific controls could be determined by the government if it so wished. The government by its decisions, especially on foreign exchange, determined the success or failure of any venture, and even an informal suggestion by a powerful government official could have the force of a regulation. Few businessmen wanted to incur a black mark that could affect their next import permit.

THE COSTS OF CONTROL

The system of detailed direct controls was very costly. It introduced inequities of its own, created political difficulties, was accompanied by economic inefficiency, and undermined the effectiveness of government.

An important cause of economic inefficiency was inadequate information and span of control when a profusion of decisions was centralized in the hands of a few civil servants. The few civil servants who made the crucial decisions just could not know enough to avoid serious mistakes, and sometimes could not get their decisions carried out. At the same time, private decision-makers, thanks to the control system, often had an incentive to make decisions that were not desirable for the economy. Thus, the civil servants could not competently make and carry out the necessary decisions, while the many private businessmen were encouraged to make the wrong decisions.

The problem of inadequate information was compounded because inevitably the civil servants had to decide on more and more detailed and complex issues. For instance, controls on the import of investment goods forced a decision on the desired capacity in different industries. To make a proper decision, government officials would have to know about the demand schedules, existing capacity, and import costs of the products involved; they needed some idea of the likely production costs of the industries that could supply the demand. And it was impossible to stop there. Since foreign exchange was cheap to the individual industrialist in terms of the rupees he had to pay for it, he asked for as much as possible. To assure that excessive foreign exchange was not allocated, officials had to examine the technical processes and the foreign-exchange costs of individual proposals. Moreover, the allocating authorities, dealing with a very scarce resource, wanted to reserve foreign exchange for those who were able to use it effectively. For each application, then, they needed to examine the financing, the experience of the entrepreneur, and similar details. Whatever limited information could be collected demanded analysis by competent people whose analyses then required hundreds of decisions which had to be carried out. This in turn required reports from businessmen, checks to see that the reports were accurate, and punishment for violators.

Inevitably the information that could be obtained and the number of competent analysts available were completely inadequate. Decisions were long delayed, sometimes wrong, and often difficult to implement. Even appropriate decisions were not always appropriately carried out, as error, incompetence, or worse intervened between the decision made at a high level and its execution by a clerk. Mistakes and delays were compounded by inexperienced controllers. The resulting costs to the economy were substantial indeed.

The costs were compounded because the control system gave private businessmen, cultivators, and industrialists good reason to make decisions which were bad for the economy. Imports, for instance, were strictly limited or entirely eliminated by direct controls through the import licensing system. With imports of some final goods unavailable at any price, the domestic producer was not under pressure to improve efficiency of investment and production for fear of losing sales to lower-priced imports. In addition, the overvaluation of the rupee meant that there was a strong incentive to use imported raw materials and machines, cheap to the private individual or firm, although the government at the same time tried to cut down on imports.

The economy paid a heavy price for the inadequacies of centralized government decisions and inappropriate, decentralized private decisions. First, there were costs due to particular incorrect decisions. Simple-minded examples include the factory forced to operate at a fraction of capacity for lack of a few imported spare parts. Since it was the only one of its kind in the country, its import licenses for spare parts had been fixed arbitrarily in the same proportion to output as the textile industry. Until an official could be convinced that this was wrong, a major investment was largely wasted. Then there is the story (117) of an investor given licenses to import most, but not all, of the machinery he required, and who was thus unable to produce anything. The coal mines produced at far less than capacity because they could not get foreign exchange from a distant official to purchase safety lamps, though the cost of lamps was a tiny fraction of the value of the mines' output. Finally, in a two-year period from 1958 to 1960, the government changed the controlled prices of textiles four times by uniform percentages for all grades. These changes inevitably caused tremendous confusion, substantial waste, and interruption in production. Firms had to change prices all along the line and shift their output mix to emphasize profitable items.

Another important loss to the economy stemmed from the delay imposed by the control machinery on the decisions of the whole private sector. Decisions that should have been made in hours or days sometimes took months if they required government approval. Individual applications for import licenses were an example. At times, such licenses were issued 3 months after the 6 months' licensing period had begun. The result was production and export possibilities foregone because delivery schedules could not be met or imports could not be bought when they were cheapest.

Substantial loss resulted also from the need for excessive stocks, imposed by the delay and uncertainty of the control apparatus. Whenever possible, industrialists imported and stored excess raw materials and spare parts since storage costs were a small fraction of the potential loss if imports were subsequently delayed. Pakistan has been desperately short of foreign exchange since 1953; yet in

1958 the foreign exchange reported to the Survey as tied up in industrialists' inventories was nearly equal to annual imports of all raw materials used by industry. Actual stocks were higher, since some industrialists probably understated their inventories of imported goods, and since the inventories of importers and wholesalers were not reported.

A fourth area of loss arose because industrialists and businessmen always pressed for more foreign exchange than they required. Since imported goods were cheap for them, importers could make large profits on their resale. Industrialists preferred to use familiar, quality-controlled foreign goods rather than deal with troublesome domestic labor or unknown domestic goods. It was impossible for officials to assure that permitted imports were no more than required. As a result, some foreign exchange was wasted for imports that would not have been used had they been more expensive. Examples are the use of imported steel beams and concrete for structures where brick would have been satisfactory, and the use of imported instead of domestic pumps.

Illegal diversion of cheap imports to low-priority uses was another cause of inefficiency. For instance, a factory producing metal products that were considered "important" would be given a license to import iron and steel. Because its output was "important" it would receive little protection from import competition and its rate of profit would be low. It could do much better by illegally selling much of its imported iron and steel to manufacturers who produced low-priority but high-profit items. The relative cheapness of some imports made illegal activities often highly profitable.

More important, investment continued in some industries despite excess capacity. Entrepreneurs invested even if they knew that there was excess capacity. Their profit was protected, and it was better to make an investment for which a permit was available than to risk waiting for permission to enter an even more profitable industry. Government regulation alone could not prevent excess capacity. In 1958 nearly 15 percent of all capital was operated at substantially less than 800 shift days for lack of imported raw materials and another 15 percent for lack of demand or domestic raw materials. Two-thirds of these firms operated only one shift per day or less. (Other firms operated below capacity for other reasons, less clearly identified with an inappropriate investment decision.) Not all of this idle capacity represented misinvestment. Some idle capacity was only temporary. Mistakes would have been made even if the control system had not distorted the incentives. Nevertheless it is clear that a substantial number of investment decisions permitted and encouraged by the government machinery created excess capacity. A poor country such as Pakistan could ill afford to put nearly one-third of its investment in industries which could not operate at capacity.

Other investments, which were not the highest priority use of scarce resources, were permitted. For instance, substantial investments were made in sugar refining, though it is high-cost and requires high protection, while there were delays in approving investment for cement where Pakistan had a real advantage. In several industries (notably textiles) many small, inefficient plants were sanctioned, rather than a limited number of more efficient, larger plants. Industrialists invested in these enterprises, which were nonetheless profitable, rather than wait around for possible permission to invest in something even better.

Additional inefficiency was guaranteed by the historical base of the allocation system. No criterion other than past imports or past consumption could be used to determine the allocation of import licenses to thousands of importers and industrialists. Many purchases, therefore, were made in very small lots as each importer separately bought his fractional share of imports. It was estimated that bulk instead of small-lot purchases would have saved 15 percent of cost for vegetable oil and about 40 percent for iron and steel imports. Quotas prevented more efficient producers and importers from expanding at the expense of less efficient ones. Since an import license generated riskless income, it was naturally felt that this gift should be widely shared. There was therefore strong resistance to concentration of imports, even though the wide distribution was at the cost of the rest of society.

Finally, the very complexity of a control system that grew by fits and starts, as policies were patched over the holes that had developed in other policies, was bound to have some internal contradictions. The most important arose in the import licensing system. Policies were designed to accomplish four separate objectives — to protect domestic infant industry, to compensate for the general overvaluation of the rupee, to influence the composition of imports, and to guide the location of investment. In practice these objectives conflicted; for instance, import restrictions were minimal for goods considered "desirable" or "essential," so that the potential domestic producer of capital goods and some intermediate products received little protection. On the other hand, curtailment of luxury imports provided a great incentive for domestic production of goods considered least desirable. In 1960, for instance, most machinery and machine tools had a tariff of 12 percent and a relatively generous import quota, while cotton cloth had a tariff of 100 percent and artificial fibers of 250 percent, with almost no import permitted. Policies which encouraged consumer-goods production were quite appropriate in the early period of industrialization, when industries with a simple technology were preferable, but later on protection ran counter to the policy favoring producer- and intermediate-goods production. Also, the restriction of imports obviously provided protection only to industries producing for the domestic market. Export industries, far from being encouraged, had to overcome the handicap of an overvalued rupee. In short, import restrictions distorted investment by favoring the production of consumer goods for the domestic market and discriminating against exports and producer goods.

It is impossible to make a convincing estimate of all the economic losses which resulted from the control system. However, if there had been no further investment in industry operating below capacity for lack of raw materials or demand, 50 to 80 crores of rupees of investment funds could have been saved. Reduction of imported industrial stocks to a 4 months' supply would have saved another Rs. 20 crores. If the losses from small-lot purchases of imports averaged only 5 percent, they would still add up to about Rs. 12 crores per year. Waste was involved also in the import of goods where domestic production could have provided the same article. Incorrect decisions and inappropriate incentives in individual cases meant further losses. Total measurable losses from all these causes were probably at least Rs. 65 crores of investment funds, representing 15 percent of total industrial assets in 1958.

The control system was not only inefficient in economic terms, it was also poorly adapted to meet the equity goals of Pakistan. In practice many of the controls proved ineffective. No government has yet been able to enforce price control or an allocation system without substantial leakages. The leakages in Pakistan were bound to be large, given poor communications, limits on available personnel, the long period during which controls operated, the severe shortage of goods, and a tradition of resistance to government. Price control and consumer rationing worked only for a small part of the population and only for part of their food and clothing needs.* Profit control could not be effectively enforced. Imports were sold for whatever the seller could get. He charged scarcity prices and pocketed the difference between what consumers were willing to pay and what the importers had to pay. Usually the importer made a high profit, sometimes the processor did; otherwise, it was the retailer or the idler who stood in line to buy the scarce goods at fixed prices and resold them at the market price. The government, relying on statistics based on official or controlled prices, might believe that its directives were effective, but for many goods the official prices were for officials only (139; 140).

Another objective of the control system was to reduce concentration of economic wealth and power, and to assure comparable economic progress in all major areas of the country. Controls were successful in keeping the inefficient producer from bankruptcy. However, they were of maximum benefit to the large, well-established industrialist, and discriminated against the small entrepreneur, the less developed regions, and the late-comer. The would-be importer or industrialist had to convince a gaggle of government officials that he was a good risk to be given scarce foreign exchange and other resources. He was in competition with industrialists who had capital and experience, who had proved successful, and who could offer connections and bribes. In the abstract, government decisions were to favor the small newcomer. In fact, they favored all established firms, especially large ones. Officials knew

---

* The Prices Commission reported, for instance, that textile mills avoided price controls by (a) introducing spurious "new" varieties on which they charged higher prices, (b) stopping production of less profitable varieties, and (c) forcing retailers through tie-in sales to take unprofitable varieties in order to obtain popular ones. (123).

they would be blamed for the failure of an unknown entrepreneur, but would get very little credit for his success. They saw little reason to take the risk. Civil servants also considered the smaller established industrialist as a greater risk, and his gratitude less rewarding, than his larger competitor. There is some evidence that the small firm was operating at a disadvantage. According to the Survey, almost one-half of the smaller firms functioned below capacity for lack of imported raw materials, but this was true for only 10 percent of the larger firms.

For similar reasons the control system also reinforced, rather than counteracted, the tendency to geographic concentration. The more pervasive the controls, the greater the advantage conferred by proximity to the government. In addition, Karachi had developed early, so it had a large proportion of well-established industrialists who received preference when import permits were issued. Businessmen from East Pakistan, furthest from the central government, found it difficult to gain the officials' ear. East Pakistan also had few early industrialists who would later look like sound chaps to government officials; both factors thus hampered its development.

Furthermore, the control system created political and economic problems by rewarding the businessman or industrialist who through historical accident or pressure could obtain permits, not the one who performed the socially most useful function. Success went to those who could extract favors from the government; industrialists devoted time, thought, and money to convince government officials rather than to improve the functioning of their firms. Import controls created large nonfunctional incomes. There developed a substantial group of essentially parasitic businessmen with guaranteed incomes, who strenuously resisted any attempts to liberalize or rationalize imports. Politically, as well as morally, wealth is slightly more acceptable if it is accumulated as a result of efficiency rather than by skullduggery or accident. A Chief Engineer, administering contracts worth millions, would see something wrong in a society which gave him an income one-tenth the size of that of his brother who imported luxury goods on a fixed quota.

Besides introducing inefficiency and falling below its social and political objectives, the control system pinned down and seriously weakened one of the scarcest and most important resources of Pakistan — its civil service. The decisions that needed to be made in administering the controls were numerous and complex. The power of those who made them was great. As a result, the control effort required a considerable proportion of the better and more senior civil servants, and absorbed much of the attention of the political leadership. At the same time it was bound to undermine the reliability of the civil service. Some recipients of an import license could afford to pay literally hundreds of thousands of rupees for it and consider this a reasonable cost of doing business. Inevitably, some civil servants succumbed to temptation. During one period, of the 1,134 persons proceeded against under the Foreign Exchange Regulations Act and the Hoarding and Black-marketing Act, 735 were government employees, 136 of them in the senior grades (7, p. 91, n. 1). When the martial-law government took over in 1958, 75 senior government officials (Class I) and 82 other officials (Class II) were dismissed. Of these, 30 were from the elite services. (These figures do not include lower level staff, nor those dismissed by Provincial governments.) Although some who were removed were not corrupt and some who were corrupt were not removed, dismissal of about 5 percent of the civil servants in each category is a useful indication of the size of the problem.

Corruption had several consequences. It re-enforced the

tendency to concentration, as the wealthy were better able to offer bribes. Bribery increased inefficiency since licenses were often issued in accordance with bribes, not national interest. The really serious consequence, however, was that it led to a further loss in the effectiveness of the civil service. Elaborate provisions to check those who made decisions led to further delay and caution and required additional people, presumably even abler and more honest than those who were handing out the licenses. Some good civil servants who might have performed well were lost forever because they did not resist the extreme temptation facing those in charge of the controls.

Even in the United Kingdom toward the end of World War II, an elaborate system of direct controls produced inefficient decisions, fell short of meeting the social objectives set for it, and required increasing inputs of administrative talent. The time period over which controls were expected to work was much longer in Pakistan than in the United Kingdom. Pakistan's civil service was stretched much thinner. Instead of the spur of war, Pakistan's control system operated under the handicap of a negative attitude toward government. In view of these difficulties the performance was more than respectable, but in comparison with its aims the control machinery had only limited success. It achieved its major purpose of allocating scarce resources in some relation to economic criteria, but its economic, social, and administrative cost was considerable.

MOVES TOWARD INDIRECT CONTROLS

The Pakistan Government was unusual in recognizing the existence and importance of these costs. In 1959 it began to replace direct with indirect controls.

To stimulate exports, it began to shift from exhortation

and export quotas to monetary incentives. To compensate in part for the overvaluation of the rupee, exporters of manufactured goods and some raw materials (including monkeys) received import permits, equivalent to 10–40 percent of the value of their exports. These "bonus vouchers" could be sold. With tight import restrictions, especially on luxury goods, the demand for these permits was strong. "Bonus vouchers" commanded a premium of 120–150 percent. In effect the scheme gave exporters additional rupees equal to 30 or 40 percent of the value of exports.

Contrary to expectations, price incentives proved effective. Over a three-year period, the net exports of the commodities covered by bonus vouchers increased by an estimated 40 percent (15). The primary effect was to stimulate exports of well established international products such as cotton and jute goods. Growth was most rapid, however, in some new industries, including those in which quality and marketing problems were important (frozen fish, metal products, paper, cement).

The effectiveness of the bonus scheme was all the more remarkable since it was not universal and there was uncertainty as to its duration and magnitude. The government never made a commitment that the export bonuses would continue beyond a few years. The commodities covered and the rate of bonus vouchers earned for a particular export could be varied quite arbitrarily. The premium which the vouchers commanded was also uncertain, since it depended on the level of regular imports. Furthermore, the government could and did restrict the use of vouchers, limiting some to imports of spare parts, capital goods or raw materials. These risks somewhat reduced the effectiveness of the scheme.

The great variety of effective rates of exchange for exports was also a drawback. Some exporters faced an effective rate of 8 rupees to the dollar, if their commodity had been assigned 40 percent vouchers, all of which could be sold in the open market. At the other extreme, exporters who received no vouchers and paid export duties faced an effective rate of less than 4.7 rupees to the dollar. Other exporters faced effective rates anywhere between these two figures. The result was to encourage some exports that might prove uncompetitive unless the scheme were continued, and discourage others that could be fully competitive with only a slightly better price. There was a natural tendency to provide maximum assistance via the bonus scheme to the industries facing the greatest obstacles in exporting, and therefore to encourage investment in industries that were least competitive and desirable. Finally, the whole system was effective only as long as the import of goods with a strong unfilled demand was permitted. Otherwise the premium on vouchers would have dropped and with it the incentive to export. Imports which could be sold at a premium of 140 percent, allowing for import duties, inevitably included a high proportion of consumer luxuries. A result of the bonus scheme could well have been the import of more luxury goods than otherwise considered desirable.

Other economic incentives were provided for exporters. They were given tax concessions and special facilities to import for their own needs. For a while some exporters, by taking advantage of all the incentive schemes, could obtain a higher value of imports than the value of their exports, thus profiting while their country actually lost foreign exchange on the transaction. The specific effect of each incentive is impossible to document, but in all they undoubtedly contributed to the marked increase in export earnings.

In short, various economic incentives which had considerable success were offered the exporter. Their limited coverage and duration, however, and the uncertainty and complexity which they introduced, meant that their effectiveness was more limited and their cost to the economy greater than with a broader, more permanent approach.

The export bonus scheme not only provided a price incentive for exports, it also represented the first step in substituting higher prices for direct controls in limiting imports. Before the scheme was introduced, there was a great deal of concern that to limit imports by higher prices would require astronomical price levels to be successful. Yet the price for bonus vouchers did not exceed 130–150 percent of their value, and this was adequate to restrict luxury imports to Rs. 2.5 crores, or less than 1 percent of total imports. The premium required to restrict the demand for luxury imports would have been even less if free imports had been continued long enough to satisfy accumulated demand, and had been guaranteed for the future.

Freeing imports from direct controls had several advantages. The number of individual decisions required of government officials was reduced, since they no longer had to determine who got an import license, for what commodity. Some windfall profits were eliminated since many importers now had to buy their import permit at market prices. Above all, free imports under bonus vouchers permitted rectification of some simple errors in the system of allocating imports. For instance, an industrialist could now import an important spare part by buying a bonus voucher.

However, for imports as for exports, the export bonus scheme and related measures had a good many shortcomings. They resulted in a complex system of multiple-exchange rates, at first even for a single commodity. The importer who could get a regular import license paid the official exchange rate (4.7 rupees to the dollar). The importer who had to buy a bonus voucher paid more than twice that amount (as much as 12 rupees to the dollar). Finally, the importer who bought a voucher restricted to the import of raw materials or investment goods, could pay yet a third rate, somewhere between the other two.*

Multiple exchange rates and uncertainty under the bonus voucher system not only reduced its effectiveness in stimulating exports, but also weakened the protection of infant industries. The domestic producer found the protection he received suddenly reduced by a fall in the bonus voucher premium or by an increase in regularly licensed imports. The bonus system also continued to provide maximum protection for luxuries. The more "useful" a commodity, the more freely it could be imported without paying the bonus voucher premium and the less the incentive for producing it in Pakistan.

More important steps than the bonus system were taken in 1964 to reduce direct controls over imports of raw materials and spare parts. Many iron and steel products, nonferrous metals, drugs, chemicals, dyes, and some other goods were placed on the "free list," and could be imported without requiring a government license. Another large group, including tractors, tires, vehicles, and office equipment, were put on an open general license. Although they required a license, it was to be issued automatically on proof that a previous license had been used. In addition, industrialists were allowed to import maintenance spares and components. Finally, many other industries were to be given more liberal licenses for requirements not covered by the free list or the open general license. The Finance Minister estimated that Rs. 100 crores of imports were included in the various liberalization measures. Total imports had been over Rs. 400 crores, of which about

---

* For a compilation of the implicit exchange rates facing exporters and importers see (116, p. 479).

Rs. 100 crores were imported by the government, so liberalization covered about one-third of private imports.

While reducing direct controls, the government increased taxes. Customs duties were raised between 5 and 10 percent on a wide variety of imports. The sales tax, levied on landed cost, automatically increased with customs duties. One estimate was that total tax collections on liberalized imports would increase by Rs. 8 crores, or 8 percent of the value of these imports. Another estimate was that the increased costs to importers averaged 13 percent (*173*). (The language used when the new taxes were imposed is worth noting: ". . . the Central Government is pleased. . . ." It conjures up a picture of some grimly cheerful soul slapping on yet another tax.)

What happened when many iron and steel imports were placed on the free list early in 1964 is interesting. The rush to open letters of credit for their import was frightening. Fortunately, reassurance was provided by the United States aid program which had underwritten the step. As imports began to flood in, prices dropped below those paid by most consumers in the past, although they remained above the officially fixed prices. All at once, various items were freely available. A number of importers, all set for the killing of their lives, found that profits were modest. A few actually faced the prospect of losing money on imports, an unheard-of state of affairs in Pakistan for more than 10 years. All were sadder and wiser men. Thereafter, importers were unlikely to order without investigation or limit, the moment the government gave them permission to do so. Imports of iron and steel on the free list actually declined in absolute terms and were a smaller share of total imports in late 1964 than they had been earlier. It became clear that the demand for imports, even in a country like Pakistan, was far from insatiable.

Both industrial production and investment seemed to respond to the liberalization of imports. The index of industrial production increased by almost 17 percent in 1964–65, compared to an average of less than 14 percent in the previous three years. "Free-list" imports into East Pakistan increased by substantially more than those into West Pakistan, while the reverse was true of controlled imports.* This development lent strong support to the contention that liberalization was particularly important for the area that was further from the government and less developed.

The shift to indirect controls over imports was very significant. However, its effect was limited by exceptions and conflicts of purpose. Direct controls had been retained on most consumer goods and on many raw materials. Goods on the open general license were supposed to be free of restrictions. In fact, the authorities found ways to slow down the issue of the supposedly automatic licenses when they feared that large imports might put a strain on foreign exchange reserves. Confusion remained about whether importing was a function or a privilege. Since direct controls remained over a wide range of imports, the importer of some goods could still make high and riskless profits. This was a privilege which naturally should be handed out equitably. Therefore not everyone could be allowed to import just because he thought he could perform the function at low cost. Would-be importers had to belong to a group which government desired to favor (e.g., they had to live in one of the smaller towns, be a newcomer to importing or have been a small importer be-

* Controlled imports into East Pakistan actually decreased between the first half of 1963–64 and a year later, while those into West Pakistan increased. Free-list imports, on the other hand, rose about 25 percent more in East than in West Pakistan.

fore, or import for their own use). Upper limits had to be placed on the quantity any single importer could bring in, in order to spread the privilege widely.

As a result, for a wide range of goods, imports were limited by the absence of a license rather than by price. Importers continued to buy in small, and therefore expensive, lots. Since there was no assurance that the government would continue even the limited freedom to import, industrialists held excessive stocks. The bulk of imports continued to be controlled by licenses, so mistakes continued to be likely in denying permission to import where it would be desirable, or granting it where it was not. The government apparatus for issuing licenses could be reduced only slightly; it could not be dismantled. Bribery to obtain scarce licenses continued, and high riskless profits continued for some goods. Consumer satisfaction was not maximized. Last but by no means least, for many manufacturers and importers the pressure for efficiency and lower prices, which imports — even at a high price — could have exerted, just did not exist.

Some steps were also taken to shift to indirect controls in guiding investment decisions. Enterprises in less developed areas were given a tax holiday for 6 to 8 years, compared to 2 to 4 years in more developed areas. However, studies elsewhere suggest that concessions on profit taxes are a weak device for influencing location decisions. They do not reduce the risk that investment in the backward area may earn no profits. Exemption from profit taxes also may not compensate for significantly lower profits in the less developed area. For example, if the expected rate of return on investment in East Pakistan was 15 percent as against 20 percent in West, and if the tax rate on profits was 50 percent, the present value of returns discounted at 20 percent would be about equal in East and West Pakistan, despite an additional 4 years of tax exemption in the former.

In 1960 the government began to publish an industrial investment schedule indicating for 1 to 5 years in advance the private investment which it expected and permitted in different industries (34; 35; 124). Until the quota for each industry or type of investment was exhausted, no special permission was required for most investments if the foreign-exchange cost was to be financed by PICIC, IDBP, or bonus vouchers. In the past, only government agencies could approve investment projects. Now two semi-independent agencies were added as channels for foreign exchange. An investor could also proceed without any screening if he paid the 140 percent premium for bonus vouchers on his imported goods. (Permission was not required if no imported goods were involved, but in the 1960's this provision was of little significance in Pakistan.)

The investment schedule proved only a modest step away from direct controls. Some items on the schedule looked highly profitable because they faced little competition from domestic production or imports. Others were risky, with doubtful profits. To assure implementation of the whole schedule, the government therefore felt it had to retain some direct controls. At best, only one-third of potential investment came under the liberalization provisions of the new investment schedule.* Even for this third it was still necessary to obtain approval of a government or semigovernment agency. (The use of bonus vouchers to avoid the sanctioning procedure was generally ruled

* In the first investment schedules, about one-third of specified investment continued to require government permission. In addition, no financial provision was made in the schedule for a number of important industries, likely to involve large units (fertilizers, other petrochemicals, air conditioners, refrigerators, radios, machine tools, sugar, cement), and these continued to be subject to government permission.

out since most firms could not compete if they had paid a premium of 140 percent for their imported investment goods.) Finally, the schedule established clear limits on the investment permitted in a particular line.

Even for the limited investment covered by the schedules, the government's purposes were achieved only in part. The regional distribution of investment remained skewed. Only Rs. 90 crores were provided for East Pakistan in the first schedules, as against Rs. 195 crores for West Pakistan; sanctions for the West were more than twice those issued for East Pakistan (366 crores against 151 crores). Clearly, measures to speed up the rate of industrial growth in East Pakistan were inadequate. There were great additional disparities between the planned schedule and actual sanctions with respect to different industries. For instance, of the allocation for chemicals and food products which was to be spread over 5 years, two-thirds had been used within 1 year. On the other hand, only one-sixth of the allocation for engineering and practically none of the large allocation for minerals and power were actually used in the same year. Some investments considered very desirable by the government were not taken up for several years.

In short, the use of an investment schedule represented only a first step toward reducing direct government control over investment. Since no indirect measures had been adopted to restrict the total amount of investment and to channel it to particular industries, the government could not leave investment uncontrolled. Instead, it limited the scope of the investment schedules and retained considerable control over decisions even for investment included in the schedules. The schedules reflected detailed government decisions on investment by industry, by location, and to some extent by technology.

Besides somewhat reducing its control over imports and

investment, and providing price incentives to exports, the government took other steps in the 1960's to substitute price incentives for direct controls. Remittance of income by Pakistanis abroad was put under the bonus voucher scheme. This resulted in a higher effective exchange rate, reduced the incentive to use the black market, and sharply increased legal remittances. Repatriation of capital was freely permitted, allowing some capital exported illegally to return to Pakistan without penalty. Some Rs. 12 crores of capital were brought in from East Africa in the early 1960's. A few excise and sales taxes were put on a capacity basis, that is, imposed on the number of machines rather than on output. This simplified tax collection and encouraged capacity use of machinery. Price controls were gradually abolished, and profit controls were effectively dropped as soon as it became obvious that they were not feasible. Export duties on cotton, jute, and other products were reduced several times, though not eliminated.

Even after the direct-control system had been partly dismantled, it continued to use considerable scarce administrative talent. In 1963 some 40 responsible civil servants (Class I Gazetted Officers) were assigned to the Chief Controller of Imports and Exports, whose primary function was to deal with import licenses. Another 80 officials were with the Department of Investment Promotion, one of whose main functions was to control investment. In addition many other able senior officials in such ministries as Industry, Commerce, Finance and the President's Secretariat spent a good deal of their time on import licenses and investment permits of various kinds.

In the 1960's Pakistan removed a number of direct controls and, to a more limited extent, substituted indirect measures. The result was a more efficient functioning of the economy. Price incentives proved effective in increasing exports and production, and in allocating and restrict-

ing imports. However, if the process of removing direct
controls is to continue without a greater use of indirect
measures, it is likely that both production and imports
will include more luxury consumer goods. The increased
availability of such goods might then tend to reduce the
rate of savings. Experience in substituting government-
manipulated prices for direct controls has been good. The
problems resulting from the remaining direct controls —
and an inadequate recourse to indirect controls — are
likely to increase in the future.

THE POLITICS OF GOVERNMENT CONTROL

The whole process discussed so far — the development
of an elaborate system of direct controls and its partial dismantling — was almost exclusively the result of decisions
taken by government officials. Economic policy in Pakistan was framed in a political context quite different from
that which prevailed in Europe or North America during
their period of development. Government dominated the
economy. It could carry out any economic policy it was
determined to follow, without meaningful opposition from
affected interest groups. (There was one major exception:
at least until 1958 the landlords of West Pakistan could
block significant land-tenure changes.) The government
was the successor of powerful Moghul and British rulers;
it had attracted some of the best minds and the most educated groups; it had at its command the machinery of the
modern state. Private businessmen and industrialists had
inherited the lowly status of their predecessors, included
few well-educated, experienced individuals, and started
with little concentrated economic power. The assumption
of government officials, businessmen, and the public was
that the government would and should dominate the economy. Even the most self-confident industrialists saw their

position vis-à-vis the government as that of supplicant,
rather than master. They largely accepted that the government was the guarantor of the social good, not that a
minimum of government activity would lead to maximum
social benefit.

Contrary to some simplified, neo-Marxist analyses, the
civil service and therefore the government were neither
subservient to nor allied with either landlord or business
interests. Nor were they drawn from these groups. As a
result, in Pakistan of the 1950's the government could
dominate significant economic decisions without extensive
ownership or direct control.

The government's freedom of action was great, since
the wishes of the large private sector could be more readily
ignored than elsewhere. For instance, even before martial
law, the central government raised tax rates sharply from
time to time; depressed food grain prices for years; reduced the rupee receipts of exporters by maintaining a
low foreign-exchange rate; drastically reduced or eliminated some imports — all actions that would have been
politically difficult, if not impossible, in most other countries. Economic policies did have to take into account the
wishes of the "New Class" of the civil service. Proposed
changes in civil servants' prerogatives were strongly resisted. However, their demands could be met without
great cost to the economy.

Shifting from direct controls, especially over imports,
to indirect tax measures in the 1960's, the government encountered a mixed reception from the industrial and business community. Private firms suffered higher taxes and
lower profits in exchange for fewer restrictions. Direct
controls had taken a large share of the businessman's time
and energy. He had also found them humiliating. Even
the most successful industrialist or trader sometimes found
himself having to plead for a permit from a low-level offi-

cial. Businessmen's complaints were frequent, loud, and often exaggerated. Actually some businessmen, especially the less efficient and enterprising, welcomed the relatively safe, though confined, existence under direct controls. They strongly opposed liberalization of imports and the consequent increase in competition. However, the more successful businessmen, pleased with the greater freedom and opportunity to expand, supported some aspects of the liberalization policy.

The reaction of the civil service and intellectual communities was similarly mixed. On the one hand, they were quite aware of the less desirable features of the direct control system and particularly sensitive to the corruption that accompanied the extreme temptations inherent in that system. On the other hand, there was the belief, for all the reasons discussed earlier, that direct controls were more equitable and efficient than indirect measures. The new elite in the civil service was naturally reluctant to give up the power which direct controls conferred on them. The reluctance, and in some cases outright opposition, of these groups might have prevented even a limited dismantling of the direct control system, had it not been for the determination and strength of the political leadership. Pakistan differed from other countries in having a government that used the abilities of the civil service but that could on occasion also overcome bureaucratic inertia and self-interest.

In the 1960's the relationship between government and business had begun to change subtly but unmistakably. Businessmen, and especially industrialists, had become wealthier, more powerful, and sophisticated. Now that they owned newspapers and financed political groups, their support was increasingly valuable in political life. The previous humility of the petty trader vis-à-vis government officials began to give way to the arrogance of the industrial magnate. Leading industrial families began to intermarry with families important in the civil service, the military, and in the landed aristocracy. Some of the bright young men no longer tried, almost automatically, for the elite civil service, but sought employment in industry. Some of the leading civil service, military, and political families began to invest in industry. The process had only begun by 1964, but the trend was clear. The pressure from business to remove onerous controls may well increase. The ability and willingness of the governing group to impose heavy new taxes as the price of dismantling direct controls may simultaneously decline.

In another decade other political forces are bound to become more prominent. The industrial labor force was of some political significance in the 1960's. With the phenomenal expansion of secondary and higher education, students, semiprofessionals, and lower middle-class groups began to play a role. As both industry and education continue to expand rapidly, these groups will soon be of major importance. Pressure from below will have to be reckoned with. Future government policy will be framed more as the result of this pressure than in conformity with the notions of equity held by the civil service.

SOME CONCLUSIONS

The performance of the Pakistan government is bound to be judged as inadequate if measured against an ideal standard; it was more than respectable if measured against the performance of other governments. Its strength came from a small elite corps of civil servants and strong technical organizations in a few fields. A major achievement of the civil service was its execution of the government investment program, which increased twelvefold in real terms over 15 years. Waste and inefficiency probably decreased at the same time. With the political leadership able, especially after 1959, to use the government apparatus effectively, the "executing capacity" or the "absorptive capacity for capital" of the government increased at a very rapid rate. In part, this resulted from Pakistan's centralized machinery for considering, deciding, and implementing economic policy. The ability of the government to develop the infrastructure was one of the essentials for a high rate of industrial growth. The government also played an important role as industrial entrepreneur, and supported two agencies which provided equity capital and credit to industry.

The government's most important economic effort, in addition to the development of infrastructure, was the establishment of reasonably effective controls over some economic transactions. Enforceable control over imports and capital exports was a necessary condition for rapid private industrial development. Effective tax collection provided the resources for the government's expanding role. Both import controls and taxes were used to influence private actions in directions that were considered socially and politically desirable.

Although some controls over private decisions were desirable, the system of detailed direct controls which developed between 1952 and 1959 was much too extensive. This elaboration of controls occurred for a number of reasons: unfamiliarity with indirect measures and the belief that they would not be successful; a conviction that decisions by civil servants would often be more in the national interest than those of businessmen; preference of the civil service for administrative devices; ideological grounds for direct government intervention in the economy. By 1958 the government made nearly all important, and many unimportant, economic decisions. This system had a substantial cost. The scope of control was too great in relation to the manpower, information, and administrative machinery available. The results were individual decisions that were incorrect, delays, excessive stocks, errors in the direction of investment and in composition of imports. The inefficiencies introduced in the economy were substantial and significant; moreover, the goal of equity was inadequately met. Price control and allocations could be only partially enforced. The system fostered concentration of wealth and economic power in the hands of a few families, and a concentration of industry in Karachi. It rewarded the person who could obtain permits, not the one whose productive contribution was greatest. Finally, there was a tremendous administrative cost. A substantial proportion of the government's attention and administrative capacity had to be used to implement the controls. The system inevitably fostered corruption.

Contrary to widely held opinions, indirect tax measures and subsidies worked well when substituted for direct controls. Improved returns greatly increased the exports of some goods; luxury-goods imports were effectively limited and allocated by higher prices; when controls were removed on some raw material and spare parts, imports did not shoot up excessively nor did their prices rise; the abolition of most price, profit, and allocation controls had no untoward consequences.

The system of direct controls had been a major consumer of government administrative talent. Even when controls were reduced in scope, their administration continued to require much scarce manpower. Pakistan had a competent government machinery, capable of carrying out a large number of tasks. However, it could not make and execute all major economic decisions. It had to perform the regular administrative functions of a government and maintain law and order. The rapidly growing development program imposed a further burden. The government machinery was already overstrained when responsibilities for a large direct control system were added to these functions. As a result, some aspects of the government investment program were poorly implemented and some activities were seriously neglected. The consequences of the neglect of a crucial activity — agriculture — are examined in the next chapter.

CHAPTER VI

PEASANTS

The Development of Agriculture

Farming is a rather morbidly dirty business that has little appeal to the . . . poet-civil servant whose interests tend more toward an ever whiter shirt and a higher capacity air conditioner. Another explanation [for the neglect of agriculture] is the sincere belief that very rapid industrialization is a cure-all that some day, in some unspecified way, will remedy the grubby, stubborn illness of low agricultural productivity.

FORMER AGRICULTURE ADVISER (128)

AGRICULTURE was the sick man of economic development in Pakistan during the 1950's. A stagnant agriculture in a predominantly agricultural country meant a slowly growing economy. Pakistan was not unique in this respect; agricultural stagnation has been a problem in all underdeveloped countries with peasant rather than commercial agriculture. Industrial development required a few hundred entrepreneurs and a limited number of technicians, some of whom could be imported. Agricultural development, on the other hand, required that several hundred thousand peasants change their behavior and adopt new techniques. During much of the 1950's, agriculture, unlike industry, suffered from low prices and great risks. Increased agricultural production was particularly difficult to achieve in a country such as Pakistan because little additional land could be brought under cultivation by the individual peasant.

THE STAGNATION OF AGRICULTURE

The facts on agricultural production are not easy to establish. Crop production in Pakistan, influenced by irregular monsoon rains, varies considerably from year to year. Since crops account for nearly three-quarters of agricultural value added, the influence of weather on total agricultural production is large. Feelings of optimism and pessimism fluctuated with the weather. When output was high, the effect of weather was not sufficiently discounted, and the assumption was widespread that the problem of agricultural production was on its way to a solution. Since years of good and bad weather are sometimes bunched and fluctuations great, even short-term averages are deceptive. In 1953–55, for instance, two good crop years caused widespread optimism, especially since the two previous years' output was below trend, and this made for a larger apparent gain. For a more reliable picture of changes in crop production, one must eliminate the effect of random fluctuations due to weather. Output data on agricultural products other than the major crops are often guesses. Still, it is reasonably sure that the output of agriculture did not keep up with population growth in the 1950's, despite statements in the first Plan that agriculture must be given the "highest priority." There is confirmation in price and import data for the belief that agriculture lagged behind population. No grain had to be imported during 1947 to 1951, while imports in 1955 to 1962 averaged 1,000,000 tons per year (nearly 10 percent of domestic production). Nevertheless, the wholesale price of agricultural products increased somewhat more rapidly than the general wholesale price index during the 1950's.* In addition, there is some evidence that part of the limited

* Imports are from (3); prices are from (30).

increase in agricultural output was due to the use of marginal land, forced by population pressure (*94*). The cultivation of areas exposed to unusual risk from flood or drought made agriculture more vulnerable to weather fluctuations.

TABLE 21. TRENDS IN CROP PRODUCTION.

Crop	1949–50	1954–55	1959–60	1964–65
	(*Crores of rupees in constant 1959-60 prices*)			
East Pakistan	550	570	640	746
Rice	429	442	513	608
Sugar cane	15	17	16	27
Jute	71	72	75	75
Other	35	39	36	36
West Pakistan	328	353	385	505
Wheat	143	138	150	181
Rice	42	45	50	74
Other grains and oilseeds	76	79	81	84
Cotton	29	38	38	54
Sugar	32	42	53	94
Tobacco	6	11	13	18
Total	878	923	1,025	1,251
	(*Rupees per capita*)			
East	128	119	119	122
West	92	88	86	98
Total	111	105	104	111

Sources and explanations: Appendix Table 6.

Agriculture stagnated although numerous investigations had reached the same conclusions: first, that increasing agricultural output was extremely important; second, that there were known techniques for achieving a rapid increase (*80*, p. 178; *33*, pp. 2–10); and, third, that a given increase in agricultural output required less investment funds and foreign exchange than in industry, if appropriate techniques were used effectively. Some government officials and outside observers argued that increased agricultural output was more a theoretical than a practical possibility in a peasant agriculture. They doubted that a large proportion of cultivators would make the necessary decisions. The social, psychological, and institutional obstacles might be too great. Change might be precluded by the peasant's fatalism, the low importance he attaches to economic as against other values, the social and political organization of the village, the hold of tradition, or the distrust of government. If it is impractical to get a substantial proportion of peasants to change their production practices in the short run, it may be very sensible not to embark on a hopeless task, but rather to concentrate on industry and infrastructure, where something can be accomplished. Confounding the pessimists, a radical change occurred in the 1960's with agricultural production increasing more rapidly than population. This spurt in agricultural production was the main difference between the Pakistan of the 1950's and of the 1960's, as well as between Pakistan and other countries. The reasons for earlier stagnation, and the causes for the change in the 1960's are clearly important for Pakistan's development.

EFFECTS AND LIMITS OF PRICE INCENTIVES[*]

The evidence in earlier chapters suggests that changes in industrial investment and efficiency were brought about by price incentives. The effect of prices on agricultural output was not as clear-cut. It has often been argued that peasants in underdeveloped countries, even more than traders, do not act as rational economic men. Agricultural price policy in Pakistan, as in many other countries, assumed that peasant production would not be affected by

---

[*] For a more extensive discussion see (40).

a reduction in prices resulting from high export taxes and compulsory government procurement.

Even in the 1950's, taxes on agricultural exports — mainly on cotton, jute, and tea — were an important source of revenue, providing between 10 and 15 percent of total government revenues. Since most agricultural exports were sold in a highly competitive international market, the effect of export duties in Pakistan was to lower prices to the producer. Jute was an exception for a while, but India rapidly expanded its production and Pakistan's monopoly position was undermined.

Prices of food grains were also depressed as the government imposed compulsory purchase, price control, and rationing, especially for wheat. Until 1960 wheat surplus areas could sell their surplus production only to the government, at a price which was lower than if it had been sold on the free market. The government then sold to the deficit areas. Government procurement efforts naturally were strenuous in years of low production, when high prices might have compensated producers for reduced output. The destabilizing effects on cultivators' income were increased by this policy. At all stages prices were controlled. In addition, the government closely regulated milling practices and distribution channels. The dual purpose of these policies was social justice and low prices. As might be expected from the failures in controlling industry, the results were smuggling, black market prices, and a disincentive to produce wheat, especially in the surplus areas best fitted for wheat.

The effect of low prices on production was ignored until impressive evidence accumulated that Pakistani peasants do act, to a considerable extent, as rational economic men. The price of tobacco rose sharply between 1949 and 1959; its output increased steadily and substantially. By contrast, average annual wholesale prices of wheat remained unchanged and so did wheat output. More sophisticated studies found that relative prices affected the cropping pattern. The short-run elasticity of supply for some crops was quite high, and was similar to that in countries like the United States. Changes in the cropping pattern occurred even if the more remunerative crop took more labor; that is peasants were willing to exert themselves for additional income.*

Two important conclusions follow. First, many peasants, even in an underdeveloped country such as Pakistan, respond to economic incentives. Tradition and ignorance are not always insurmountable barriers to the use of economic policies in changing peasant behavior. Second, prices can be used to change cropping patterns and, by causing a shift from low-value to high-value crops, to increase the value of total agricultural output. For instance, a 10 percent increase in the relative price of cotton, obtainable by abolishing the export duty and providing an export subsidy, can be expected to increase cotton acreage by about 4 percent, mostly at the expense of crops with a lower value. A shift to an optimal cropping pattern could produce dramatic results. One purely theoretical estimate, for a sizable area in West Pakistan, was that such a shift could increase the value of output over 50 percent without any major change in techniques or inputs (33, pp. 2–10).

However, there are very severe limits on the effectiveness of relative prices on cropping patterns. First, there are physical limits. Significant options are open only in some areas; in others, the development of irrigation or drainage facilities is required before there can be an alternative to the low-value crops.

More important, most of the high-value alternatives require a shift from production for local consumption to

* Information and conclusions on cropping patterns are drawn from (38); (39); (32); (111); (99); and (159).

production for a wider market. This shift cannot be made unless the increased output can be marketed and the risks of the shift are within acceptable limits. For instance, growing vegetables may be a good linear-programming solution, but it is not a real possibility unless the output can be taken over good roads to sizable markets. The risks of producing for the market are important deterrents to a change in cropping patterns. Producing for their own consumption or for barter, peasants have only to contend with the risk of weather; for a cash crop there are the additional risks of a drop in its price, or of a rise in the price of the food the peasants would have to buy. Those who live on the edge of real starvation, with few reserves, appraise such risks differently from those who are less vulnerable. Cash crops are grown on large farms or on land which is not needed for the peasant's own consumption requirements. This pattern will remain unless the risk of price fluctuations is reduced, or unless the difference in return between cash and food crops is very great, so that the risk becomes acceptable.

Although changes in relative prices induced shifts from one crop to another, the effect of the level of agricultural prices as a whole on total agricultural output is less clear. A change in the terms of trade for agriculture, that is, in the relationship between the prices of the goods bought and sold by the peasants, did not seem to induce much change in the land under cultivation or in the use of labor or of improved techniques. The response of most peasants was limited by inadequate capital, inadequate knowledge, and high risk.

Little unused cultivable land remains. Water-control measures — irrigation and drainage — could increase the effective cultivated area by permitting double cropping or the use of idle land. However, many water-control projects depend substantially on government or government-

organized action, not on the response of individual peasants. Other steps to increase agricultural output required a
major change in techniques which seemed little influenced
by price levels. Peasants were quite prepared to shift to a
crop requiring more work, but on a particular crop the
amount and kind of labor applied was largely governed
by tradition. Whether new technology was adopted depended in large part on the producer's knowledge of the
technique and on the risk involved. It depended equally
on the availability of credit and of the required supplies.
For many changes in technique, for instance in the use of
fertilizer, the returns (ex post) would have been far above
the cost, even at the terms of trade for agriculture prevailing in the 1950's. But this was of little significance so long
as cultivators were ignorant of the technique; or had little
confidence, because of an uncertain water supply, that the
returns would actually be forthcoming; or could not obtain the fertilizer when and where it was needed.

The prices of agricultural products did affect the peasant's appraisal of the risk of some innovations. Investment
in pumps or purchase of fertilizer were more attractive if
the ratio between cost and return was improved by higher
prices for agricultural products. Other constraints, especially inadequate distribution, might still be decisive.
However, if these were not too severe, relative prices did
affect the use of these inputs to some degree, in the judgment of knowledgeable people.

The response of agriculture to price incentives therefore differed fundamentally from that of industry. Peasants responded by adjusting their cropping pattern and
by changing the use of some inputs, but there were severe
limits to both tendencies. In addition, the smallness of
units and the inherent risks of agriculture meant that price
stability was particularly important.

Government policies took increasing account of these factors. To encourage production of export crops, export duties on cotton, jute, and other products were progressively reduced, although they had not been eliminated by 1965. (For cotton, the duty was reduced from Rs. 115 per bale in 1958 to Rs. 25 per bale in 1964–65.) In 1960, amid dire predictions of profiteering and food riots, all restrictions on the price and movement of wheat were removed. The government undertook to sell wheat at Rs. 16.0 a maund (82 lbs.) and to buy at Rs. 13.5. Predictably, prices rose above the official level as soon as controls were removed. They were quickly stabilized, however, in a range below the previous black market price. Fears of an astronomical price increase proved groundless because wheat was released from stocks built up by large shipments from the United States, and decontrol made for more efficient distribution. Price differences among areas and between years were reduced, the black market disappeared, and smuggling declined. The elaborate machinery required to enforce distribution and price controls could be dismantled.

Unfortunately, storage facilities were inadequate to carry out fully the wheat-price guarantees. In addition, the government remained unsure of the effectiveness of its own machinery and was not always willing to release stocks when needed. As a result there were temporary shortages, and prices rose above the guaranteed maximum. For instance, early in 1964, the government underestimated the need for imports, and stocks were inadequate to compensate for the error. More serious, when there was a particularly good harvest in 1962–1963, the government simply was not able or willing to maintain prices at its guaranteed minimum. There was no place to put the stuff. Peasants who have found that the government guarantee works only when they do not need it are bound to be even more suspicious than peasants traditionally are about government guarantees.

Rice prices were also stabilized somewhat, although without a guarantee. Variations in the import of rice and in the release of imported United States surplus wheat reduced price fluctuations. These measures have been generally successful in preventing large price rises. Between 1961 and June 1965, with 1959–60 as base 100, the index for East Pakistan rice prices has been above 110 for only 3 months. The government, however, was less successful in assuring minimum prices. During the extraordinary harvest of 1963–64, wholesale prices dropped from an index of 112 to 74 in 9 months, a fall of over one-quarter. The government simply did not have the facilities to store, or the ability to export, the rice.

The price policy, which was gradually developed in the 1960's, substituted market incentives with stabilized prices for direct controls over distribution. It improved the distribution of food grains and provided some incentive for the production of cash crops and export commodities. By reducing the risk of large fluctuations in food grain prices, it increased the willingness of peasants to shift from subsistence to cash crops, to use fertilizer, and to develop irrigation. It was a move in the right direction.

The government had to play an important role in raising and stabilizing the prices received by the cultivators. To make price guarantees effective, a large-scale government storage, purchase, and distribution system was necessary. To make the increased production of cash crops marketable required government improvement of the transport and communications systems. The role of the government in creating the infrastructure for agriculture was especially important in Pakistan because there was little private activity in this area and because the control of water, largely a government function, was of unusual importance in a country consisting of part desert and part swamp.

RURAL INFRASTRUCTURE

The government's increasing competence in developing the infrastructure has already been discussed. Roads and water-control projects were crucial to agricultural development. Expenditures in these fields increased more than tenfold in constant prices between 1949–50 and 1964–65. However, the contribution to economic development of many of these projects was less than planned. The government's ability to carry out engineering works was not matched by a capacity to organize and administer the more diffuse, widely distributed, and complex task of maintaining roads, developing local water distribution and drainage systems, and settling people on the land. For instance, it is typical that during the first Five-Year Plan the construction of irrigation works in the Indus Basin proceeded largely as planned, but the area actually irrigated was only two-thirds what had been planned (*150*). In the first 3 years of the second Plan, expenditure on water development was 54 percent of the 5-year target, but the area irrigated was less than 25 percent of the target (*152*).

The costs to the economy are obvious. A large proportion of the government's total investment (over one-quarter of total public investment went to irrigation alone in 1964–65) was unproductive for 1 to 3 years after completion of the engineering works. If one assumes a 15 percent rate of return, and if returns from half the water investment are delayed 2 years, this would mean an annual loss of income approaching Rs. 15 crores ($30 million) in the middle 1960's. Yet this particular loss was not inevitable; it was due, at least in part, to a failure in administration. The elite civil service had demonstrated that it could solve more complex problems in other fields. A greater allocation of administrative resources to this aspect of rural development could have reduced the losses from inefficient use of construction projects.

In the 1960's the contribution of the government's development program to agricultural output was more effective than earlier. For one, the engineering effort was much larger. Between 1954–55 and 1959–60 the real expenditure for water, power, and roads tripled. In the next 5 years it nearly tripled again over the new level. In addition, there was a significant improvement in administration. Two semiautonomous Water and Power Development agencies (WAPDAs) were established, one in each Province. They were less bound by rigid bureaucratic practices than were normal government departments. Good staffing and the heavy use of outside consultants added to their effectiveness. Both agencies benefited from the almost unprecedented decision of the new military regime to ignore rigid seniority in order to appoint first-rate men to crucial positions, although this was considered sacrilege by some civil servants. Government actions indicated that the water control and engineering aspects of agriculture, at least, were being taken seriously. As a result, land reclamation in West Pakistan was accelerated. The vast Indus Basin Replacement Works was ahead of schedule in the mid-1960's and presumably so were the considerable, though incidental, development benefits. In East Pakistan, WAPDA was slower in getting started, but by the middle 1960's it was beginning to show progress.

The government's transport-development program was also accelerated and improved, but a large proportion of it continued to cater to the urban, industrial and commercial sector. In 1961 cultivators in East Pakistan reported that, in order to reach a surfaced road, a steamer stop, or a railway station, about one-half of them had to go 11 miles or more (25). To market some produce, a distance of 5 miles or less may be the limit.

The government's direct-investment program still left much to be desired in the 1960's — water use continued to lag behind water engineering works, road maintenance behind construction, and land settlement behind land availabilities. But, compared to the 1950's the government investment program had substantially improved. The irrigated agriculture of West Pakistan benefited especially from an expanded and more efficient government water development program. East Pakistan, on the other hand, was more successful in developing a large number of local public works projects under decentralized administration, a cooperative effort between the government and local committees.

THE WORKS PROGRAMME[*]

This effort, the Works Programme of East Pakistan may be the major contribution to economic-development techniques which Pakistan has made. A substantial modification of programs tried in a few other countries, it is a locally administered, rural public works program, financed largely but indirectly by imported surplus agricultural commodities.

Perhaps the outstanding feature is its local administration. Public works programs have been restricted in scope because they are difficult to administer. To take advantage of farm labor, part of the year, on a few large projects, vast numbers of workers would have to be moved from their farms to the construction site, and returned home at

[*] Factual material in this section is taken from (132); (133); and (53).

planting and harvest time. At the project site, housing and other facilities would be called for — a costly undertaking. A solution is hundreds or even thousands of small, scattered local projects. But most governments find it impossible to administer such a program centrally. It would be a tremendous administrative task to plan several thousand projects, design them, organize the workers, supervise the work, prevent excessive waste and corruption, and finally make payment. Decentralization of management was adopted in Pakistan because a large local works program could not be carried out otherwise. It was widely assumed that substantial waste would result, but that it could be accepted since the real costs of the program were small. In fact, there was waste. Funds were misappropriated, factional disputes prevented work from going forward, many projects were delayed by inadequate management, and design or engineering was sometimes poor. On the whole, however, the program was carried out with less waste and at substantially lower cost than comparable projects run by government departments through contractors. Decentralization proved successful in part because it was accompanied by detailed instruction manuals; by short but intensive training of the local government officials in charge; by insistence on open meetings to discuss projects, and the publication of booklets on the work accomplished; by the requirement that three local government officials certify work done; and by detailed reporting and inspection of records after the work had been completed. Compulsory publicity was crucial. When word spread on funds available, villagers had a pretty shrewd idea of what could be accomplished with them. Political or personal enemies were sure to point out any failure to give a community its money's worth. The post-audit system made it possible to dispense with detailed controls before and during the execution of the projects, which would have delayed progress. Technical manpower was made available by government departments, but management was local. (The program used a few Peace Corps volunteers with technical training. It could have used many more.)

The second basic principle was that labor would be paid for. It was to be neither voluntary nor compulsory unpaid work. For one, unpaid work is very difficult to organize on a large scale. Besides, unskilled workers usually need additional food to work effectively. Most rural areas are too poor to support community investment with their own resources. There was no need to insist on unpaid work; a large proportion of any pay received would be spent on basic foodstuffs, and the United States was prepared to make available its food surpluses. Workers were usually not paid directly in surplus commodities. This would have required a substantial administrative apparatus, some workers would have refused such an arrangement, and most would have resented it. Instead United States surplus commodities, especially wheat, were imported in large quantities and sold. The money from the sale was used to pay the workers, at a rate appropriate for off-season, local, and largely unskilled work.

The surplus wheat was sold at prices sufficiently below the price of domestic rice to induce large numbers of consumers to overcome their strong prejudice in favor of rice. In 1956–57 East Pakistan produced and consumed only 20,000 tons of wheat. By 1962–63 it used over 600,000 tons. A simple study suggested that wheat purchases were closely related to the ratio of rice to wheat prices, thus destroying the myth that rice eaters would rather starve than shift to wheat (47). The time period is short for quantitative conclusions, but it is clear that some people's consumption patterns were remarkably flexible, given adequate price incentives.

The physical accomplishments of the East Pakistan Works Programme were impressive — greater than even its advocates expected. In the first year of full operation (1962–63), it built 3,600 miles of new earth roads, and 17,000 miles of existing ones were repaired. In addition, 1,300 miles of channels were excavated, new embankments were built, and so on. This whole program cost Rs. 10 crores ($20 million). Accomplishments in the second year were also considerable, although affected by the 1963–64 election when the energies and attention of the local leadership were naturally divided. In 1964–65 emphasis on roads continued strong (29,500 miles constructed, reconstructed, or surfaced), but there was an important shift to water-control projects. The excavation of channels to speed drainage (5,400 miles) and the construction of embankments for flood protection (3,700 miles) were obviously important for agricultural production in East Pakistan, where some of the most productive areas suffer regularly from floods (*14*). Estimates suggest that annual returns were several times the investment cost. There were some obvious problems. Earth structures of the kind built need substantial maintenance and rebuilding in East Pakistan because they are partly washed away by each year's rains and floods. Of the 28,300 miles of roads and embankments included under the 1963–64 program, less than 4,000 involved new construction. The great bulk of work was repair of existing structures. The first years saw the very simplest structures built; in the future more technical knowledge and coordination will be required, especially since the program is to be rapidly increased five-fold.

The second benefit was in providing income and employment. An estimate of the effect on employment is only a rough guess. It would appear that in 1964–65 employment was between 2 and 10 million man-months (*14*), substantial by any measure. About three-quarters of total expenditures were for wages.

The program also reinvigorated local governments, who finally had something important to do, and the resources for doing it. For the first time, they were effectively enlisted in an important, massive development effort. New leadership developed. Local government officials had a new sense of purpose. The workers' attitude toward government changed. They will be more receptive to other programs to increase agricultural production.

The effect on agriculture is difficult to demonstrate in quantitative terms. Agricultural output in East Pakistan reached unprecedented levels in 1963–64 and remained high in 1964–65. Those close to the Works Programme consider it a significant factor in this performance. Some of the added income was used to reduce indebtedness, and a heavy debt burden is widely regarded as discouraging to increased output. They argue that the Works Programme added to rural purchasing power, some of which went to agricultural inputs; that the expanded rural road network reduced the price of inputs, improved the prices received by the farmer, and encouraged production for the market; that the roads built under the program sometimes acted as embankments to protect land from floods, while the ditches dug to provide soil for the roads helped with drainage; and that drainage channels and embankments constructed under the program alone made a significant contribution to production. Local works, especially drainage channels and coastal embankments, probably deteriorated after 1947 with the exodus of many Hindu landlords who had organized maintenance. With land reform, holdings were too small for individuals to remain responsible for maintenance. The Works Programme may be a good device for organizing and financing on a community basis the maintenance of thousands of local works and for constructing new ones. There is little question that the program contributed to increased production in East Pakistan, but it is too early to be sure that it was a major factor.

The success of the East Pakistan Works Programme provides further evidence that a peasant society is not completely stagnant and tradition-bound. In Pakistan the government was able to mobilize and organize the peasants to participate in the change. The Works Programme also showed that the government can carry out a massive program to develop the rural infrastructure by working through existing institutions.

The situation in West Pakistan was different. Larger holdings meant that a communal works program was less necessary. Local government units were less well developed. Unemployment was less of a problem. Decentralization of management was carried less far. For all these reasons, the Works Programme was neither as large nor as successful in West as in East Pakistan.

THE ROLE OF GOVERNMENT
IN PROVIDING TECHNOLOGY AND WORKING CAPITAL

So much for the environment in which cultivators made their decisions. The prices they faced had been depressed by the government in the 1950's, but had been raised and stabilized in the 1960's. The rural infrastructure had been substantially improved by a larger and more effective government investment program. The development of major irrigation works was particularly important in West Pakistan. The Rural Works Programme was of special benefit to East Pakistan. While prices and infrastructure were important, a large increase in agricultural output depended at least as much on changes in agricultural technology, combined with the increased use of various inputs. Improved technology and the greater use of inputs required both government and private actions.

Throughout the 1950's, the government's role in inducing a change in peasants' behavior was emphasized. It was widely accepted that yields could be doubled, without much additional fixed investment, by inducing the peasants to use fertilizer and improved seeds, by pest control and weeding, and by improved techniques in planting and water application (*33, 80*). It was widely agreed that this required the government to improve the extension system, provide credit, reorganize its own administration of agriculture, organize the villages for joint effort, distribute fertilizer and seeds at low prices, and so on.

It is clear that widespread government action is necessary to increase agricultural output. The market alone is inadequate to bring about technological change in peasant agriculture. For many aspects of agricultural development, there are substantial external economies, great differences between private and social costs and returns. The government universally carries much of the cost of agricultural research and its dissemination to cultivators. Supplying goods and credit to millions of small buyers and borrowers who are not aware of the increase in output they can achieve and who are a substantial credit risk requires government subsidies at least, and usually some government management besides.

In the 1950's, the government in Pakistan was not geared to such actions. Failures in this respect are widely documented. For instance, by 1960 only 10 percent of cultivators had visited demonstration plots and less than 5 percent had used the services of the extension staff (*25*). Guaranteed and improved seed for jute, the most important of Pakistan's exports, was sufficient for less than 2 percent of total acreage in 1960 (*122*). Many government seed farms were reported to provide inferior quality seed;

and nearly half of all cultivators reported that the government stores did not have seed when it was needed. About a quarter reported trouble with price or credit. Ignorance and complaints were frequently expressed about the government plant-protection service (25). Even discounting for the fact that some people are never satisfied and that others rationalize their own failures by blaming the government, these figures should have caused some concern about the adequacy of the government effort.

Three-quarters of all cultivators in East Pakistan, and an even higher proportion in West Pakistan, said they knew about and believed in the use of fertilizer. Yet less than a third of these had actually used it in 1960–61. The main reasons given for this discrepancy were that credit was not available, that prices were too high, and that the authority to issue permits for subsidized fertilizer was too far away (25). Some of the explanations may be rationalizations — many cultivators may consider it good practice to tell government questioners they belive in progress and therefore fertilizer — but even discounting for this, there was a startling discrepancy between cultivators' willingness to use fertilizer and government's ability to make it readily available on credit. The complaints are substantiated by the reports of outside observers. Credit facilities were completely inadequate to finance desired investment and current inputs, and government or government-supported credit facilities provided only a small fraction of the limited credit which was available (109).

These examples concern only the simple problem of making sure that the government had made appropriate services and supplies available. It is "a record of insufficient supplies, insufficient manpower, insufficient transport, insufficient coordination. It is a record of too few men with too little material trying to deal with too large a problem. No wonder that the results have been so meager" (33). Although the government managed to build 15,000 houses in 6 months, it failed to get 25,000 acres of improved jute seed planted in a dozen years.

There were a number of well-known reasons for the inadequate attention paid by government to agriculture. Until the middle 1950's, Pakistan was believed to have an exportable surplus of agricultural products. Later, official pronouncements emphasized the high priority of agriculture, but it remained low in practice. The government's agricultural program had little prestige and offered an unattractive career, with lower pay, perquisites, power, and responsibility than other fields. For instance, a Province had a single Director of Agriculture, the highest post a technician could reach. He was paid Rs. 1,250, or $266. a month. The same Province would have about 50 officers in the elite civil service, mostly younger than the Director, with much of their career still ahead, and whose income equaled or exceeded his. There were another 120 or so professionals (doctors, police officers, engineers) and administrators with higher pay (82). Most of these were engineers, whose opportunity for supplementary income was legendary. Similar differences existed at all levels of the hierarchy. Most young men, contemplating their careers, would judge the priority given to agriculture not on the basis of the Planning Commission's statements, but by the low pay and prestige actually accorded that profession.

The frequent shifting of professional personnel was widespread in government, but seemed to be especially damaging in rural development. In one district, the average tenure at a single location of Union Agricultural Assistants, Thana Agricultural Officers, and District Agricultural Officers was 4.5, 5, and 12 months, respectively (48; 179). Presumably all they could do was to recommend the same practices wherever they went, however inappropriate they might be. In three years, there were

4 different Secretaries and 3 different Directors of Agriculture in one Province.

In addition, an assignment in agriculture was likely to leave a black mark on the record of any administrator. Even a lazy, not-too-bright civil servant was capable of handing out import licenses to eager businessmen. On the other hand, an administrator in charge of developing cooperatives, settling peasants on new land, or distributing fertilizer usually had clear-cut, quantitative goals. Unfortunately, since the objectives were often unattainable with the available resources, the administrator in charge of an agricultural program was almost certain to fail, and his failure would be obvious.

One need only read the 500 pages of the Report of the Food and Agriculture Commission of 1960 to find many examples of inadequate performance (*80*). A dozen years after Independence, and several years after agriculture theoretically was given the highest priority by the government, there were failures in the agriculture program which the government simply would not have tolerated elsewhere.

By the middle 1950's, some improvement in the government's performance in agriculture became noticeable. Progress became more rapid in the 1960's. According to one study, the government's effort in agriculture doubled in the four years between 1955–56 and 1959–60. During the subsequent four years it increased more than sixfold from the higher base.

Not only was more being done, it was also better focused. Earlier, the limited resources allocated to agriculture had been widely dispersed with little sense of priority. Veterinary medicine had been well developed under the British; therefore much more attention had been devoted to livestock disease-control than to measures that

TABLE 22. GOVERNMENT EXPENDITURE ON
AGRICULTURAL DEVELOPMENT.[a]

Year	Expenditure (crores of rupees)[b]
1955–56	2
1959–60	4
1961–62	12
1962–63	23
1963–64	29

Source: (4).

[a] Expenditures are actuals for the first three years in this table, revised budget and budget figures respectively for the last two.

[b] Current prices.

promised greater returns. Gradually, there was increased attention to the crucial inputs and somewhat less emphasis on useful, but not essential, measures. Research, for instance, had not emphasized application in the early years. While the development of new seeds could contribute quickly to increased output, it had not received adequate priority in comparision with more esoteric but perhaps more fascinating matters. By the middle 1960's some government officials began to encourage research to develop new seeds.

The land reform program carried out by the government after 1959 was expected, by some observers, to have a major impact on agricultural output. Because changes had taken place in East Pakistan much earlier, in large part as the result of the exodus of Hindu landlords at Partition, the 1959 land-reform program affected only West Pakistan. The program was not conceived as a radical reform. In execution it was further affected by exceptions. Only a small fraction of the land in West Pakistan was redistributed under land reform. The program did provide increased security of tenure in some areas and may thereby have made a contribution — though neither measurable nor documentable — to increased output.

Another innovation in the 1960's was administrative. The success of semiautonomous agencies in industry, and in water and power, suggested that the same approach was desirable for agriculture. For some years observers had despaired of effective performance by the regular Agriculture Departments, especially in partly commercial tasks — producing and distributing improved seed, distributing insecticides, fertilizer, and irrigation pumps. A semiautonomous Agricultural Development Corporation (ADC) was set up in each Province. They were something of a disappointment at first since the neglect of agriculture could not be reversed overnight. However, by 1965 the ADCs were beginning to overcome their teething troubles. In addition, their establishment provided new room for experimentation. The ADCs, without sufficient staff and swamped with work, were quite willing to indulge private initiative. Private effort was particularly effective where economies of scale and external economies were not important, but where decentralization was vital. The installation of wells and pumps, and the distribution of fertilizer were the most important instances.

PRIVATE INVESTMENT AND TRADE — PUMPS AND FERTILIZER

While most irrigation developments required either government effort or the cooperation of many cultivators, wells and pumps often could be installed by the individual cultivator. A large part of the growth in agricultural output of West Pakistan was due to the rapid increase in private tube wells. One source estimated that over 31,500 tube wells had been installed in West Pakistan by 1965, most of them since 1959 (*41*). By the mid-1960's, about 6,500 wells were developed annually (*126*). These tube wells were financed chiefly by the cultivators and installed with a careful eye on costs. More important, the private owners wanted to maximize the returns from their investment. They sold any water which they did not need and adopted other practices to produce higher yields. As a result, the gross value of crops on land irrigated by private tube wells averaged nearly twice that on comparable land (*126*). In areas having a suitable underground-water supply, tube wells were highly profitable.

Several factors may explain the rapid increase of tube wells in the 1960's. The risk of shifting from subsistence to cash crops, which were more heavily irrigated, had been reduced by the guaranteed maximum price for wheat. Second, installation and operating costs of wells had declined. This was due in part to the gradual increase in the capacity of the Department of Agriculture and of private firms for drilling tube wells. More important, in the 1950's tube wells required diesel engines, with high capital and operating costs and maintenance problems. By 1964 about half of all wells were powered by electricity from the government grid (*126*). In addition, it became cheaper and easier to obtain materials needed for wells. During the 1950's import controls, combined with low priority for agriculture, made it difficult to obtain the imported materials required for wells. There was a black market for pipe, with prices twice the official ones. With a higher priority for agriculture and liberalization of imports, it became much easier to acquire such equipment. Third, there is always a time lag in the diffusion of agricultural innovation. In 1952 only the most venturesome and affluent cultivators risked making the investment. Gradually, as the wells' profitability was demonstrated, the word spread. Even for such simple practices as line sowing, which requires practically no capital, the average delay between awareness and trial adoption was 3 years for a small sample of cultivators (*160*).*

The rapid spread of tube wells in the 1960's accounts for a large share of the increase in crop production in West Pakistan. It also supports the argument that some peasants do look out for their economic advantage. They will even find the capital to invest if the risk is not too great and necessary facilities are available. Tube wells turned out to be a strategic innovation. Cultivators with access to reliable tube well water could adopt other improved practices, especially chemical fertilizers, with less risk that water shortage would mean losses from these practices. Those with wells also had a strong incentive to adopt other practices in order to obtain maximum benefits from their investment. As a result of both factors, tube well areas led in the adoption of other improved practices. Also remarkable is the rapid growth of private industry to drill and service the wells. Over two-thirds of the wells were being installed by private firms which developed in response to the profitability of the tube well trade.

The other major area of private initiative was in the distribution of fertilizer. Various trials had suggested (*80*) that the return on one rupee spent on unsubsidized fertilizer ranged from 4 to 6 rupees for rice, jute, sugarcane, and oilseeds, to more than 10 rupees for potatoes and tobacco. Obviously this was highly attractive, yet little fertilizer was used despite heavy subsidies. Although fertilizer use nearly tripled in the 5 years ending in 1963–64, still the area covered was less than 10 percent of sown acreage for most crops. Two major causes of inadequate fertilizer use were administrative failure to provide credit, and failure to make fertilizer readily available. Occasionally the

---

* See also the discussion on the shift to sugarcane in (*38*).

high cost of fertilizer also played a role. Peasants again demonstrated that they were rational economic men and that the cost of fertilizer made a difference to them. Whenever the government subsidy on fertilizer was changed — and it ranged from 25 to 60 percent — the amount of fertilizer which was bought changed also.

Fertilizer was often costly to the cultivator, despite the subsidy, because the distribution system was inefficient. Distribution was in the hands of government agencies, semiautonomous corporations or cooperatives. That these agencies were often inadequate in performing their task is obvious from letters in newspapers, sample surveys, and field observations. Some distribution points were closed for days; fertilizer was often out of stock; there was red tape in obtaining it; and stores were too far from many villages. The distribution system was simply inadequate. It was therefore argued that the use of private dealers would improve distribution, and in 1963 some private agents were appointed to sell government-produced fertilizer. But fertilizer distribution was made unattractive to the private dealer. Gross markup was limited to an average of 10 percent so that, after meeting costs, the rate of profit was only a fraction of profits available in other activities. The distributor's own funds were tied up by a requirement to post a bond and by difficulty in obtaining credit. Since money could often be lent at 5–10 percent per month, tying it up in fertilizer was not very attractive. Moreover, the distributor could not legally increase his profit margin if he moved the fertilizer from the railhead, so he had no inducement to go to the trouble and risk of selling away from the railway line. Finally, the government could change its mind about using private dealers, so he was wise not to develop his facilities or his market. As a result, private distribution of fertilizer remained limited. In about half of all districts in West Pakistan, there was only one dealer for 10,000 or more farms, and one district averaged nearly 200,000 farms per dealer; over 400,000 farms were located in districts with no dealer at all.*

Even with these restrictions, distribution improved rapidly when private participation was permitted. In East Pakistan, fertilizer sales doubled in one year. Part of the increase was due to the greater effectiveness of the newly organized Agricultural Development Corporation, but part was due to the use of the private trade. The Districts with a large number of private dealers used much more fertilizer per acre under crops than the Districts with few dealers.† In 1963 West Pakistan reported excess stocks of 250,000 tons. In part as the result of the change in distribution policy, by November, 1964, there were unfilled orders for 125,000 tons (*41*).

In June, 1965, the government again eliminated private trade from fertilizer distribution in West Pakistan. Demand for fertilizer had increased rapidly, domestic supplies were suddenly inadequate, and orders for imports had not been placed in time. Given the scarcity of fertilizer, it was argued that public or cooperative distribution would assure a fair allocation, reasonable prices, and greater equity. The more cynical Pakistanis assumed that the major purpose was to take advantage of scarcity to enrich and strengthen the political position of those who control distribution. When supplies improve it may be possible to return to a system in which private, public and cooperative agencies are all allowed to distribute fertilizer.

---

* Unidentified, typed compilation, probably West Pakistan PIDC, 1964.

† Four Districts, each with 300 private dealers or more, used 45 percent of all fertilizer in the Province on 29 percent of the cropped area; ten Districts, each with 100 dealers or less, used 36 percent on 48 percent. (*120*).

EXPERIMENTS TO CHANGE PRODUCTION PRACTICES

The discussion so far has largely ignored general efforts to bring about a rapid change in the whole range of production practices, primarily because these efforts were effective at best only in limited areas. Two experiments undertaken in East Pakistan are examples. One was carried out in Mymensingh District, the other by the Academy for Village Development at Comilla. The Comilla experiment, started in 1960, aimed at a fundamental reform in village life, with agricultural change a consequence (*134*). A number of innovations characterized Comilla's approach. The main vehicle for disseminating knowledge was not the outside field worker going into the village, as in most community development projects. The individual field worker was not sufficiently well trained to deal with the wide variety of technical problems encountered. He could reach only a limited number of cultivators. Typically he was a young outsider, whose information and support might be welcome, but whose advice was often regarded with skepticism. Instead, the Comilla experiment had the village itself designate a representative who came to the Academy for training once a week. There, he was exposed to a concentrated and specialized technical staff. The staff could train 20 persons at a time and through them reach several hundred villagers. Most important, this agent of change was to be a respected villager, whose example and advice would be followed.

The second innovation was the organization of cooperatives to provide credit and encourage savings. The village cooperatives — in a more centralized system than usual — pooled resources, encouraged farm planning and savings, and carried out some of the simpler administrative tasks. They were not burdened with technical and accounting jobs, for which they did not have the skill, nor with management responsibilities, which in the past had aggravated factional disputes and led to dishonesty. The burden of management, of safeguarding funds, of audit and control was transferred to a Central Association, organized and largely supervised by the Academy.

The Comilla approach also called for the central pooling of some equipment (pumps and tractors) that was costly and inefficient to own, even for a whole village. To reduce risk, cooperative rice storage facilities were developed; credit was provided, with stored rice as security; and cooperatives were required to set aside disaster reserves of grain before loans were granted.

The program also brought together in one place and under some central guidance three functions and groups: the general administrator, usually the most powerful representative of government in the area, the professionals of the various government departments, charged with programs in agriculture, irrigation, road construction, health, and education; and the local self-government units, representing the political leadership of the area. Unlike previous rural-development programs, the Comilla project wanted to cooperate with the three most powerful influences in the area, not to set up a mechanism that would be regarded as a rival. This meant that information, supplies, and supervision were available in a single place, cooperation among agencies was facilitated, and different programs were reinforced.

There is some evidence that the new techniques were effective. Membership in cooperatives increased rapidly; the loan repayment rate was 99 percent, compared to 20–40 percent in other credit programs; cooperative processing plants and distribution channels were established; considerable use was made of pumps to permit double-cropping, and of tractors for early planting. Considerable data are available on the rapid increase in agricultural inputs. In 1963 the technique was extended to three new areas, and in 1965 to much of Comilla District. In a few years, the extent to which the institutional changes and increased inputs in Comilla depended on the dynamism of the director and the size and devotion of the staff should be measurable. The effects on output should also become clear. So far, crude measures, comparing production increase in the Comilla area with neighboring areas, show no measurable impact on acreage or yield (163). While there may be some question on the cost-benefit ratio, the Comilla experiment does provide evidence that change can be brought about in a peasant agriculture in a relatively short period of time.

Similar conclusions can be drawn about another pilot project in East Pakistan, in Mymensingh District (48, 179). The approach was different. Comilla aimed at a fundamental reform in village life, with agricultural change expected as a consequence; Mymensingh concentrated on agricultural change, with a reformed village life to follow. Existing agricultural personnel were given practical training for short periods, and then expected to organize local committees for various activities. The Mymensingh approach covered a wider area and operated at a higher administrative level than Comilla. It sent agricultural workers to the village, rather than bringing selected cultivators to a center. Because dissemination of new technology was the core of the program, with credit less important, it reversed the Comilla approach. Above all, the Mymensingh project worked within the traditional machinery. It demonstrated that agricultural development is possible, even by relying on the existing bureaucracy. In a period of two years almost a third of the District was organized. Improved practices were adopted on nearly 200,000 acres. Yields on demonstration plots were nearly twice those on other plots owned by the same cultivator, and were three times the average in the District. Over 1,000 pumps were used to irrigate about 60,000 acres. (The District has 285,000 cultivated acres.) This one District used almost half of all pumps in the Province in 1963–64. Areas were drained, roads built, irrigation channels dug. However, again unusual human resources were brought to bear on a rather limited area. Only an expanded program will show whether the results were another example — as in British days — of a dedicated and strong government official able to make a success of a "village uplift" program, or whether the techniques used can be duplicated widely.

The success of Comilla and Mymensingh is further evidence, indirect though it is, that rapid and widespread change in rural areas is not out of the question. In a few years there will be more direct evidence on the ability of the government to help bring about widespread change in technology over large areas. Until the middle 1960's, however, the increase in agricultural production which occurred was the result not of widespread improvement in technology, but rather of the effect of government programs on the one hand, and of changes introduced by the larger cultivators on the other. An unfortunate by-product probably was growing inequality in rural incomes.

GROWTH AND EQUITY

First, there were differences in regional growth rates. Tube wells were sunk primarily in West Pakistan, where the soil and water conditions are more favorable than in East Pakistan, and where more land is held in large enough units to make private development of wells feasible. In East Pakistan the development of tube wells and

the use of movable pumps was too limited to have a measurable effect on output. The difference in the development of wells largely explains the higher growth in agricultural output in West Pakistan.

In addition to Provincial differences, there are differences among areas and among individual units in the use
of fertilizer and well water, and in the impact of government programs. Institutional obstacles prevented progress
in some areas. There are still areas, especially in West Pakistan, where insecurity of tenure and lack of incentives
for the tenants make it difficult to achieve much change
in agricultural practices. In other areas in both Provinces,
the consolidation of tiny plots is a prerequisite to many
innovations.

The major difference, however, was between large and
medium-sized units on the one hand and small units on
the other. In general, only the former had the capital, or
access to credit, required to make some investments or to
step up the use of working capital; generally only the
former had holdings of adequate size for some investments and technological changes; generally only the
former had ready access to information and to government assistance; only the former could take the considerable risk of changing technology, increasing the use of
purchased inputs, or of producing for the market.

The ability to sink private tube wells differed greatly
with size of unit. It is estimated that nearly 80 percent of
all tube wells were sunk by cultivators with holdings of
25 acres or more (127). The smaller peasant did not have
enough cash to pay for a tube well, nor enough land to
use it effectively. Government or cooperative credit played
only a small role in enabling poorer peasants to raise the
capital for tube wells or in paying for privately distributed
fertilizer.

In addition to regional and size differences, social and historical factors also made for persistent differences in development among groups of cultivators. Some groups of poor or highly tradition-bound farmers did little to increase output. Others had less interest in income than in factional disputes, or in social and religious activities. Of course, there were also areas where little could be done because of poor land and scarce water. Tube wells naturally were concentrated in areas with a good supply of sweet underground water. In areas or among groups with none of these problems, there were individuals who were lazy or stupid or improvident. Programs to increase production could not be equally useful and attractive to all farmers. Studies at Comilla suggested that even a highly concentrated effort was effective with only some groups and individuals, chiefly middle-income cultivators (98; 9). The relatively rich presumably felt they could do better outside an organized program, and the very poor were too ignorant, or could not save, or could not afford risks. The Comilla program also was frustrated by factional disputes in some villages.

The selective impact of agricultural programs is not surprising. Even in countries where agricultural production has increased rapidly, areas and individuals have been left behind. The substantial rate of over-all growth in the 1960's was achieved only because resources, including government help, were available to those able to use them most effectively. Increasing disparity in income probably accompanied higher total production. There are serious moral and political disadvantages to programs which concentrate on those who can best take advantage of them. A conflict exists here between the aims of growth and equality, which parallels the conflict in industrial development.

THE DETERMINANTS OF AGRICULTURAL OUTPUT
AND THE ROLE OF GOVERNMENT

If one reviews the discussion thus far, it is clear that the use of price incentives, sensible policies, and effective government action achieved a respectable rate of growth in agricultural production. As a guide to future strategy, it is useful to quantify the contribution of different factors to increased output, though obviously any such estimate has to be very crude. More important, it does not take account of the interaction of factors, but arbitrarily assigns the increase in output which results from several factors combined to a particular input.

No detailed analysis has been made of factors responsible for the slower rate of growth in crop production in the 1950's, nor for important aspects of agriculture other than crop production — livestock, fisheries, fruits. For the crucial sector of crop production some conclusions can be drawn:

1. In West Pakistan the most important difference between the 1950's and 1960's was the increase in the number of tube wells sunk. About one-third of the additional water from wells was provided by the public sector; in the 1960's this was largely due to the improved performance of the Water and Power Development Authority (WAPDA). Private wells contributed over two-thirds of the water. The speed-up in drilling seems to have been the result of higher and more stable prices for cash crops and wheat, improved supplies of imported equipment, more widespread electric connections, drilling facilities and credit, and the gradual spread of technical knowledge and information. A very large share of the increased production in West Pakistan was due to tube wells.

2. In both Provinces fertilizer use increased in the

TABLE 23. CAUSAL FACTORS IN INCREASED CROP
PRODUCTION 1959–60 TO 1964–65 (APPROXIMATE
ANNUAL PERCENTAGE CHANGE).

Factor	East Pakistan	West Pakistan
Fertilizer	0.5	1.0
Irrigation — wells and pumps	–	2.0
Irrigation — surface water	–	0.7
Plant protection	0.3	0.4
Improved seeds	0.5	0.2
Increased labor, improved technology, and residual	0.8	0.6
Increase in cultivated area (including effect of irrigation)	1.3	–
Total	3.4	4.9

Sources: Adapted from (*43; 44; 41*).

Note: The growth rates for crops shown in this table differ from those in
Tables 1 and 6 for several reasons: (a) Trends in the above table were
estimated by the formula: $\log y = a + bt$, where y is value added and t is
time; whereas the equations estimating the trends in major crops in Tables
1 and 6 were of the form: $y = a + bt$, where y is gross output and t is time.
(b) In the above table, the trend was calculated for all major crops taken
together (the trend of the sums), while in the other two tables, trends in each
individual crop were calculated and then added together (the sum of the
trends).

1950's, and was accelerated in the early 1960's with improved distribution through the Agricultural Development
Corporations. (ADCs). There was further acceleration
when private dealers were allowed to participate in local
distribution. Increased fertilizer use "explains" something
like one-sixth of increased production in the two Provinces.

3. In both Provinces the improved performance of government machinery — the WAPDAs, ADCs, and Agriculture Departments — resulted in more effective programs
for improved seeds, plant protection, and water management. The West Pakistan program to develop surface-
water supplies was accelerated. Improvement in govern-

ment performance reflected the relative priority assigned to agriculture. Another quarter of the increased production in both Provinces can be arbitrarily assigned to such government programs.

4. In East Pakistan a significant, but not presently quantifiable, contribution was made by improvements in technology, concentrated at Comilla and Mymensingh, and by the development of protective levees, drainage channels, and roads under the Works Programme. These factors were of less importance in West Pakistan. In both Provinces part of the investment in local infrastructure only made good the deterioration caused by Partition. A very rough guess would be that one-fifth of growth in East Pakistan could be "explained" by improvements in technology and by local works.

5. East Pakistan's output increased because more labor and land were employed. Over one-quarter of the increase in output in that Province may have come from these sources. Further significant increases in production from these sources is strictly limited because the agriculture of East Pakistan is already labor-intensive and nearly all cultivatable land already produces at least one crop.

The impact of these factors resulted in a higher rate of growth of crop production in West than in East Pakistan. Since some inputs which are important in West Pakistan — tube wells, for instance — can be readily increased while the limits of other inputs — land and labor — may soon be reached in East Pakistan, only a special effort can raise the rate of agricultural growth in East Pakistan to that realistically planned for the West.

A basic change in government policy in the 1960's encouraged the increase in inputs and the shift to higher value cash crops. In the 1950's, the government depressed most prices of agricultural products by export duties and controls on food grains; in the 1960's export duties were reduced, food grain prices and distribution were freed, and the government stabilized wheat and to a lesser extent, rice prices. The terms of trade for agriculture as a whole improved, and the relative prices of higher value cash crops especially rose. Subsidies on inputs continued to be high. The evidence is strong that many of the peasants of Pakistan, with a largely noncommercial agriculture, behaved substantially as economic men. Within limits imposed by lack of knowledge, lack of capital, and inability to face large risks, they responded to price incentives. The change in governmental price policy was therefore a major, though not quantifiable, factor in the rapid increase of agricultural production in the 1960's.

Both the government and the private sector played a role in expanding agricultural output. The larger units could more readily take advantage of opportunities to produce for the market, to develop their own wells, and to increase the use of such inputs as fertilizer and improved seeds. Quite naturally these units needed less assistance from the government than the small cultivators. The larger number of medium-sized holdings in West Pakistan may help explain the more rapid growth in that Province compared to East Pakistan. The fragmented holdings in East Pakistan require that the development effort in that Province involve more cooperation among individual owners, and more participation by the government. The Works Programme is the prime example of such an approach.

The explanation for the remarkable agriculture development over five years can be summed up as: higher and more stable output prices and some subsidized inputs; improved government performance to provide water, transport, seeds, and other inputs; and a larger role for private initiative in distribution and investment. The key to increased production in the short run was water and fertilizer, with private initiative of great importance in expanding the use of both. However, it is doubtful that progress, even in the use of these inputs, would have been great without support from government price policy, infrastructure development, and distribution policies. As the obvious sites for tube wells and the obvious areas and crops for fertilizer are exhausted, the government will have to further expand its efforts in research, extension, and credit in order to change technology.

The success of Pakistan in increasing agricultural production has been due in large measure to the same pragmatic mix of government and private enterprise which explained much of industrial growth. The government concentrated on a large range of functions which it alone could perform effectively — major infrastructure development, provision of credit and subsidies, price stabilization, production and distribution of some agricultural supplies, research, demonstration and extension — while leaving largely to private initiative the functions where decentralization is important — management of farms, investment in wells, local distribution of fertilizer, and marketing of products.

CHAPTER VII

SQUEEZING THE PEASANT

Savings

In underdeveloped countries, the rate of voluntary saving is low.

Upper-income groups often assign considerable prestige value to conspicuous consumption. This propensity seems to be re-inforced by . . . the "demonstration effect."

Moreover, the saving of the upper-income groups in these countries is seldom channeled into developmental investment.

In sum, the social and political context of some newly independent countries is hostile to the accumulation of capitalistic profits of the kind that played an important role in financing economic growth in the West.

TEXTBOOK ON DEVELOPMENT (95, pp. 480–82)

SO FAR, the rate of investment has been discussed, but the sources of savings and the factors influencing savings have figured in the drama only by implication. The implications have to be made explicit and the pieces pulled together, even if this process inevitably involves some repetition of earlier discussion and is of interest primarily to the economist.

It is sometimes argued that achieving a respectable rate of domestic savings (say 10 percent of domestic product or more) is one of the most difficult problems for an underdeveloped country. Only a very ruthless dictatorship can obtain significant savings in the public sector. It is equally difficult to increase private savings, because the wealthy are presumably subject to two "demonstration effects": first, the consumption levels of developed countries motivate imitation; second, industrialists and businessmen aspire to the consumption patterns of the traditionally prestigious groups — landlords and aristocracy — notorious for high living. Besides, conspicuous consumption differentiates the well-to-do from the "common folk." For the rich, the desire for modern forms of consumption, added to the traditional forms of displaying wealth, is supposed to make for a very high propensity to consume. The middle class tries to imitate the rich in both respects, and they too save little. The poor have little to save, and any income above subsistence goes for ceremonials and entertainment.

The outlook for private savings is therefore considered discouraging, unless religion or ideology intervenes. Supposedly Protestantism and Communism are the only strong ideological movements to stress austerity, savings, and productive investment. This is unfortunate since no underdeveloped countries are Protestant, and few authors of such arguments advocate Communism. The Japanese experience does not fit neatly into this scheme, so it is usually ignored or ascribed to unusual circumstances. There seems to be no disposition to elevate the Buddhist or Shinto ethic to the esteem enjoyed by the Protestant ethic in encouraging austerity in consumption, high savings and productive investment as a causal factor.

Even more discouraging is the argument that the small amount of available savings contributes almost nothing to economic growth. Part is exported, since there is considerable insecurity in underdeveloped countries. What remains is invested largely in land or in gold. This form of investment produces no increase in production. People sell land in order to consume the proceeds, and thus the purchasers' savings are dissipated. Gold is smuggled in, so its purchase does not increase the country's output.

One would expect Pakistan to find it especially difficult

to provide capital for investment. Per-capita income is low, even by comparison with other poor countries. To divert resources from consumption to investment, therefore, involves a difficult sacrifice. And Pakistan does not have a high-income enclave of raw-materials exporters to provide investment funds. Thus, it would appear that inadequate savings should be added to a poor physical and human resource base as a serious obstacle to Pakistan's growth.

Yet inadequacy of domestic resources was in fact not a limiting factor to Pakistan's growth. Imported capital goods were the constraint; private savings were remarkably elastic. Domestic resources were adequate to support the investment that could be undertaken. This bold statement must be somewhat modified and justified, but it is a reasonably adequate generalization.

THE SOURCES OF INVESTMENT FUNDS

Data on savings are particularly unreliable and their usefulness can be debated at length. Gross domestic savings were calculated by subtracting from estimated gross investment the estimated inflow of foreign resources. Both estimates have a considerable margin of error, so the estimate of domestic savings is not likely to be very accurate. There are also vexatious questions of definition which greatly affect savings calculations. Finally, in an economy such as Pakistan's, considerable investment and saving is nonmonetary (for instance, peasants who dig a shallow well). However, since estimates of nonmonetary investment are largely guesses, only monetary savings will be discussed.

Although the reliability of savings data is very low, some general conclusions can be drawn. In the first few years of Pakistan's Independence gross investment was low. It

TABLE 24. FINANCING OF GROSS INVESTMENT
(CURRENT PRICES).

CATEGORY	1949–50 Crores of rupees	1949–50 Per-cent of GDP	1954–55 Crores of rupees	1954–55 Per-cent of GDP	1959–60 Crores of rupees	1959–60 Per-cent of GDP	1964–65 Crores of rupees	1964–65 Per-cent of GDP
Import surplus	35	1.7	9	0.4	104	3.2	315	6.7
Public saving	−12	−0.6	4	0.2	8	0.2	37	0.8
Private saving (monetized)	53	2.6	149	6.9	238	7.4	460	9.8
Private saving (nonmonetized)	19	0.9	32	1.5	48	1.5	58	1.2
Total gross investment	95	4.7	194	9.0	398	12.3	870	18.6

Sources: Appendix Tables 2 and 7.

was financed in large part by drawing down the foreign-exchange reserves created by wartime savings. Current domestic saving during the period was very low.

The import surplus actually declined from the late 1940's to the middle 1950's. Foreign-exchange reserves were used up and foreign loans and grants were still small. Thereafter, however, the import surplus rose consistently and rapidly. By the middle 1960's, it was almost 7 percent of GDP, and that had grown substantially over 10 years. On the other hand, the import surplus was beginning to decline as a proportion of gross monetized investment.

Government savings — that is, the surplus of revenues over current expenditures — remained negligible until the middle 1960's and even then it was very small, despite successful measures to increase tax and other revenues. The government's current expenditures increased as rapidly as revenues.

The greatest change took place in (gross) private monetized savings. In the early 1950's, as the result of high export earnings, imported capital goods were readily available. Profits on investment in industry were high. Would-be investors had a strong incentive to save. During the Korean boom, high profit rates on exports and imports made it possible for those in foreign trade to save. At the boom's end, industrial profits and savings by industrialists increased very rapidly. If the figures are to be believed, real monetized private savings tripled between 1949–50 and 1954–55.

Later in the decade, the availability of imported capital goods to the private investor was reduced. Foreign-exchange reserves had been depleted, goods on order had been delivered, and the government took an increasing share of foreign exchange earnings for its own use. Investment, therefore, became more difficult and costly, and the incentive to save in order to invest was weakened. At the same time, the terms of trade for industry worsened and industrial profits declined. With savings incentives reduced and profit rates declining, gross private monetized savings stagnated after 1955.

In 1959 there was another sharp reversal of the situation. Imported capital goods became more readily available as the result of increased export earnings and foreign aid. There was also some increase in domestic production of capital goods. For the first time it seemed possible that the limit on investment would be savings, not foreign exchange. Would-be investors again had a strong incentive to save. At the same time, the industrial sector had grown rapidly. Even with a lower rate of profit, its potential for generating savings had improved. Agricultural savings probably increased as rural incomes improved and wells became an attractive investment. Real, private monetized savings almost doubled in five years.

The experience of the 1960's contradicts the argument

that savings are likely to be hampered by the development of domestic consumer goods production. The argument assumes that it is much more difficult to restrict the availability of consumer goods when they are domestically produced and do not have to be imported (157; 107). This may well be true, all other things being equal, but they never are. In Pakistan, one of the things that did not remain equal was per-capita income. The development of domestic consumer-goods production also raised incomes. It was easier to tax and easier to save when per-capita income was increasing than when it was stagnant. Increased national income also meant increased investment incentives and greater availability of capital goods, both of which provided further incentives to savings. At a given income and with given incentives, savings would probably decrease as domestic consumer goods became more abundant. With higher incomes and greater incentives, savings actually increased with the availability (or perhaps, despite the availability) of domestic consumer goods.

By the middle 1960's Pakistan's gross domestic savings clearly exceeded 10 percent of the GDP. The specific reasons for higher savings are of considerable importance for understanding the role of private enterprise and government.

GOVERNMENT SAVINGS

One of the criteria for United States foreign aid is the effort made by the recipient country, especially in increasing taxes and raising them equitably. Pakistan could meet this criterion admirably: tax rates were progressive, taxes were paid, and their amount rapidly increased. The authoritarian aspects of the political system made it possible to increase tax revenues very sharply in some years. The increase in central government tax collection over the respective previous years was nearly 25 percent in 1955–56, over 10 percent in 1960–61, and 20 percent in 1963–64. Unlike some other countries, Pakistan did not heavily subsidize its public enterprises. True, the railways, the PIDC, and other government enterprises probably did not cover their depreciation requirements (much less finance their capital needs), and were in effect dissaving; but they did not impose a large, continuing drain on government funds to meet operating costs. (It is difficult to be sure. The accounts are designed less for economic analysis than to show a current surplus.) Other government subsidies were also quite limited.

Despite a relatively good tax-collection system, sharply increased tax rates, and only modest subsidies, the government in Pakistan was unable to save significant amounts. Its revenues were enough only for current expenses.

The reasons are not difficult to discover. The functions which government performed before Independence were quite limited and the revenues which it raised were just adequate to finance them. Comparable levels of government in the United States, for instance, collect something like 4 times the proportion of GDP that the Central and Provincial Governments collected in Pakistan. With Independence, the government's role expanded tremendously: in defense, in foreign affairs, in administering rehabilitation and welfare measures, and above all in administering a rapidly expanding development program. It was inevitable that the cost of government would increase with its functions.

It took strenuous efforts to increase revenues. There is, after all, something to the argument, old in writings on development, that it is politically, administratively, and morally harder to squeeze taxes out of a population close to subsistence than one several notches above it. (This is

TABLE 25. GOVERNMENT REVENUES AND EXPENDITURES —
CENTRAL AND PROVINCIAL GOVERNMENTS
(CRORES OF RUPEES — CURRENT PRICES).

Item	1949–50	1954–55	1959–60	1964–65
A. Revenues				
Customs revenues	46	46	56	108
Excise and sales taxes	22	36	68	152
Income and profits taxes	12	23	36	63
Agriculture taxes	16	18	33	35
Other taxes	6	11	17	46
Total taxes	102	134	210	404
Other revenues	25	43	71	101
Total	127	177	281	505
As percent of GDP	6.4	8.4	8.9	11.3
B. Current Expenditures				
Defense	77	75	112	134
Administration, etc.	61	97	150	289
Debt servicing	4	13	25	43
Total	142	185	287	466
Accretions to reserve funds	−3	−12	−14	2
Net current (noninvestment) expenditures	139	173	273	468
C. Gross Public Savings (A minus B)	−12	+4	+8	+37

Sources: See Appendix Table 7 (GDP from Table 2).

only one of the reasons why a mechanical comparison between rates of savings in different countries shows little or nothing about the nature of their development effort.) If in a generally poor country there is some readily taxable income concentrated in a few hands, from oil, or plantation crops, or mineral exports, the governments find it easy to raise revenues, despite general poverty. But Pakistan had few highly profitable exports. Incomes in industry and business were sometimes high, but these sectors were small. Tax rates were in theory highly progressive. To raise income or profit-tax rates further, or to collect these taxes more effectively, would have been difficult and would have reduced both private savings and industrial investment.

It was politically difficult to collect more revenue from agriculture. The major direct tax on agriculture was on land, varying with its quality, and was designed originally to reflect the income that could be derived from the land. However, rates had hardly increased for a decade or two in most areas and, since the general price level had risen sharply from the prewar period, taxes had become a very small share of agricultural product. To increase the rate of land taxes posed obvious administrative and political problems. No government wanted to make itself unpopular with the overwhelming majority of the population. In West Pakistan there were a limited number of landlords with high agricultural incomes which could have been taxed. The political difficulty of doing so was due not to the number of landlords but to their power. Given the importance of agriculture in the economy, the result of stagnant agricultural taxes was an increasing burden on other sources of government revenues.

Income and profit taxes, collected mainly from industrial and commercial incomes, rose rapidly. Collections, however, lagged behind the rapid growth of value added in industry, the sector on which these taxes substantially fell. In part the lag was due to various tax concessions to promote investment; in part it was the result of an increased ability to avoid or evade taxes. There was a sharp rise in collections in 1958–59, when taxpayers feared the martial-law regime. New exemptions were subsequently granted, and the fear of drastic penalties diminished, so that revenues from these direct taxes again dropped behind the growth in industrial output. Income and profits taxes are widely considered a desirable way to raise government revenues, since they can be made equitable and progressive. In theory the Pakistan system was a good one; in practice various exemptions and tax evasion meant that, according to one estimate, only 10 percent of actual industrial profits were collected in taxes. At that level it is unlikely that these taxes were in fact sharply progressive or did much to reduce inequality in incomes.

The shift from imports to domestic production of consumers goods meant a rapid rise in revenues from excise and sales taxes and a much slower increase in customs-duty collections. Together these commodity taxes tripled between 1949–50 and 1964–65. However, during the same period, value added in large-scale industry increased nearly 15 times and commodity imports almost 5 times in current prices, although exports increased only 3 times. Therefore even revenues from commodity taxes were a declining share of the value of available goods. One reason is that many taxes were specific, not ad valorem, so that when prices rose, the impact of taxes declined. In addition there was a shift in the composition of imports as capital goods and intermediate products with low tax rates became more important.

While it was not easy to raise government revenues, it was even more difficult to restrain current government expenditures. The very poverty which made it difficult to raise taxes also made for strong pressures to raise spending. Government employment provided security and was much sought after. Salaries outside the elite service were often incredibly low and it was not only politically desirable, but often administratively important and morally imperative, that they be raised. For instance, at one time a large proportion of teachers in East Pakistan were paid less than 20 rupees (about $4) a month. At that salary, they naturally did little that was worthwhile. Raising their salary was an essential but costly step to improve education.

Expenditure for what is now everywhere euphemistically called defense, was always a heavy burden for Pakistan. Given the disparity in the size of the economies of India and Pakistan, any defense expenditure designed to approach India's in absolute terms would be relatively very large for Pakistan. Over 3 percent of national income has regularly gone to this purpose, a high percentage for an underdeveloped country with a very low income (although the military regime in Pakistan may have been unique among its kind in not raising that percentage).

In short, the government's current expenditures rose rapidly, while some revenues proved quite inelastic. That the government covered its current expenditures was due chiefly to the taxes collected from industry. Manufacturing contributed only 6 percent to gross domestic product in 1958. Yet, of total tax revenues of about Rs. 180 crores, some Rs. 47 crores, or one-quarter, came directly from industry in the form of excise, sales, and profits taxes. In addition, an unknown but substantial share of the Rs. 15 crores of income tax and profits tax was paid by individuals out of distributed industrial profits. Finally, a substantial proportion of the more than Rs. 40 crores of import duty were levied on industrial raw materials, spare parts, and capital goods. Administratively and politically, it proved much easier to tax industrial production than agriculture or commerce. Taxes were often passed on to the consumer, which meant that the peasant paid a large share ultimately, but industry proved an excellent device for collecting the taxes.

PRIVATE SAVINGS — INDUSTRY

Industry not only collected the taxes, industrial profits also provided a large proportion of private savings once a substantial industrial sector had developed. Initially, however, and through the early 1950's, investment in private industry was largely financed by profits from trade. Some figures may be apropos.

TABLE 26. SOURCES OF FINANCING FOR INDUSTRIAL ASSETS
WHICH EXISTED IN 1959 (AT COST).

1. "Initial" investment to establish particular units		*(crores of rupees)*	
(a) Indigenous private investment			
Pre-partition industry — owned by Pakistani citizens		26	
Trade — import		25	
Trade — export		13	
Trade — internal and government contracting		25	
Agricultural land and real estate — sale or income		7	
Commercial banks and other creditors		33	
Other sources		8	
Subtotal — indigenous private	137		
(b) Government and foreign investment			
Government equity investment (through PIDC or directly)		55	
Government credit (through PIFCO, PICIC)		1	
Indian citizens — pre-partition industry		12	
Other foreigners		11	
Subtotal — government and foreign	79		
Subtotal — initial investment			216
2. Later investment from outside industry — for expansion or modernization of existing units (net of disinvestment)			63
3. Industrial earnings reinvested in industry			221
Total assets			500

Source: Survey.

The initial investment in any particular unit often called for more entrepreneurial activity than investment in its later expansion. For the private, indigenous enterprises existing in 1959, such initial investment at cost totaled roughly Rs. 137 crores. (This excludes PIDC, government, and foreign investment.) Of this, about Rs. 26 crores was from pre-Partition industry, largely factories that already existed in Pakistan. Rs. 33 crores were provided by commercial banks and creditors but an examination of asset structures suggests that this mainly financed working capital, and was provided only when factories were in operation. Of the remaining Rs. 78 crores, 80 percent came from trade earnings, much of it from profits on imports. Importers directly earned about Rs. 25 crores. In addition, until the early 1950's much of the internal trade involved goods that were originally imported, such as textiles. Part of the profits of government contractors derived from sales of imported goods to the government. A rough guess would be that 10 to 15 crores of rupees from internal trade and government contracting represented profits on imported goods. Therefore approximately 35 to 40 crores of rupees invested in industry came from profits on imports.

Using these and other data, one can make a very rough guess at the rate of savings out of importers' profits. One first has to guess the profits of importers. Most imports in the period which was crucial for initial industrial investment (1947 to 1953) were consumer goods, and consumer goods had a much higher rate of profits than other imports. Import statistics show that in the period under review about Rs. 270 crores of consumer goods were imported. One can speculate — it is no more than that — that something like 20 percent, or Rs. 54 crores, of the total value of imports represented profits (the period under discussion was mostly before sharp import restrictions made for high profit rates). The rough guess above suggested that investment in industry out of import profits was 35 to 40 crores of rupees. Import earnings also financed investment in real estate, commerce, service industries, and transport. Some profits from imports were diverted to savings in foreign banks, though later a part was repatriated. If these guesses are even reasonably accurate, then the proportion saved (say Rs. 40 crores) out of import profits (say Rs. 54 crores) must have been very high.

While profits from the import trade were important in financing initial industrial development, subsequent expansion depended on a high rate of reinvestment from industrial earnings. If the figure for reinvested industrial earnings in Table 26 is correct (Rs. 221 crores), reinvestment in industry must have averaged over 10 percent of capital per year between 1950 and 1958.

There is further confirmation for a high rate of saving and reinvestment in the earnings reported by industrialists to the Survey. Of course the figures reported, especially for profits, were substantially lower than actuals. The interviewers' assurances notwithstanding, industrialists were afraid that tax authorities might obtain access to the Survey. This may not have affected the reported relationship between distributed and reinvested profits.

If the proportions are reasonably accurate, profits reinvested somewhat exceeded profits distributed. The picture becomes sharper if total returns are considered. Depreciation as reported bore little relation to actual depreciation on physical capital, but depended on tax laws. The great bulk of depreciation, often all of it, was reinvested. The management fees were largely profits paid to the managing agency as its share of the return, and were often partly or largely reinvested. Most of the interest charges went to banks, some for distribution to the owners, some for reinvestment. Some of the profits distributed were of course saved and reinvested by the shareholders.

If the assumption is made that undistributed profits and depreciation allowances were saved, the reported rate of gross savings between 1947 and 1959 was over 8 percent of industrial assets. This is an extremely conservative figure

TABLE 27. BREAKDOWN OF INDUSTRIAL RETURNS —
1947 TO 1959[a]

| CATEGORY | 1958 | | OTHER YEARS |
	Crores	Percent of assets	Percent of assets
Profits distributed	12.3	2.6	2.6
Profits undistributed	13.1	2.8	3.2
Profits taxes	16.8	3.5	6.5
Management fees	2.4	0.5	1.3
Interest charges	2.1	0.4	0.9
Depreciation charges	16.3	3.4	5.6
Total returns	63.0	13.2	20.0
Profits undistributed plus depreciation	(29.4)	(6.2)	(8.8)

Source: Survey.

[a] Data for 1958 are separated out because they are comprehensive, covering practically all firms in the Survey. For other years information was obtained only from some firms, mostly the larger units, and the results are therefore less reliable.

because reported profits are greatly understated. In addition, assets include "reserves," a large part of which were held as cash balances for future investment and were not really part of industrial investment. The "reserves" were one-fourth of industrial assets, but some were used as working capital. Subtracting "reserves" not used as working capital from assets, the rate of reinvested earnings as a percentage of capital used in industry is about 10 percent. This estimate is similar to one made earlier, based on the growth in industrial assets.

THE DETERMINANTS OF INDUSTRIAL SAVINGS

While the figures for reinvestment in industry are not exact, it seems fairly clear that well over half of industrial returns after taxes were saved and reinvested in industry.

Adding other forms of saving out of industrial profits — the funds exported, used to buy gold, or invested in real estate, land, trade, insurance, or banking — total savings may well have been at a rate of 60–80 percent of returns in industry. Evidence was cited earlier that traders, and especially importers, also saved substantial amounts and invested heavily in industry.

The reasons for this departure from expectations are complex. The attitude of Pakistan's industrialists did not conform to some authors' stereotype. These men had worked for their wealth, not inherited it, and they were little inclined either to waste it, or their precious time, by high living. Many seemed to have the Muslim equivalent of the Protestant ethic. Or rather, many had been used to a frugal existence and their wants increased much more slowly than their income. Industrialists probably had a standard of living which was traditional and changed slowly; they took from profits whatever was required to maintain this standard, and reinvested the rest.* This supports the argument that great inequality of incomes is conducive to increased savings. This, of course, is likely to be true only in the short run. By the 1960's in Pakistan, the expenditures of the newly rich seemed to be catching up with their income, and the political strains of inequality were being felt. But at least in the 1950's, regardless of the underlying psychological or sociological factors, many newly rich industrialists continued to live austerely in relation to their income, although not in comparison with those around them.

* There is evidence of this in the close correlation between absolute profits and the proportion reinvested. Smaller firms reported a higher rate of return after taxes than larger firms (12.5 percent as against 9.8 percent). But the larger firms reported reinvesting 57 percent of total profits, with smaller firms reinvesting less than 30 percent. Also, in years when profits were high (e.g., 1954 and 1959), firms reported that they reinvested a higher proportion of total profits.

The natural frugality of some industrialists may have derived support from the appeals by political leaders for austerity after Independence, from the obvious plight of many refugees, and from the egalitarian philosophy of Islam, although appeals for austerity might not have been very effective if it had been possible to indulge a taste for extravagance. Unfortunately for the potential profligate, government controls over investment assured that practically no luxury goods were produced in Pakistan. Import controls assured that few were imported and that these were extremely expensive. The newly rich industrialist could hire large numbers of servants or buy local rugs, but he could not throw away his new wealth on a fleet of cars, air-conditioners, or Dior gowns. Large houses were difficult to build, because imported steel, fixtures, and cement were hard to obtain. Travel abroad required special permission, and little foreign exchange was made available even for permitted travel. In short, the government's restriction on imports, travel, and domestic production of luxury goods discouraged the use of high incomes for consumption.

Restrictions on consumption not only discouraged the would-be consumer, they also changed the atmosphere in which the individual operated. The nouveau-riche businessman did not have to compete strenuously with other wealthy men in terms of travel, housing, or consumption. All of them were handicapped by the lack of goods, so none was under strong pressure to match the expenditures of others.

While consumption was frowned on and restricted, investment in industry was highly profitable and applauded by government. Investment, however, had to be largely self-financed since the capital market was rudimentary. The industrialist therefore faced strong incentives to save, and little encouragement to consume more than a limited fraction of his very high profits.

Industrialists continued to save, although profits declined and restrictions on consumption were maintained for a long period. Again one can only speculate on the incentives involved. Some industrialists wanted to increase their power, prestige, and influence by expanding their empires. Others may have labored under a kind of "income effect," enjoying an expanding income even if they could not or would not spend it in Pakistan's austere economy. Still others may have wanted to increase their income in anticipation of the time when consumption would be less restricted. The basic reasons for the behavior of Pakistani industrialists are undoubtedly complex. Many studies in other countries have shown that businessmen do not respond solely or even principally to the incentive provided by higher consumption. They may respond to outward measures of success, even if their consumption hardly changes. In this respect, Pakistani industrialists are probably not very different from Western ones. They too seem to be willing to exert themselves, to take risks in order to expand their empires, their profits and their power, even if they are not able to acquire a second or third car.

The explanation suggested should not be misunderstood. It is not argued that ideology, religion, the social system, or institutional factors were not important. It is suggested that strong economic incentives compensated for an unfavorable social and political environment. Though the social and political situation in Pakistan in the abstract may not have been very favorable to savings, just as it was not to entrepreneurship, government policies made for very strong economic incentives which resulted in a high industrial savings rate. The rate of savings in industry may have been determined largely by the incentive to invest and the disincentive to consume, both resulting from a scarcity of appropriate consumer goods.

Few data are available on savings outside the industrial sector. Savings from trade invested in industry have already been discussed. They were clearly substantial during the period when import trade was important. Industrialists reinvested some of their distributed profits via the stock market as new issues were floated. Investment in industry by "scattered shareholders" was therefore in part financed by savings out of industrial earnings. Industrialists in 1959 had assets outside of industry of over Rs. 100 crores, much of it (Rs. 46 crores) in banks and insurance companies, and some in land and real estate (Rs. 10 crores). Since the large industrialists derived their income primarily from industry, their acquisition of non-industrial assets was probably financed by industrial profits. Annual investment of industrial earnings outside of industry could be guessed at 5 percent of the stock of industrial capital.

Various surveys provide some slight, indirect information on saving by industrial workers, owners of small industrial firms, and lower-paid government and commercial employees. The results differ but they all lead to the conclusion that these groups saved very little. If the survey figures are reasonably accurate and typical, total net savings by industrial workers would be between 2 and 4 crores of rupees in the late 1950's. The savings of owners of small industry would be Rs. 4 crores, while savings for lower-paid government and commercial employees would be negligible. Compared to total savings of over Rs. 200 crores, the contribution of these groups was not significant.

Almost nothing is known about private saving and investment in agriculture. Some evidence that peasants save

TABLE 28. ESTIMATES OF PERSONAL SAVINGS
(AS PERCENT OF INCOME).

Coverage	Average	Lowest[a] income	Highest[a] income
Four cities, West Pakistan — workers (1958)[b]	4	−20	–
Karachi — workers (1959–60)[c]	6–8	0	20
Karachi — workers, government and commercial (1955–56)[d]	negligible	–	1
Karachi — owners of small industry (1959–60)[c]	7–13	–	–

[a] The definition of the lowest and highest income group varied among sources.
[b] (12).
[c] (162).
[d] (23, pp. 31, 56, 81).

under certain circumstances was mentioned in discussing programs to increase agricultural output. To finance the 3,000 private tube wells sunk per year on the average in the early 1960's required savings of over Rs. 3 crores by West Pakistan's cultivators. To finance the wells developed in the middle 1960's, savings of well over Rs. 6 crores per year were needed.

Over-all surveys suggest that agricultural savings may be quite significant. For East Pakistan, calculations from one survey give an average agricultural savings rate of over 3 percent (108). Another source of sample surveys reports the following personal rural savings rates (25):

1960:	East	7%	West	−1.2%
1961:	East	0.5%	West	5.5%

If one averages these figures on the assumption that variations are due to fluctuation in output, one also finds average savings rates of around 3 percent, or savings of about Rs. 50 crores.

A detailed study of five small areas in East Pakistan showed highly variable gross savings (89). It suggests typical per-family savings of Rs. 60–70 per year. This rate, extended to 10 million rural families, implies gross annual savings of 60 to 70 crores of rupees.

One survey (25) indicates that about 40 percent of rural savings was used directly for productive investment by the peasant. Almost a third was savings in kind (presumably stocks), and another quarter took the form of cash. If total savings were Rs. 50 crores, the share directly invested would be Rs. 20 crores.

It is difficult to know what the estimates of agricultural saving rates mean. The Central Statistical Office, commenting on its own surveys, suggests that the results should be taken "with a pinch of salt" (24). The salt dosage seems inadequate. Few peasants have reliable information on their income, and even fewer will give it to outsiders. There may be great variations in savings with the vagaries of the weather. If the crop has been good, cultivators may store some of it for a few months or a year, thus saving although without investing to increase future production. There is therefore little one can say with assurance about agricultural savings, one of the most important determinants of growth in an economy dominated by agriculture. If one accepts the results of the various sample surveys, ascribing the fluctuations and inconsistencies to fluctuations in output, prices, and investment incentives, one could guess that savings in agriculture have averaged Rs. 50 crores per year in the 1960's. Of this amount, some Rs. 20 crores would be invested directly by the cultivator, Rs. 13 crores would represent accumulation of cash, and the remaining Rs. 27 crores would be absorbed by changes in stocks.

The discussion of agricultural savings has been of gross savings. A great deal of investment in rural areas is offset by depreciation of houses, roads, irrigation and drainage channels, wells, and levees. It is likely that deterioration

in the years after Independence exceeded gross investment, as the result of the disruptive effects of Partition.
Net investment and savings in the rural areas may have
been negative in the early years. This is very likely since
the terms of trade sharply turned against agriculture in
the 1950's; savings must have been particularly difficult
during this period.

By the 1960's, the deterioration resulting from Partition
may have been largely made good. The terms of trade for
agriculture sharply improved. It was easier for cultivators
to save out of increased income, and they had greater incentives to save in order to invest in wells, pumps, and
other measures to increase production. Increased savings
in agriculture may to some extent have compensated for
declining savings rates in industry in the 1960's.

Another estimate of private savings has been made from
a different point of view. It covers the whole noncorporate
sector, that is, households and noncorporate business
(113). This estimate, in which currency holdings are the
largest single component, shows large fluctuations from
year to year, without any definite trend. For this reason,
a nine-year average may be more reliable than any single
year's data.

TABLE 29. ANNUAL AVERAGE OF NONCORPORATE PRIVATE
SAVINGS, 1954–1962 (CRORES OF RUPEES).

Currency holdings	19.3	Life insurance	3.3
Bank deposits	11.4	Corporate shares	10.6
Postal savings	6.9	Cooperatives	0.9
Provident fund	4.8	Deductions (loans)	−4.0
		Total	53.2

Source: (113).

THE SOURCES OF TOTAL SAVINGS

Putting all of the speculation in the past few pages together, one can arrive at an approximate picture of the

sources of savings. At best, this indicates orders of magnitude; and even this claim is not too well founded.

TABLE 30. A GUESS AT THE SOURCES OF GROSS PRIVATE
SAVINGS (CRORES OF RUPEES — 1958).

1. Industrial returns reinvested in industry (10% of industrial capital)	51	
2. Industrial returns invested outside industry (5% of industrial capital)	26	
Industrial returns saved		77
3. Additions to agricultural cash holdings	13	
4. Increase in cooperative assets	1	
5. Agricultural income directly reinvested	20	
Agricultural savings		34
6. Personal savings of industrial workers	3	
7. Personal savings of government officials, businessmen, professionals, and others, plus savings from trade, commerce, and small scale industry	29	
Commercial and urban household savings		32
Grand total by sources		143

If these figures have any validity, savings originating in industry account for over half of total private, monetized savings. Direct agricultural savings are much less important, despite the fact that agriculture's contribution to domestic product was several times that of industry. Indirectly, however, the peasants paid for industrial development. They made up the bulk of the consumers who paid prices far above those in the world market, thus providing high profits to industrialists and tax revenues to government. Only a fraction of what was extracted from agriculture in high prices came back directly in the form of government subsidies for fertilizer or water, or indirectly through government investment in water control, agricultural technology, or rural infrastructure.

Saving in Pakistan, as in most underdeveloped countries, involved squeezing the peasant. Because more than half the national income was generated in agriculture, the bulk of savings had to come from that sector. In Pakistan, however, squeezing the peasant did not mean direct taxes on agriculture; administrative and political problems were too severe for that. Instead, the terms of trade were turned against agriculture during the 1950's. Food prices were kept low while the prices of industrial products rose. Out of these high prices, the government took its share in the form of commodity taxes and import duties, the industrialists in the form of depreciation allowances and profits. For industry as a whole, the cost of production, despite inefficiency, was less than 80 percent of the sales price; nearly 10 percent went to the government in the form of excise, sales and income taxes, and at least 13 percent was the industrialists return. Value added by industry was roughly divided into three equal shares: for labor, the government, and the industrialist.

One can only speculate why this system was politically feasible. A complete answer requires a separate study by a competent political scientist. Undoubtedly the spirit engendered by Independence and Partition played a role. Later, the severe limits on democracy, and the effectiveness of the state's police power, were factors. But the use to which taxes and especially profits were put must have played some part. The tremendous disparities in income which resulted from the Pakistani pattern of development were not translated into equally wide disparities of consumption. The extraordinarily high incomes of the new industrial entrepreneurs were not as visible nor as galling when they were invested rather than consumed. The pri-

vate sector, particularly industry, was a superb machine
for squeezing resources out of a poor society, but it took
government-imposed restrictions on consumption to assure
that returns from industry were saved, not consumed.

As a result of the high propensity of industrialists to
save, combined with the shortage of foreign exchange, industrialists accumulated substantial cash reserves. They
held these in anticipation of foreign exchange for investment. In 1958 the estimated reserves amounted to Rs. 80
crores, or about one quarter of the book value of all industrial investment. That such tremendous sums were held
with little return, in large part in anticipation of an opportunity to invest them, tells a good deal about the willingness of Pakistan's industrialists to save in order to invest,
and their reluctance to fritter away their profits on high-
cost consumer goods.

INFLATION

The accumulation of capital reserves also helps to explain the absence of inflation in Pakistan, despite the very
rapid industrialization and the sharp increase in government development expenditures. Unlike many underdeveloped countries, especially those with a sharp increase
in development, Pakistan has not had a continuing, substantial general price rise. Some prices have risen. The
prices of manufacturers went up sharply when imports
were curtailed in the early 1950's. Devaluation in 1955
further increased the domestic price of imports. Other
goods, particularly crops affected by the weather, have
shown sharp temporary fluctuations in price. Changes in
world market prices affected Pakistan, especially through
changes in the prices of agricultural exports. The fall in
world agricultural prices with the end of the Korean boom
largely explains the decline of nearly a third in Pakistan's

wholesale price index between 1951–52 and 1954–55. Subsequently, with poor crops, devaluation, and a curtailment of imports, the index rose by over 60 percent in two years. Inflation seemed a real threat. Both the drop in the early 1950's and the later rise were much greater in East than in West Pakistan. However, from 1956–57 to 1964–65, Pakistan's wholesale price index increased by only 20 percent, and almost half of the increase was in the final year. The average annual increase in wholesale prices of less than 2.5 percent was one of the lowest in the world.

This stability has existed despite a rather rapid increase in the money supply. Currency in circulation and demand deposits increased from Rs. 300 crores in 1951 to Rs. 500 crores in 1957, and Rs. 800 crores by 1964 (93; 165), or an average compound annual increase of about 8 percent. Part of the increase in money supply was absorbed by an increase in goods and services available, part by an increase in cash balances.

The major reason for price stability after 1956–57 was the very rapid increase in the goods and services produced by and for the monetized part of the economy. It is a commonplace that the money supply can increase as the goods available increase without causing a rise in prices. In Pakistan the very rapid growth of industry increased the supply of goods for the market. There was therefore a rapid increase in the transactions demand for money. The almost limitless availability of wheat from the United States stabilized the prices of food grains, an important determinant of the general price level.

Cash balances increased rapidly and absorbed part of the increase in the money supply. Proceeds from the sale of surplus commodities partly accumulated in idle balances. Another part of the money supply was held by industrialists in the form of reserves for later investment. Finally, the increased monetization of the economy ab-

sorbed some of the increase in the money supply as working balances. If the previous guess about rural cash holdings is reasonably accurate, rural areas alone could have
absorbed over a third of the increase in the money supply.

Price stability resulted in part from the high rate of
industrial growth, combined with a high rate of savings
out of industrial profits. Price stability in turn encouraged
savings and made it possible to avoid the distortions in
investment patterns which can result from rapid inflation.

THE LIMITS OF SAVINGS AND AUSTERITY —
FOREIGN EXCHANGE AS THE LIMITING FACTOR

Clearly Pakistan had done well in the 1960's to step up
savings and investment without major price increases. The
question remains whether savings could have been increased further, both in the 1960's and earlier, and
whether as a result a higher rate of investment and growth
could have been attained. What, in short, were the limits
on savings and on austerity in consumption?

It was contended earlier that investment in Pakistan
was limited, especially in the 1950's, by the inadequacy
of foreign exchange, not by inadequate savings. That contention is open to challenge. Neither the foreign exchange
available for investment nor the foreign exchange required
for a given rate of investment are fixed by immutable
laws. More foreign exchange can be made available for
investment by increasing exports or curtailing imports for
current use. More investment can be undertaken with a
given amount of foreign exchange if the composition of
investment is altered to stress projects requiring less foreign exchange or if domestic goods and services are substituted for imports in the case of a particular investment.
A more realistic foreign-exchange rate might have simultaneously encouraged exports, discouraged imports, and

reduced the use of imported goods in the investment program. A more realistic exchange rate might also have made total savings, rather than foreign exchange, the limiting factor in investment. In view of these possibilities, can it be argued that foreign exchange was really the crucial limiting factor in Pakistan? To answer the question, the short-run possibilities and limits for (a) increasing exports, (b) reducing current imports, and (c) reducing the import component of investment need to be examined in turn. (The concern here is not with the possibilities and nature of an appropriate long-term development strategy for Pakistan, but with policies that affect savings and foreign exchange availabilities in the short run, a few years at the most.)

To achieve greater exports, or reduced current imports, or a reduced import component of investment, involves either the diversion of resources from consumption to investment, or the use of idle domestic resources, or more efficient use of available resources. The diversion of resources from consumption to investment was limited by political constraints. The only significant idle resource in Pakistan was labor, and its use was limited by institutional and administrative problems, by ignorance, and by the absence of suitable technology. More efficient resource use was possible, but difficult in the short run.

In the very short run, curtailing consumption would have been the most effective means to increase the foreign exchange available for investment. Consumption could have been reduced by various measures, including direct controls, devaluation, or specific taxes on domestic consumer goods. By reducing the domestic consumption of goods that could be exported, export earnings could have been increased. For instance, an increase in the price of cotton would have increased its production and therefore the amount available for export. A rise in the excise tax on cloth for domestic consumption would have increased the proportion exported at the expense of domestic cloth consumption. The same is true of tea and hides. On the import side, curtailing consumption could have freed foreign exchange for investment. Imports of consumer goods were already extremely low, but further reduction was possible. For instance, imported cars were few in number, but they could have been eliminated. Imported parts for car assembly could have been reduced. Gasoline for private cars could have been made more expensive. Imported raw materials for the production of consumer goods could have been further reduced or eliminated (for instance, rayon, plastic powder, and finer yarn).

In the 1950's, when the economy was growing slowly and per-capita consumption was stagnant, it is at least questionable whether consumption could have been curtailed further to make foreign exchange available for the import of investment goods. The temptation is great for the foreign observer or adviser to see few limits to austerity. Unlike the bulk of the indigenous population, austerity is not imposed on him; unlike the elite of a country, the foreigner is unlikely to be the victim if excessive austerity leads to the overthrow of the elite. Pakistan had already gone very far in imposing austerity in the middle 1950's. Imports of consumer goods and raw materials to produce them averaged Rs. 100 crores per annum before the Korean boom. Value added by industry then averaged Rs. 35 crores per annum. Together (Rs. 135 crores) they give a rough measure of the availability of (non-food) manufactured consumer goods during that period. In the middle 1950's, corresponding imports had declined to Rs. 35 crores. Value added by industry had risen to Rs. 95 crores, some of it in the capital goods industries. The total availability of consumer goods was then at most Rs. 125 crores. Prices of Pakistani manufactures were much higher than equivalent imports had been, so in real terms there was a significant absolute decline in the availability of manufactured consumer goods. Over the same period, population increased by 10 percent. If these figures are roughly correct, Pakistan's consumers experienced a considerable drop in their consumption levels, rather than the increase that most people demand. This was all the more serious because Pakistanis were already among the poorest people in the world, because rapid urbanization made for a sharply increased demand for manufactured goods, and because the decline in consumption levels was very unevenly distributed.

It is not possible for an economist to say whether further austerity could have been imposed. The incentives to save, to invest, to produce for the market might have been affected. The administration of further restrictions would have been increasingly difficult. But the real question is whether greater austerity would have been politically feasible. Would administration and security have broken down if the civil servants, police, and military officers had been denied even a limited quantity of luxury goods? Would peasants have retreated into the subsistence sector or reduced output if available consumer goods had been further reduced and their prices increased? Would workers have revolted if their level of living had been further depressed? All one can say is that austerity in Pakistan was substantial, that a very poor country had been induced to save 7 percent of its income, that average consumption per capita had probably declined and inequalities in consumption had increased, and that it was the implicit judgment of all governments to 1959 that it was politically impossible to increase austerity further in order to increase foreign exchange for investment.

The second method for increasing investment — using idle resources — in the short run meant employing more labor, the only significant idle resource. Some industrial capacity was also idle, but in general this was due to inadequate supplies of imported goods, so to use this capacity would mean a worsening, not improvement, in the foreign exchange situation. Labor could have been substituted for imported goods in the operation of existing units, or in investment. In addition, higher costs for imports could have led to a shift in the composition of investment to industries requiring more labor and fewer imported goods. It must be stressed that Pakistan's investors had already made a considerable adjustment to the availability of labor and the scarcity of foreign exchange by concentrating on labor-intensive industries such as cotton textiles. Where available, they had bought semiobsolete and second-hand machinery, which requires more labor per unit of capital. Construction exhibited a high labor- and low foreign-materials component.

The limits to increased labor use are well known. In some investment, increasing the amount of labor would not have reduced the need for other inputs (e.g., the chemical industries). In other instances, the technology required for greater labor intensity was not available or not known in Pakistan. Some labor-intensive industries did not have an adequate market in Pakistan. Other labor-intensive alternatives required much skilled manpower, or an extensive infrastructure. In short, many alternative labor-intensive technologies or investments were likely to result in such a low rate of return that they would not have been attractive, even at a higher foreign-exchange rate. Pakistan, with a limited market and a rather primitive economy, had only limited options for industrial development in the 1950's and the labor-intensive options were mostly taken up. Finally, labor-intensive methods of production could increase the risk and uncertainty facing the industrialist. A greater use of unskilled labor might increase the chances of strikes and riots, not an unknown experience to Pakistani industrialists with large numbers of workers. Some industrialists would be unwilling to take this risk, even if the relative cost of labor had been reduced by higher prices for imported capital goods. More labor could have been used in civil works, but here the limiting factors were administration, inadequate government revenues, and lack of demand. In addition, even civil works required some scarce capital goods, and some (e.g., housing) were considered of such low social priority that no additional allocation of scarce resources to them was warranted.

The third method for dealing with the foreign-exchange constraint — more efficient use of resources — in theory had the greatest promise. In practice some limited improvement could in fact have been brought about quite readily. If the price of foreign exchange had been raised, for instance, resources would have shifted to the production of export goods, with a higher social value than some goods produced for domestic consumption behind high protection. (A shift from grains and sugar cane to cotton is one example. The argument here is not that exports could have increased at the expense of consumption. On the contrary, with increased exports, it would have been possible to maintain imports of consumer goods and still have funds left over to import some capital goods.) Simultaneously, a higher price for foreign exchange could have somewhat improved the efficiency with which imports were used — discouraging excessive stockpiling, reducing the pressure for excessive imports which were cheap to the importer, and reducing the need for inefficient direct controls.

The effects on resource use of a higher foreign exchange cost would have been limited by the time required to shift resources from one industry or product to another; by inertia and ignorance; and by the fact that much inefficiency was quite unrelated to the cost of foreign exchange. Nevertheless, a higher price for foreign exchange would undoubtedly have reduced the severity of the foreign exchange constraint by increasing the efficiency of resource use.

One can speculate on the effect of a higher price for foreign exchange. It would certainly have reduced the foreign-exchange gap, but it is doubtful if it could have eliminated that constraint on investment. Austerity in consumption in a stagnant economy had been carried very far. Therefore, the most effective means for expanding exports and reducing current imports — a reduction in consumption — was largely ruled out because of its political and economic effects. Some additional labor might have been used, but again Pakistan's investors had already gone quite far within the limits imposed by technology, trained manpower, and administrative ability to adjust to an abundant labor supply. The efficiency of the economy might have been improved, subject to inertia, prior commitments, and technical and administrative limitations. It is unlikely that somewhat greater use of labor and somewhat greater efficiency in resource use would have eliminated foreign exchange as the crucial limit to investment.

This "two-gap" model for Pakistan of the 1950's — with the foreign-exchange gap larger than the savings/investment gap — does not explain why would-be investors did not bid up the price of capital goods. If capital goods were the real constraint in the 1950's, and potential (or ex ante) savings exceeded actual (or ex post) savings, why did the excess savings not disappear as savers tried to obtain capital goods by paying a higher price? Instead, it was contended earlier, they held some of their savings in cash.

Until the late 1950's the price of domestically produced capital goods could not be bid up, since production was negligible. When domestic machinery became available in the late 1950's, it did not compete effectively with imports so far as many would-be investors were concerned. Imported machinery was familiar, was presumed to be of high quality, and required a minimum of labor. With devaluation ruled out, and low import duties on machinery, imported capital goods were cheap to the industrialist. The alternative, locally produced machinery, was sometimes higher priced and required more skilled labor and better organization. Industrialists were not familiar with it, and suppliers of the machinery could not provide the necessary technical help. As a result, many industrialists ignored domestic machinery and did not compete for it in the market. Imported machinery was not generally sold in the domestic market. Permits to import machinery were given directly to the investors, and government controls were quite effective in assuring that the importer was also the user. In short, the market for both domestic and imported machinery was highly imperfect. In the 1950's, the industrialist often preferred to hold some funds almost idle until permission to import machinery was granted, rather than buy locally produced machinery (if any) or pay black-market prices for imported equipment.

Building materials were a somewhat different story. The sale of imports was more difficult to control, a higher proportion was produced domestically, and quality differences between domestic and imported goods were less significant. A flourishing black market developed, as potential investors bid up the price. However, the expected return on buildings was much less than in some industries, and would-be investors shifted only some funds from industry to construction. They preferred to keep other funds essentially idle, waiting for the opportunity to invest in high profit industry.

The relative scarcity of savings and foreign exchange began to change in the 1960's. The government clearly felt that austerity had to be relaxed somewhat. Imports of such goods as cars, refrigerators, air conditioners, rayon yarn, and cosmetics more than doubled between 1958 and 1960, and have continued their rapid increase since. There may have been several reasons. With a rising per capita product, some improvement in consumption could be permitted. The relaxation seems to have been largely in goods bought by the middle class — the civil servants, military officers, professionals and businessmen — whose support was important to a military government. Previous governments were more concerned with the votes of the many than the support of the elite. Restrictions on consumer goods became more difficult as a higher proportion was produced domestically rather than imported. Finally, drastic austerity may have been difficult to maintain over time. In order to provide incentives for professional, industrial, and business groups, a slight relaxation was desirable, and Pakistan could afford it more readily in the middle 1960's.

A relaxation of austerity, however slight, is likely to increase the difficulties of raising the rate of savings in the future. It may prove more difficult to step up the rate of private savings for other reasons as well. Per unit profits will continue to decline as competition from imported and domestic goods increases. In addition, there probably has been a decline in the propensity to save. By the middle 1960's, some of the nouveau riche had had 15 years to become used to affluence. Their wants increased to match their incomes. The sons and grandsons of the original entrepreneurs inherit wealth; they do not grow up in an environment where frugality is a cardinal virtue and hard work essential to earn a good living. They have expensive tastes. No longer do they sit in an open office with everyone else, use the business car for personal transportation after work, and make long-distance calls only at night, when rates are lower. They have private, air-conditioned offices, drive personal Mercedes, and take annual trips abroad. With many of them following this pattern, there is strong pressure on others to follow suit. Finally, restrictions on private investment are weakening one of the strongest incentives to savings — the opportunity to invest in a highly profitable undertaking. In the middle 1960's, the government tried to discourage further investment by the dozen leading business families. This policy is designed to restrain, albeit very modestly, concentrations of income, wealth, and power. It is also supposed to reduce the domination of industry in East Pakistan by families from outside the Province. If this government policy becomes effective, the leading families are unlikely to save in order to invest in enterprises controlled by others. They are more likely to reduce their savings and increase their attempts to export capital.

While savings rose in the early 1960's, export earnings and foreign resources available to Pakistan rose even more rapidly, reducing the severity of the foreign-exchange constraint. It was much easier to step up exports in this period than earlier, since a rising per capita product meant that this was not done at the expense of consumption, but rather accompanied increasing consumption. Also, the government in effect gradually raised the price of foreign exchange, by providing an indirect subsidy for most manufactured exports (the export bonus scheme) and raising tariffs on imports. In part as the result of the higher price for foreign exchange, in part as the result of other policies, the domestic capital-goods industry expanded; idle labor was increasingly employed as normal investment and the Works Programme were rapidly expanded; efficiency of resource use was improved. If, in the future, it proves more difficult to raise savings rates while the ambitious export targets in the Plan are met, it is conceivable that inadequate domestic savings will be substituted for foreign exchange as the decisive constraint on investment.

However, in the 1950's, and to a decreasing extent in the 1960's, limited foreign exchange to purchase capital goods was crucial in determining the rate of investment. Foreign "aid" was extremely important in determining the size of the foreign-exchange gap and therefore the feasible rate of investment. As a matter of fact the argument is sometimes advanced that foreign public transfers were crucial in Pakistan's economic growth. The significant difference between the 1950's and the 1960's, it is argued, was not a change in Pakistan's policies, but the increase in foreign resources available to Pakistan in the latter decade.

FOREIGN RESOURCES

Foreign resources financed over 30 percent of gross investment in 1959–60, and nearly 40 percent in the middle 1960's. In the 1960's, a large share (20 percent) of foreign resources financed the Indus Basin Works, very largely in the nature of replacement. The share of foreign resources in net investment in the 1960's was therefore significantly less than in gross investment.

Clearly, foreign resources were extremely important in Pakistan's development from 1955 on; but it was equally clear that they were only one factor. If foreign support for the Indus Basin Works is subtracted — as essentially designed for the political purpose of reaching a settlement between India and Pakistan rather than for development — the inflow of foreign resources in 1964–65 amounted to over $500 million and financed about 30 percent of all investment. (All data for foreign resources include agricultural surpluses under U.S. Public Law 480.) As a proportion of total investment, Pakistan received somewhat more foreign resources than such neighboring countries as India, but both in proportion to investment and on a per-capita basis it received less foreign resources than many countries, most of them with a lower growth rate.

Pakistan was able to obtain foreign resources in part because it used them effectively. The first spurt in foreign public loans and grants came in the middle and late 1950's, because aid to Asian countries was increasing in general, and because Pakistan had especially close relations with the United States. The next major increase occurred, however, in the 1960's when Pakistan's political relations with major donors were getting worse rather than better. This increase can, in large part, be attributed to Pakistan's improved economic performance. Pakistan became one of the cases cited when foreign-aid administrators spoke of countries willing to help themselves, able to use loans and grants for development, and able to absorb effectively additional resources.

In addition, specific increases in foreign resources sometimes came as the result of specific changes in economic policy. The clearest example was the reduction in direct controls in 1964–65. It would have been difficult for Pakistan to take the risk of liberalizing imports if the United States, which strongly supported a shift from direct to indirect controls, had not provided $100 million to underwrite this move. The Works Programme was financed by special shipments under PL 480. The increased uses of government credit institutions (PICIC and IDBP) to finance the foreign exchange costs of private industrial investment also increased foreign resources available to Pakistan. For ideological reasons, the United States, Germany, the World Bank, and others have been strong advocates of private enterprise. A country that caters to this preference is bound to profit. (The use of a phrase like "a dash toward freedom" should be worth its weight in capitalist gold.) More important, some donors have implicitly assumed that pursuit of profit assures that private firms choose sound investments and avoid waste. Donors therefore provided funds with less investigation or conditions to agencies funneling credit to private projects than they required for public projects. This reduced delay and administrative effort for the government of Pakistan, which did not have to prepare and negotiate detailed project proposals.

While foreign public transfers kept increasing until the middle 1960's, they were significantly less than they could have been, as the result of inadequacies in administrative machinery. The "pipeline" of committed but unused funds keeps increasing; by 1964–65 it reached Rs. 400 crores ($800 million), almost twice the annual inflow of foreign loans and grants. Some delays in the use of funds are inevitable. As the size of the aid programs increased, there was bound to be a simultaneous increase in the pipeline of committed but unspent funds. National and international donor agencies have regulations and a cumbersome bureaucracy of their own, which slows decisions. But part of the delay is the result of Pakistani action, or inaction. It is another example of the inability of government to do all things well. There were inevitably some agencies that could not prepare specific project proposals in the detail demanded by donors. Above all, available funds were often used slowly because procurement was inefficient or construction was delayed or project planning was weak. For examples, one has only to read the amazingly frank and well done reports on foreign aid, prepared by the Government of Pakistan itself.

In short, additional foreign public resources were an important factor in the more rapid rate of Pakistan's growth in the 1960's, but they by no means fully explain that growth. The sensible policies and programs adopted by Pakistan were the major reasons for the increase in resources available. In large part, causality runs from improved policies and performance to increased aid, not vice versa.

Foreign private investment has provided a very limited addition to the available resources. It was estimated at Rs. 8 crores ($16 million) annually in the early 1960's. The sheer complexity of the government control apparatus has been a significant deterrent to some investors, since there were other countries in Asia with fewer obstacles. Limited raw-material resources and a limited market were more significant in making Pakistan less attractive to foreign investors than other countries (its national income is less than that of many states in the United States), despite strong attempts to attract foreign investment. Convertibility, tax concessions, and guarantees were as good as or better than in most underdeveloped countries. If Pakistan's economy continues to expand at a rate of over 5 percent per year over the next decade, it will offer an attractive market to foreign companies. If access to that market is limited to companies that invest in Pakistan, the rate of foreign private investment could well be stepped up considerably in the future.

CONCLUSIONS

Despite a powerful and relatively effective government, Pakistan found it difficult to generate public savings. Taxes were increased almost every year, sometimes by substantial amounts. However, the general poverty of the country, the political and administrative difficulties of raising taxes on agriculture, and the need for increases in the nondevelopment expenditures of government were serious handicaps. As a result government revenues did not exceed current government expenditure by a significant amount.

Government revenues came largely from taxes on consumption — import duties, excise and sales taxes. These, as well as profits and income taxes, were substantially collected through the industrial sector. Ultimately they were paid by the consumer, who was charged prices substantially above those in the world market. The consumer meant primarily the peasant. Although direct taxes on agriculture were difficult to collect, indirectly agriculture was a large contributor to government revenues.

The bulk of private savings came from industry. Able to make large profits, unable to spend them because of restrictions on luxury imports and luxury goods production, on capital flight and foreign travel, industrialists reinvested well over half of their profits. Undoubtedly other factors also made for high savings, including wants that grew more slowly than rapidly increasing incomes, and the emphasis on austerity. Inability to spend, however, may have been the most important cause of high savings. Government tax measures, import restrictions, and controls over domestic production made consumption difficult and were essential for the high rate of private savings. The industrialists' high incomes were politically more acceptable because a substantial proportion was reinvested or collected in taxes; because riotous living was restrained by government action; and because great inequalities in income were not expressed in equally great inequalities in consumption.

The government financed its development program in part by a substantial increase in the money supply. Pakistan had no inflation, however, because this was offset by an inflow of foreign resources, especially of surplus food which stabilized food prices; by a transactions demand for money that grew with the industrial sector; by increased cash holdings in the rural areas; and, to a lesser extent, by the willingness of industrialists to hold large sums of money in anticipation of investment opportunities.

Foreign aid contributed significantly to Pakistan's growth, from the late 1950's; without it, the rapid increase in development in the 1960's would not have been possible. But increased aid in the 1960's was largely the consequence of improved economic policies and management.

Contrary to some theories, private businessmen and industrialists did save and reinvest their earnings in industry; investment increased rapidly without inflation; and high consumption taxes and profits were possible without political disaster. But by 1965 the very rapid increase in foreign resources seemed to be slowing down and profit rates were declining. To raise investment in the future may require a corresponding increase in savings, and to raise savings while profit rates decline may be difficult, especially in view of pressure to relax the policy of austerity.

CHAPTER VIII

THE SOCIAL UTILITY
OF GREED

. . . there are . . . only two ways to develop [a] country.
First . . . the way of the market. Second, a fully controlled
economy. . . . The way to get a maximum rate of "Economic Growth" . . . is to maintain a free market. . . .
PAKISTAN INDUSTRIALIST M. A. RANGOONWALLA, S.K., J.P.
in (52)

Competition is cutting each other's throat. Competition is
annihilation of the weak.
DIRECTOR, STEEL SALES LIMITED
A. K. SUMAR in (52)

. . . in all material and economic matters our attitude should
not be doctrinaire but one dictated by the basic requirements of the situation.
PRESIDENT AYUB KHAN'S MANIFESTO

THE ROLES played by government and private enterprise in Pakistan had much to do with the success of its
development. The pattern which has evolved goes far in
assigning to each the functions it can best perform. Policies have been framed to assure that the government intervenes in the economy when such intervention is in
theory desirable, while leaving in private hands decisions
which, according to theory, should be left to private initiative. The pattern which has developed was successful because some Pakistanis have behaved like economic men,
responding to economic incentives — a development which
should gladden the heart of both the confirmed Marxist
and the confirmed private enterpriser.

OBJECTIVES

To justify these statements and to appraise what has happened in Pakistan requires that progress be measured in terms of the country's own objectives. All three Five-Year Plans discussed ultimate goals. So did President Ayub Khan in his election manifestos and on various other occasions. Pakistan's economic objectives do not differ fundamentally from those of many underdeveloped countries. Foremost is an explicit commitment to rapid economic growth or economic development. The second, widely shared goal is for some measure of equality and equity in the distribution of economic benefits and costs of development. In Pakistan equity refers to the well-being not only of different groups in the population, but also of the major regions of the country, especially East and West Pakistan.

These two interrelated goals, and the belief that their achievement requires widespread government intervention, often go under the name of "socialism". In many countries there is an additional qualifier, be it Islamic socialism, Arab socialism, Indonesian socialism, African socialism, or Christian socialism.

THE ROLE OF PRIVATE ENTERPRISE

It is obvious that in Pakistan the great majority of enterprises in agriculture, industry, trade, commerce, and services is in private hands. Most decisions on production, investment, and prices are taken by private individuals. Pakistan's economy apparently could be called a private enterprise or free enterprise, or capitalist, or market system. ("Free enterprise" is the term preferred by those who like the system, "capitalism" by those who do not.)

The advantage of such a system, with decisions decentralized and made in response to market forces, are well known. A system based on private enterprise is supposed to be efficient and sensitive in meeting the wishes of the individuals who compose it for the following reasons.

First, the consequences of any decision are on the decision-maker. Enterprises that produce the wrong goods or services, that use wrong methods, or act at the wrong time incur losses. Those that persist in inappropriate actions are eliminated. The right decisions, as well as effort and ability, are rewarded by profits and growth. Strong incentives are therefore provided to encourage desirable economic behavior, and an automatic system operates to reduce the economic influence of the lazy, the incompetent, and those who make the wrong decisions.

Second, under a market system, decisions are decentralized. The individual decision-maker, concerned with a limited range of problems, has more of the relevant information available to him than if he needed the wide range of information required for centralized decisions. Much of the required information is conveyed through known market prices, and the decision-maker is also well informed about his own enterprise.

Finally, decentralization of decisions reduces their complexity and facilitates their execution. It reduces opportunities for human error in transmission, for time lags, resistances, and friction, which tend to increase with the number of persons and layers involved in a decision.

It has been argued that the advantages of a market system are particularly important for underdeveloped countries. In these economies, ownership and control of enterprises is rarely separated; therefore the incentives of private ownership are powerful. Underdeveloped countries have few experienced civil servants to operate a planned economy. They also lack the statistical, communications, and other auxiliary services required for centralized decisions. Finally, underdeveloped countries face a rapidly changing economic situation, calling for widespread experimentation, rapid transmission of information, quick adaptation, and improvisation which is more readily accomplished with the incentives and decentralization of a private system. It makes little difference, it is argued, whether General Motors is owned by the government, or by several thousand stockholders and managed by a professional group. It makes a good deal more difference whether a newly established textile mill in the hinterland of Pakistan is run by its owner on the spot or by the government, located some hundreds of miles away at the end of a poor telephone connection.

Pakistan took advantage of the claimed strengths of a market system. For a wide range of economic activity, in which strong incentives and decentralization of decisions were important, Pakistan relied on private initiative. In hundreds of thousands of economic units, private owners made decisions on labor and other inputs, on techniques of production, and on composition of output. Most decisions on investment in industry, agriculture, trade, and services also were made by private owners of individual firms. They decided what industry to invest in, what technology to use, and what location to select.

Private, decentralized decisions are efficient in economic terms only if they are responsive to economic incentives. In any economy, some decisions are made to satisfy prestige, honor, whim, tradition, the local astrologer, or his equivalent. But if many decision-makers use these criteria, the economy will not be very efficient. The extensive scope for private decisions in Pakistan was possible because, contrary to widespread expectations, a large proportion of decision-makers often behaved as economic men. Industrial development could be left largely in private hands because an adequate number of private traders were willing to shift to industry so long as economic incentives were adequate, although this involved a major change in occupation and in behavior, and considerable risk. Continued private industrial development was possible because industrialists responded to economic incentives by investing in complex industries and by improving the efficiency of their plants. Traders' behavior was also quite finely attuned to changes in the economic environment. Their responsiveness to economic incentives, even in rural areas, made private fertilizer distribution and grain purchases possible. That economic incentives affected the behavior of peasants runs counter to much conventional wisdom. Yet there was good evidence in Pakistan that many peasants shifted quickly from one crop to another in response to relative prices, especially if the risk of price fluctuation was limited, and that they increased the use of inputs if the price of the input was reduced by a subsidy.

Changes in behavior were often a response to economic disincentives as much as to incentives. Traders may have become industrialists more because profits in trade dropped sharply than because profits in industry increased. Industrialists may have become concerned with efficiency more because they feared large losses than in order to increase their gains.

While the responsiveness of private behavior to economic incentives made it possible to rely widely on private initiative to achieve an efficient growth process, this does not mean that noneconomic factors were negligible in determining behavior. Of course tradition, values, and motivations affect economic behavior. However, if economic incentives were sufficiently strong, they did seem to affect and alter the economic behavior of some Pakistanis. Like people in developed countries, they did not all behave chiefly or wholly as economic men, but enough behaved sufficiently in that way so that strong economic incentives usually called forth appropriate economic behavior.

THE ROLE OF GOVERNMENT INTERVENTION

In Pakistan it was possible to rely on private initiative to carry out many functions that required decentralization. However, the government had to assure that the incentives and disincentives facing private decision-makers were appropriate from society's point of view, and it had to carry out directly activities not suitable for private decisions. To a large extent, the government in Pakistan followed the standard recipe for government intervention in the economy. The need for centralized, government-planned decisions is argued on a variety of grounds.

First, in a private-enterprise economy, the decision-maker inevitably lacks knowledge and foresight about some changes outside his enterprise. Decentralization in a market system means that the decision-maker is well informed on his own enterprise, but learns about changes elsewhere only with a considerable lag, as prices gradually reflect developments. More important, he is hampered in foreseeing changes because the plans of other decision-makers are kept from him. This results in inappropriate decisions and reduces growth. In a market economy, individuals save and invest to obtain an acceptable rate of return. The rate of return, however, depends on the actions of others, which are neither predictable nor assured. Many who would be willing to save and invest at a given rate of return, will fail to do so simply because they are not sure that others will take the decisions required to insure that rate of return.

The second argument attacks the market system with respect to efficiency. That a perfect market system is efficient in economic terms is rarely questioned, but actual market systems are far from the perfect model. Sensible decisions in a private-enterprise economy depend on the signals given by market prices, adjusted by the decision-maker to reflect the changes he foresees. Inefficient decisions are taken for several reasons.

1. The decision-maker in a market system may fail to act appropriately because the stimulus provided by prices is too weak to overcome habit, tradition, or other non-economic factors.

2. The actions of one enterprise affect other decision-makers. Able to control only their own enterprise, decision-makers cannot take into account these external economies and diseconomies. For instance, plants may be established in different locations as each owner makes a sensible independent decision, though a joint decision to locate together could produce savings on transport, specialized services, housing, and common training facilities.

3. Finally, inefficiencies arise in a market system from prices that are fixed by monopolies, are distorted by collusion, or are affected by tradition, institutions, or other factors.

The third argument says that the market system is not appropriate for expressing the wishes or values of a society. Without government intervention, the individual's influence on economic decisions depends on his economic power. Government decisions are preferable for many aspects of the economy, but four are particularly significant:

(a) There would be differences in the time horizon, or in the value placed on current as against future consumption, and therefore the rate of growth. The result or sum of many individual decisions to save and invest is not likely to be identical with a conscious group decision on how much should be saved and invested. The majority of a society may decide to impose a much higher rate of savings on itself than the same society would achieve if each individual made a separate decision between saving and consumption from his own income. This is especially true if the planned decision is made on the basis of individual franchise or some other political process, in which the deciding is done largely by one group and the increased saving largely by another.

(b) There would be differences in the goods and services made available. If decisions are made by the government, the production of luxury goods for the few may receive less priority than if the decision is via the market, where the consumers of luxury goods have a disproportionate influence.

(c) There would be differences in the method and location of production. Society may attach independent values to employment or to particular locations and may be willing to bear higher costs in order to employ more people, or develop a particular area.

(d) There would be differences in the distribution of disposable income and wealth. In a market system these are related in part to ability, enterprise and effort, in part to luck, dishonesty and ruthlessness. The affluence of one's ancestors is a significant element. Most societies wish to modify this distribution to compensate in part for fortuitous circumstances, to assure a minimum level of consumption for all and to achieve in general greater equality of incomes.

The final argument for government intervention, then, is that the unplanned, market system expresses a set of values which may differ from the values of society. In order to implement this second set of values, the government must intervene in the economy.

Several arguments for government intervention apply with particular force to the establishment of pioneer firms: lack of information, differences in time preference, existence of external economies, and inadequacy of price incentives. If many pioneer firms are to be set up, the government must protect these infants from foreign competition.

Looked at in another way, government intervention is supposed to be necessary to step up the rate of growth, to implement social values, and to improve the current efficiency of the system by correcting imperfections of the market.

Government intervention is considered particularly important in underdeveloped countries. Growth is both more important and more difficult to attain in these countries. The need to achieve the values of society is greater in underdeveloped countries. The poor are truly poor and inequality means real misery for those at the bottom. The argument for government intervention in the economy is much stronger when its purpose is to divert resources from Cadillacs to rice for starving families, than if it is to redistribute income among the affluent. Finally, the inefficiencies of a market system are especially serious for underdeveloped countries who can least afford a waste of resources. Development requires structural changes, not marginal adjustments, and an underdeveloped country is likely to have fewer decision-makers who respond quickly and correctly to the clues and incentives provided by the price system. It will have many industries with only one or a few units, and therefore decisions will be more distorted by monopoly elements. Development also involves drastic changes and substantial risks which complicate the problems of decision-makers and increase the importance of external economies or diseconomies.

Much of the intervention of the Pakistan government in the economy was for the theoretical reasons discussed above. An over-all plan, and more detailed programs for public and private investment in particular fields (the government's annual development budget, the industrial investment schedules, and the import budget), provided considerable information to decision-makers on likely developments outside their firm. Since the government had an extensive arsenal to influence private decisions, the businessman could assume that actual developments in the economy would bear some relation to plans.

Far-reaching government intervention assured a high rate of savings, investment, and growth. There is no need to repeat the earlier argument that it was government measures which made for high, concentrated incomes that could not readily be transferred abroad or used for consumption. Although specific decisions on how much to save were left to private initiative, the government provided the incentives to achieve a planned rate of over-all saving and investment higher than would have resulted in a market economy.

It was argued that greater social equality requires government intervention for its achievement. An important step in this direction in Pakistan were tax, tariff, and direct-control measures which, though they restricted all consumption, impinged most severely on the consumption of the upper-income groups.

Direct government investment and management were used extensively to improve regional equity and to deal with industries in which external effects were important, monopoly positions were likely, or price incentives seemed inadequate. The infrastructure — transport, communications, power, large-scale irrigation, urban facilities — was in public hands, since external economies were usually large and monopoly inevitable. The PIDC undertook investment in industries that temporarily occupied a monopoly position, and in industries or locations where the government would find it difficult to provide adequate price incentives to induce private investment.

In the 1950's direct government intervention went far beyond the measures described above. When, however, many direct controls were abandoned in the 1960's, the government reverted toward the above pattern, while its effectiveness increased in administering a more restricted program of intervention.

A "MODEL" OF PAKISTAN'S DEVELOPMENT

The process of Pakistan's development can be summarized in a different dimension, stressing the relationship over time between different sectors of the economy, rather than the relationship between government and private enterprise. In the five years after Independence there were substantial economic opportunities in trade, in agriculture, and in the professions — and some opportunities in industry — simply in filling the vacuum created by Partition. The Korean boom naturally increased the scope of these opportunities. Development took place in all fields, but was largely replacement of the losses caused by Partition. Gross investment was substantial, the development effort was even larger, but net investment was probably quite small.

The next period covered the middle 1950's. The terms of trade were sharply turned in favor of industry and against agriculture. Restrictions on competing imports of manufactures, particularly consumer goods, meant high prices and profits for some industries. Capital goods and raw material imports were cheap because of an overvalued rupee. Depressed agricultural prices and a large supply of labor kept urban wages low. Incentives were strong to invest in industry, and high profits made it easy to save the necessary capital. In response to powerful economic incentives, a number of industrial entrepreneurs developed. At the same time consumers, who were primarily peasants, had to pay much higher prices for industrial goods than in the late 1940's. The prices received by agricultural producers were generally kept low, as a result both of government action and the overvalued rupee. Agriculture had been substantially disrupted by Partition and was neglected in terms of government service and assistance. Not surprisingly, the period was one of high industrial growth and agricultural stagnation.

Some changes, heralding the next stage, occurred in the middle 1950's, but the next period did not fully arrive till the 1960's. The internal terms of trade gradually turned in favor of agriculture and against industry. Competition produced sharply lowered prices for some manufactured consumer goods. Starting in the 1960's, increased imports also played a role. After 1959 the government abandoned the policy of depressing agricultural prices. Instead, the farmers' returns were raised by lower export duties and some guaranteed prices. Subsidies to agricultural inputs remained extensive and private enterprise was substituted for government direction in their distribution. The government devoted more attention and energy to agriculture and stepped up its investment in the rural infrastructure, especially irrigation. The Works Programme employed idle rural labor for investment. These changes were a major cause of the growth of agricultural production in the 1960's.

It might be expected that the industrial growth and savings rates would decline at the same time. Many feared that industrial growth would be limited by the slow growth of the internal market, since simple import substitution had pretty well come to an end, and Pakistan's industry was too inefficient to compete extensively in the world market. They argued that as firms competed for a larger share in a slowly growing market, the terms of trade for industry would worsen. As a result, profits and savings out of profits might decline. Personal savings were supposed to decline as well, since it would be more difficult for political, administrative, and economic reasons to restrict consumption when most consumer goods were produced domestically. The balance of payments would also worsen. Increased consumption would require greater imports of raw materials and semimanufactures and would reduce exports as more cotton, tea, hides, rice, and fish were required for the domestic consumer. There were some gloomy prophecies about the economic future of Pakistan in the late 1950's.

But the economy confounded the prophets with accelerated industrial (as well as agricultural) growth, and an increased rate of savings. A basic reason was the increased efficiency of the economy in the early 1960's. The market for manufactures expanded because, with higher productivity and output in agriculture, farmers could afford more consumer goods and agricultural inputs. Industrial wages were stabilized, because increased productivity and more efficient distribution also restrained the rise in prices of agricultural products. Industrial investment remained high, as a well-established group of industrialists continued to invest although profits in some industries had declined. Import substitution continued, because industrialists had gained sufficient experience and confidence to invest in industries producing complex intermediate and capital goods. A further outlet for Pakistan's industry came from foreign markets; exports of manufactures increased more than expected, because industry had increased in efficiency, accepted lower profits, and received greater returns under the export bonus scheme. The market for manufactures was widened further, as a result of lower costs following the reduction in direct controls and other improvements in government policies. Finally, the improved functioning of the economy attracted greater foreign resources and made it possible to absorb them. In turn, the availability of foreign resources helped make possible increased efficiency by underwriting steps to reduce direct controls, in one of the beneficent cycles which could be as prominent in discussions of development as the popular vicious cycles.

Savings continued to increase. The cultivator's ability to save grew apace with agricultural production. He had a stronger incentive to save, since he received better prices, had greater knowledge of the benefits of investment, and could take advantage of a better rural infrastructure. In the middle 1960's, the government was able to increase its revenues sharply with a noticeable increase in per-capita income. Thereafter, public savings became a significant addition to private savings. Savings out of industrial profits probably increased as well. Although the average rate of profits as a percentage of capital may have declined, total industrial output increased rapidly, compensating for any lower savings rate. Since the rate of saving in industry was higher than in the rest of the economy, total savings would increase also because the industrial sector represented an increasing share of the economy. In short, it proved to be easier to squeeze a rising rate of savings out of a rapidly growing economy than out of a stagnant one. Investment could increase much more rapidly than savings, because the inflow of foreign resources continued to be stepped up. The foreign resources devoted to the Works Programme, by employing an idle and cheap resource for investment, had a particularly great impact.

There is no obvious reason why Pakistan's growth should not continue to accelerate. With increased efficiency and lower prices for manufactures, the domestic and export market can continue to expand. Import substitution for some complex manufactures can continue. The process of applying improved technology and additional capital to agriculture has by no means reached diminishing returns.

POVERTY, INEQUALITY, AND INEFFICIENCY

Progress in the 1960's has been great, but the millennium has not yet arrived in Pakistan. Serious economic problems remain. For one, a process of significant growth has barely begun; it can still be aborted. At best, Pakistanis will remain among the poorest people in the world during the next couple of decades. Further, the growth process has allowed serious economic inequalities to remain between areas and groups. Finally, the shift from direct to indirect controls remains incomplete and subject to reversal. Economic inefficiency remains a problem.

Significant per-capita growth has gone on for less than a decade. Even should growth continue for the next 20 years at the ambitious rate projected by the Planning Commission, the per-capita income in Pakistan by 1985 will only reach that already achieved in 1965 in most of the Middle East, Far East, and Africa, and will not even approach the 1965 per-capita income of most Latin Americans. And this surely modest goal depends for its achievement on continued restraint in defense expenditure and a continued inflow of substantial foreign resources. Until 1965, Pakistan had devoted a small (3½ percent) share of its national product to defense, with less than 10 percent of available foreign exchange used to import defense goods. Any substantial increase in these proportions over the next decade could have a serious effect on the resources available for development. Over the same period, foreign loans and grants are projected to provide more than one-third of total investment funds. According to present plans, foreign resources are not expected to decline in absolute amounts until 1975. At least over the next decade, an end to loans and grants would stop any substantial increase in per-capita income under Pakistan's present economic and political system.

Even if foreign resources are made available as projected, and defense expenditure is restrained, it will not be easy to achieve the planned rate of growth. The necessary import substitution and growth in manufactured exports will require the development of technically very complex industries. Policies will have to be carefully framed to provide incentives for the development of such industries and to avoid their being highly inefficient. The planned export of rather sophisticated manufactures, obviously, can be achieved only if costs and quality are kept competitive internationally. In agriculture much of the recent development, especially in West Pakistan, occurred on the better land, and was carried out by enlightened farmers operating medium-sized holdings. Future agricultural development may be more difficult if it involves less enlightened cultivators, or poorer land, or small holdings. As profit rates drop in established industries, and if new industries involve long gestation periods and complex technologies, it will not be easy to increase internal savings as planned. Because extreme austerity is hard to enforce for a long period of time, it may become more difficult to restrict internal demand. Pressure from the domestic consumer could create problems with savings and the balance of payments. In short, despite significant achievements, Pakistan's goals have to remain modest and its development will be precariously based for some time. It cannot afford many mistakes or much economic waste in the next decade or two.

Inequality between the Provinces and different economic groups also remain of great concern. Per-capita income was lower in East than in West Pakistan at Independence. The development of industry, infrastructure, and commerce was concentrated in West Pakistan, especially in Karachi, in the 1950's. Therefore, per-capita income rose significantly in West Pakistan but stagnated in

the East, and the resulting tensions between the two
Provinces were serious. Per-capita incomes increased in
both Provinces in the 1960's. Since the Constitution requires equality in income, however, the rate of growth will
have to be further stepped up in East Pakistan, until it
exceeds growth in the West, to wipe out the differences
between the two Provinces gradually.

Unlike inequalities between the Provinces, the great
inequalities in personal income and wealth were rather
directly the consequence of Pakistan's pattern of development. The newly rich industrialists are the most obvious
example of a group which benefited from the private enterprise, or capitalist, form of development. A few families
became absolutely quite rich, their wealth all the more
obvious relative to the poverty around them. On the
other hand, the new urban proletariat, crowded into the
slums and shantytowns of the big cities, benefited little
from development. Less obvious, but no less important
are the inequalities in income in the countryside. The
poorer peasants and landless laborers bore a disproportionate share of the high prices of cloth and other
consumer goods. It is the wealthier cultivators, the "ku-
laks," especially those producing cash crops, who install
tube wells, buy subsidized fertilizer, or take advantage of
the extension service. The private development of tube
wells, which requires a substantial investment, particularly benefits the middle-income and wealthier groups of
cultivators.

The problem of inequality exists, but its importance
must be put in perspective. First of all, the inequalities
in income contributes to the growth of the economy,
which makes possible a real improvement for the lower-
income groups. The concentration of income in industry
facilitates the high savings which finance development.
Allowing the more enterprising and wealthy peasants to

sink tube wells is a major factor in expanding agricultural output. In turn, growth of the economy means cheaper cloth, cheaper food, and more adequate supplies for the bulk of the population. Great inequalities were necessary in order to create industry and industrialists; but to maintain industrial growth after the first 5 to 10 years does not require the same high rate of profit and therefore does not imply the same inequities. Greater equality during the early period at the cost of growth would probably have left the poorer groups in a worse position absolutely, though they would have been better off relatively. This argument holds true, however, only because inequalities in income result substantially in inequalities in savings, not in consumption. High incomes are more acceptable, politically and morally, because they are used chiefly for investment, rather than for conspicuous consumption.

In assessing inequality, it is often overlooked that the greatest inequality can be between the person who is unemployed and the one who has work. The poorest of the poor are the families of landless laborers who work only a few weeks per year and of the urban shantytown dwellers who subsist on occasional day labor. Unemployment and underemployment in Pakistan is measured in the million man-years. The informal social-security system of the extended family only mitigates the condition, because often the whole family has little work or little land. It is the unemployed who have benefited most from the phenomenal expansion of industry, and from the large-scale employment provided by the rural Works Programme. Full employment now seems a reasonable long-term goal for Pakistan's economy. If it is achieved in two or three decades, Pakistan will have taken the most important step to moderate income inequalities. Even before this goal was reached, there was evidence that real wages rose in the 1960's with diminished unemployment, though they remained unchanged or declined in the 1950's.

Finally, since 1960 some steps have been taken to deal with inequalities. In the 1950's, an essentially stagnant economy offered little scope for dealing with disparities in income, and the direct control system was kind to the wealthy and powerful. With rapid growth in the 1960's, resources can more readily be found to deal with inequality. The rate of growth in East Pakistan has been stepped up by diverting a larger share of government investment funds to that Province, and by offering tax and other concessions to investors there. Government credit agencies have begun to assist newcomers and medium-sized investors in industry in order to diminish concentration of industrial control. The reduction in direct government controls makes it easier for the newcomer to enter trade and industry. Finally, growth means that the country can afford some welfare measures: more housing, more health services, more education. Further improvement in the well-being of the lower income groups may receive higher priority in the future than in the past. The improvement of urban housing and facilities is probably Pakistan's most crucial social problem. Greater educational opportunities may be second. This is not simply a question of more primary schools, but the development of a system which gives the bright child from a poor family a reasonable chance to obtain an adequate education. Clearly, Pakistan will have to do more to meet these and other needs of lower income groups if the social and political system is not to be severely strained.

Development not only provides the wherewithal to improve the situation of the poor, it also creates the political prerequisites for such action. As Pakistan's industrial labor force increases rapidly, and the rural labor force finds greater employment opportunities, they are bound to press their demands more vigorously and effectively. In the past, social welfare measures and policies to decrease inequalities were often the result of the social conscience of government officials; in the future, pressure from below will be important. Trade unions, for instance, were severely limited in number and effectiveness, so long as "the reserve army of the unemployed" was ready to supply several candidates for any job. Union effectiveness is beginning to grow, as unemployment declines and as a stable labor force becomes important in competitive industries.

The continuing deep poverty of Pakistan, the vulnerability of its development process, and the economic, political, and moral imperative to improve the situation of poor people and regions, make it essential that Pakistan's limited resources be used more effectively. The shift from the rigid, costly, and inefficient direct control system to flexible, indirect, government intervention was an important reason for higher growth in the 1960's. Yet more can be done. In 1965 the government still exercised direct control over most investment decisions, most imports, and some prices. Some groups constantly urge a return to direct controls. Some businessmen and industrialists, who were comfortable in their monopoly positions, argue against "wasteful" competition from would-be newcomers. Some government officials, part of the "new class" of powerful administrators, miss the power and income that direct controls gave them. Others condemn the profits made by selling tube well water and suggest that private tube wells be regulated or prohibited. In West Pakistan fertilizer distribution by private dealers was cut off to assure its "fair distribution." The reimposition of direct controls was extremely modest. However, there remains considerable scope for Pakistan to carry its highly successful experiment further, to substitute indirect for direct government controls even more widely.

AN INDIRECT CONTROL SYSTEM

Almost all the purposes of government intervention in the economy can be achieved by a system of over-all planning and indirect fiscal measures — mostly taxes, some subsidies — accompanied by some direct government investment. Such a system would represent a logical extension of the steps taken by Pakistan in the 1960's.

Pakistan already had prepared plans and forecasts. Its government commanded adequate instruments to assure that most major decisions would not deviate too radically from plans. The Pakistan government therefore discharged quite well an important function: to *provide information* to private and public decision-makers on the general nature and direction of expected changes in the economy.

The most important instrument in the government's hands for assuring desired decisions has been its control over foreign trade and payments. This control is in part exercised by direct means (specific import licenses), in part by a mixture of direct and indirect measures (licenses freely available plus special tariffs), and in part by indirect means (tariffs on free list imports and the export bonus scheme). Controls over foreign trade and payments are designed to accomplish a variety of purposes: to compensate for the undervaluation of foreign exchange, to protect infant industries, to increase savings and reduce consumption, to reduce the consumption of the rich relative to the poor and of luxury goods relative to necessities, and to encourage investment in "backward" areas. Most of the remaining direct controls over foreign transactions could be eliminated if suitable indirect measures are substituted, with improved efficiency in the allocation of Pakistan's scarce resources.

The *undervaluation of foreign exchange* could, of course, be eliminated by devaluation. This could be combined with export duties on goods which have an inelastic foreign demand, or where there is danger of retaliation by competitors. Devaluation, as such, has been ruled out in Pakistan, but its purpose could be accomplished by a general import surcharge and export subsidy. This is a less obvious form of partial devaluation, which can be introduced gradually, and should reduce the risk of retaliation and loss of confidence.

The purpose would be only to compensate for the general undervaluation of foreign exchange, not to protect domestic industry or discourage imports of particular commodities. Therefore all transactions requiring foreign exchange could be subject to the same import surcharge, including foreign services, foreign travel, the transfer of profits and capital abroad, and the remittance of salaries by foreigners. (Food imported by the government under the United States surplus disposal program is a special case. Any increase in its book price as the result of the import surcharge could be offset by a greater book subsidy, simply a compensating entry.)

Similarly, a uniform, basic subsidy rate could compensate all sources of foreign exchange for the general overvaluation of the rupee: exports, services supplied, or foreign investment. However, for several exports, the price policy followed or the quantity exported by Pakistan substantially affects the international price. Their export subsidy obviously should maximize the return to Pakistan, given alternative uses for the resources required to produce the export, and applying a suitably high discount to future returns.

The general import surcharge and export subsidy should be identical, to make investment in import substitution and export production equally attractive alternatives. In order to reduce uncertainty, neither should be changed frequently. Because they should reflect the foreign-exchange rate required to achieve a balance in the foreign accounts over a number of years, frequent changes should not be necessary, though in the first year or two it might be necessary to experiment a bit with different levels. The level of the surcharge and subsidy need not be very high to compensate for the general undervaluation of foreign exchange.

Pakistan has already gone quite far toward an appropriate foreign-exchange rate by imposing tariffs on most imports and providing a bonus on non-traditional exports. The advantages of the next step, a general surcharge on imports and subsidy on exports, would be reduced uncertainty, greater simplicity, less administration, and wider coverage. Potential exporters could count on a subsidy. They would not need to apply for it specifically, nor fear its later withdrawal. Domestic producers would similarly be assured of general protection. Potential importers would know that the cost of imports would remain high and would have an incentive to look for domestic alternatives.

Two problems should be mentioned. An import surcharge and partial export subsidy might run into strong opposition from East Pakistan, since the subsidy would provide only limited benefits to that Province's major export (the elasticity of world demand for jute is low), but would increase the price of imports just when East Pakistan expects to obtain an increased share of imported goods. Other policies to provide direct benefits to East Pakistan would need to be introduced as part of the same package. Another side effect would be to raise the cost of investment, since investment has a particularly high import component. But in Pakistan the number of potential private investors, and the funds available to them, have exceeded foreign-exchange availabilities for a decade.

There is no need to encourage or stimulate investment in general.

The government has intervened very little to correct another inappropriate factor price. While foreign exchange has been undervalued, unskilled *labor has been overvalued* relative to its marginal productivity. Pakistan has considerable urban unemployment. There has been disagreement whether some workers in agriculture are actually redundant, but there is wide agreement that a substantial proportion is not needed part of the year. For institutional reasons, the urban wage rate exceeds the marginal product of labor and the cost of transferring redundant workers to new jobs. Therefore, fewer workers are employed outside agriculture than would be desirable. The result is an inefficient allocation of resources and lowered employment. Elaborate proposals have been made for government intervention to increase employment, mostly by direct subsidies to industry. Subsidies, however, present serious administrative problems and, if they draw labor from agriculture for the year around, might reduce agricultural production. Their most important drawback, however, is ineffectiveness. Pakistan's industry employed half a million workers in 1958. For some industries even a large subsidy will not lead to much increase in employment. (For example, in the production of chemicals, the factor proportions are almost wholly fixed by technology.) There are only a few industries and some functions (mainly materials handling) in which labor is readily substitutable for capital, and most labor intensive opportunities in industry have already been exploited. If a subsidy were to increase industrial employment by 10 percent, this would hardly affect the large number of unemployed and underemployed.

Alternative means for increasing the use of labor are

preferable. Idle seasonal rural labor can be directly employed through an expanded Works Programme, where unskilled labor can substitute for machinery almost without limit. Labor-intensive techniques would also be encouraged, especially in civil works, by various proposals for increasing the cost of capital. Finally, the use of unskilled labor could be subsidized indirectly, by government programs to subsidize their housing, which would be desirable for the sake of equity. All these measures would go far to provide employment and to bring labor costs and productivity into balance, without the need for subsidies or direct government intervention.

Capital is the final factor of production which is *undervalued.* For institutional reasons, the interest rate is too high for some borrowers and too low for others. Large-scale private enterprise, governmental bodies, and those borrowing from government-supported institutions pay a rate of interest substantially lower than rates prevailing in developed countries. On the other hand, the rate charged to peasants, and to newcomers in industry or commerce, is often very high. This duality is a standard feature of a poorly developed capital market. The results are as expected. On the one hand, government agencies and a few large firms tend to use more capital than is desirable. The inability to obtain loans and the extremely high interest rate asked of other potential borrowers discourage innovation, reduce competition, and keep the size of some units below the economic optimum.

The government can increase the rates paid by government agencies and the State Bank, thus forcing them to increase the interest charged to their borrowers. The disadvantages of a higher discount rate are small, and the arguments against it largely spurious. To provide credit to newcomers and smaller cultivators at a rate of interest lower than that prevailing now is more difficult. Government-supported credit institutions are the major instrument. Their limited effectiveness in the early stages of industrialization has already been discussed. The usefulness of industrial credit bodies was later limited by the influence of leading industrialists on their boards. It would be inhuman to expect dominant industrialists to make a special effort to provide government-subsidized credit to potential competitors. However, government pressure to improve credit facilities to newcomers seems increasingly effective. A combination of higher interest rates for borrowers favored in the past, and lower rates through government institutions to the rest, should go far in making the price of capital a more nearly appropriate one.

So far, the discussion has dealt only with the general price of labor, capital, and foreign exchange. Additional measures are required to protect domestic industry, for the familiar *infant-industry reasons* discussed earlier. There are no wholly satisfactory solutions to the simultaneous need for infant-industry protection and for maintaining competitive pressure. A significant improvement would be to give more uniform assistance to all infant industries — subsidies if they produce for export, tariffs if for domestic consumption. These would be in addition to tariffs and subsidies used to compensate for the overvaluation of the rupee, discussed earlier. Differences in social utility would be dealt with separately, since they are irrelevant for infant-industry protection. For instance, the tariff on textile machinery and luxury cars should be the same if they require similar infant-industry protection. The system would therefore differ from one which gives greater assistance to industries producing for the domestic market or producing goods considered socially less useful.

The same rate of assistance could be provided for broad groups of commodities with similar technological characteristics. This would avoid the need for individual decisions and might reduce the effectiveness of political pressure for differences in tariff rates. One or two dozen basic categories, rather than several hundred individual items, would also simplify administration and changes in rates. Commodities could be included in the assistance schedule even if they are not produced in Pakistan, so potential entrepreneurs would know the level of protection or subsidies they could expect. Subsidies for exports could become effective the moment exports take place; tariffs only when the domestic production has reached a specified proportion of past imports.

Finally, the length of time for which full infant-industry assistance would be available could be made known when it is provided, together with a schedule for gradual reduction. Such a schedule would have several advantages. It would continuously increase the pressure on firms to improve efficiency. It would reduce the danger of monopoly by encouraging investment in an industry as soon as possible after the first unit has been set up, since a delay would mean reduced infant-industry assistance. A definite time schedule could also ease the political problem of reducing concessions. Infants are notoriously reluctant to forego assistance, regardless of their age and argue that the time has not yet come for the weaning process to start. If that time has been specified in advance, the government's hand might be strengthened in resisting pressure. The administrative burden of constant review of tariffs and subsidies would also be lessened by an automatic process, though it would be naive to suppose that the process would be always automatic in practice.

A third major reason for government intervention in Pakistan's economy — besides inappropriate factor prices and infant-industry protection — is the need for *implementation of social values.* No government in Pakistan could allow private choice to determine the composition of imports and of domestic production. The government now deals with this objective by a combination of direct controls over imports, direct controls over investment, differential taxes and tariffs, and government investment. The indirect devices could become a more important instrument of policy. Decisions on the extent to which various kinds of goods should be made available to consumers can be implemented through excise taxes on both domestic production and imports. (Domestic production would still be favored by the general import surcharge and infant-industries protection previously discussed.) All consumer goods could be divided into a few — say half a dozen — groups of commodities, varying from complete luxuries to necessities, with different taxes for each category. Fine distinctions among commodities are neither necessary nor desirable. Once it is decided, for instance, what total amount of luxuries should be made available the exact composition within that total is of less importance. Consumer preference would dictate what goods are produced or imported in each category.

Taxes could range from several hundred percent for expensive cars and travel abroad, to no taxes on food grains, medicines, and textbooks. To limit consumption even of luxury goods to acceptable quantities would not require taxes higher than a few hundred percent, since the import of a limited range of luxuries was kept in bounds by premiums of 120–150 percent on bonus vouchers plus import duties of 80–250 percent. No taxes to implement social values would be required on most intermediate goods, raw materials, or investment goods. Their import and domestic production would be influenced by the taxes on the consumer goods for which they are used.

The resulting tax system could be progressive. Highly taxed luxuries are a greater proportion of total expenditure for upper than for lower expenditure groups, so the rich would be paying a much higher rate of tax on their consumption expenditures.

Another reason for differential taxes for different industries is the need to compensate for *external economies and diseconomies* — that is, if an investment affects the cost or returns of other enterprises, yet pays no penalty or obtains no benefit because the other enterprises are under different ownership. However, unless the external economies or diseconomies are so large that ignoring them would significantly affect investment decisions, no government intervention is necessary. Many industries for which external economies and diseconomies are really important, such as utilities, are already in the public sector in Pakistan. Firms in new industries would receive infant-industry protection or subsidies, to compensate in part for the external economies sometimes produced by pioneers (e.g., training workers that may subsequently be hired away by latecomers). For some external diseconomies, an enterprise can be made to pay directly through appropriate charges for land, or real estate taxes. Where significant external economies (e.g., investments which sharply reduce risk and uncertainty for other firms) or diseconomies are not otherwise compensated, lowering or raising the excise taxes imposed for other reasons could be the solution.

There is one large sector in which external economies are important — *agriculture*. In Pakistan, as elsewhere, most operating units are small and unable to do their own research, training, purchase of supplies, or sale of product. In addition, noneconomic factors and market imperfections are particularly important for agriculture. Natural risks are great and, for institutional reasons, access to capital is limited for most peasants, so they have only limited ability to engage in activities which carry with them additional risks. The need for government intervention is therefore especially great in agriculture.

To extend maximum and minimum price guarantees to additional crops would be a major government contribution. This requires improved storage and purchasing facilities, and a careful working out of price policies, particularly for export crops. Greater price stability would reduce the risk of shifting to higher-value cash crops and of purchasing inputs to increase production. Local purchaser monopolies would also be weakened. Not incidentally, a widespread price guarantee program would particularly help the smaller cultivator. Finally, price policy can be used to induce further shifts to a cropping pattern which will yield the highest social returns, since peasants respond readily to relative prices once risk is held in reasonable bounds.

A major effort would be required to carry out widespread price guarantees. But the government also needs to do more in research and in extension; to assure that supplies of seeds, insecticides, pumps, and spare parts are available for those cultivators already prepared to use them; to expand the Works Programme; to speed up major irrigation, power distribution, flood control, and road-building works; and to improve the availability and repayment of credit. The government effort required to step up the rate of agricultural growth beyond that achieved in the mid-1960's would be greater than anything so far tried in Pakistan. The most important requirement would be for more leadership and administrative capacity. For instance, to expand the Comilla approach to all of East Pakistan would take about 500 senior and experienced administrators, plus some 50,000 other staff members. The program recommended in the Revelle report (33) for West Pakistan would require 1,000 senior technicians and administrators. Plans call for more than

50,000 tube wells in West Pakistan and another 15,000 in East Pakistan in 5 years. To provide credit and electricity for a large proportion of these wells, and maintenance services for those in East Pakistan, would not be easy. These figures are only illustrative, but they do suggest that agricultural development will need increased government attention and manpower. It obviously makes sense for the government to concentrate on activities it can perform effectively, and to leave to the private sector activities it can carry out efficiently. Allowing private dealers to participate in fertilizer distribution worked well. Private development of tube wells, added to government development, has greatly increased the availability of water. Fertilizer distribution and the installation and operation of wells or pumps are highly decentralized activities which are done effectively by private people. It would be well to enlist private initiative, in addition to government and cooperative efforts, in supplying other agricultural inputs, notably seeds and pest control materials.

The indirect measures so far adopted to increase agricultural production could be carried further. The advantages of stabilizing prices of additional crops have already been discussed. Lower prices for inputs have proved effective in increasing their use, and subsidies could be extended. Those on fertilizer are high and are being continued, but it may be desirable to subsidize irrigation quite heavily. In East Pakistan a high, say 50 percent, subsidy for investment may be necessary to encourage the wide use of pumps. In West Pakistan subsidies on tube wells may eventually become necessary to encourage their development in less favorable areas and by less progressive cultivators. If substantial subsidies are provided and agricultural output continues to increase, many cultivators should be able to pay higher taxes. A tax on land has none of the disincentive effects of taxes on output or export. It can have positive effects by encouraging more effort and a shift to higher value crops, and by discouraging underutilized land. There are obvious political difficulties in raising land taxes, but these might be minimized by raising taxes while introducing additional subsidies and price guarantees. The aim and result of agricultural price policy would not be to turn the terms of trade further in agriculture's favor. It would provide incentives for increased production by raising and stabilizing the price of output and subsidizing the price of inputs. At the same time resources from agriculture would be obtained through taxes on land and consumption.

Continued concentration of effort is a necessity in agriculture. The government effort needs to be concentrated on the inputs that will give the highest immediate returns (e.g., water, fertilizer, seeds), and on the activities that are crucial (e.g., research, credit). The areas that have serious problems with waterlogging, drainage, drought, or flood should be given lower priority than the better-endowed areas — the resources required to reclaim land can be several times the resources required to make good land more productive. Reliance on private initiative will automatically assure concentration of effort as the more energetic cultivators, on better land, will be be the first ones to take advantage of the opportunities offered.

The final major reason for government intervention in the economy in Pakistan has been the political imperative, and the social and economic need, for more rapid *development in the economically backward regions,* especially in East Pakistan. Policies adopted so far have had some success. East Pakistan's share in total government investment has increased in the 1960's. In addition, East Pakistan and the less-developed areas of West Pakistan have benefited from longer tax holidays on profits, lower import duties on machinery, and other minor inducements. However, concessions on profits taxes have had only a weak influence on location decisions, and private investment continues to be heavily concentrated in West Pakistan.

To increase the rate of growth in East Pakistan, more of the measures adopted in the last few years will be needed. The increased allocation of government funds to this area is a clear-cut step, and much of the political pressure from less-developed areas has focused on their share of government expenditure. But there are limits and dangers to such a course of action. For one, the very visibility of the process means that it will generate maximum resentment in the developed areas, and will call forth countervailing pressure. This is especially serious when public investment in the more developed area is threatened with slowdown if pressures from the backward area are successful. Second, a large part of government-developed infrastructure has heavy maintenance expenditures (especially roads, schools and hospitals). The backward regions can least afford an infrastructure which is large in relation to the directly productive sectors. Third, and most serious, infrastructure development may not be a very effective lever, in the short run, to produce a higher rate of general development. Government investment in infrastructure in East Pakistan can and should be stepped up. However, excessive preoccupation with the most visible aspect of the regional problem could produce an extensive and costly transport system, power grid, education and health system, superimposed on stagnant per-capita agricultural production and slowly growing industrial output.

Fearing such a development, Pakistan's Plan provides for a rapid expansion of industry in East Pakistan. The political imperative in East Pakistan is for industrialization to be dominated by Bengalis, natives of the Province. That industry has been largely owned and managed by non-Bengalis is widely resented in East Pakistan. In addition, it means that any conflict between labor and management is often exacerbated, becoming also a conflict between Bengalis and non-Bengalis. Whatever one may think of the widespread Bengali feeling about outsiders, it exists and has to be taken into account. It could be the major reason for allocating, in the Third Plan, half of all industrial investment in East Pakistan to its PIDC. This assures that industrial growth will be controlled by the East Pakistan government. The PIDC has an important and logical function to perform as entrepreneur, but there are limits to the size of the task it can handle well.

To reach planned targets for industrial development in East Pakistan without exceeding PIDC management capacity, private investment will have to increase rapidly in the near future. In addition, the investment will have to be substantially in Bengali hands. East Pakistan, unlike less-developed regions in other countries, is a clearly demarcated area, distant from the rest of the country, and with its own international frontiers. It is therefore possible to apply policies to encourage private investment in the Province such as separate tariff, tax, and subsidy rates — without insurmountable administrative and policing problems. Imports of manufacturers into East Pakistan can be specially taxed and exports subsidized, whether their origin or destination is another country or West Pakistan. Alternatively, production of manufactures in East Pakistan can be subsidized by reducing the excise tax imposed on all nonessential consumer goods, and by providing a subsidy on goods that do not carry an excise tax. Subsidizing production, unlike taxes on imports, would not affect the price to the East Pakistan consumer, would be effective only when production actually takes place, and would have obvious and measurable costs. Its major drawback would be administrative complexity. The best solution might be to use different techniques — import surcharges, export subsidies, and reduced excises — for different commodities. Prices received by producers in East Pakistan, net after taxes, could then be higher than in West Pakistan by a uniform percentage. The investor in East Pakistan would find his risk reduced and his rate of return increased from the moment he begins production.

Since industrialists have previously responded to similar economic incentives, these measures should encourage private industrial investment in East Pakistan. The incentives are likely to be effective also for Bengalis. In the 1960's there emerged a number of Bengali businessmen and industrialists who could be expected to try to take advantage of opportunities similar to those which faced their counterparts in West Pakistan earlier. However, unlike their counterparts, the Bengalis face tough competition from established non-Bengali firms and need special help to meet it. The PIDC can take Bengalis as partners in joint ventures, including ventures with foreign investors. It can also sell enterprises to Bengalis, even at a price below their market value. (It would be important to abandon any policy of setting the price of PIDC enterprises in relation to the investment cost and to adopt instead prices related to market value. Cost-pricing means that some favored investors get profitable plants after the government has taken all the risk, while the PIDC is stuck with the plants that do not turn out to be profitable.) Government-related credit agencies can support Bengalis. These special steps are already being taken, but could be extended.

Discrimination in favor of East Pakistan and Bengalis clearly has undesirable aspects. There would be costs to the consumer and to the economy, and political and moral drawbacks. However, if it is accepted that steps must be taken to speed up industrial development in East Pakistan, the choice of alternative tools is limited. Direct government intervention is costly and difficult to administer, distorts investment, and has not worked. Minor concessions in taxes have only limited effect. The proposed special subsidy should be uniform to reduce distortion in investment patterns. It should be limited in time, inducing a badly needed spurt in investment to overcome East Pakistan's handicap with respect to skilled labor, overhead facilities, and complementary industries. Since the special assistance would be obvious, and opposed by the powerful industrialist of West Pakistan, there is a good chance that it would expire as planned. Most important, it should be effective in providing incentives of the same order as those facing the small traders of West Pakistan in the early 1950's — assured high profits, reasonable risks, and available capital.

It is equally important to step up the rate of agricultural growth in East Pakistan. The arithmetic is obvious and disquieting. Well over half of East Pakistan's product is contributed by agriculture. Unless agricultural output increases more rapidly than population, per-capita income in the Province is unlikely to increase significantly; unless growth in agricultural output at least approaches that in West Pakistan, East Pakistan is not likely to catch up with the other Wing.

In West Pakistan the prescription is relatively simple. With a moderate expansion of the existing programs to provide water, fertilizer, and seeds, one can predict a satisfactory increase in crop production with a good deal of assurance. Not so in East Pakistan. The potential of fertilizer is similar to West Pakistan, but water-control measures are more difficult and their results less certain. For one, holdings in East Pakistan are much smaller than in the West, making private water development more difficult. For another, the flood control, drainage, and irrigation projects in the public sector involve a technology that is more difficult, with less information available, and are in the hands of agencies that are less developed, than in West Pakistan. Lower incomes in East Pakistan make it more important that credit and knowledge be made available by the government (and cooperatives), but this involves difficult administrative problems.

To increase the rate of agricultural growth in East Pakistan, the government may need to subsidize very heavily both the sale and rental of pumps for irrigation. Because units are small, peasants are poor, and East Pakistan lacks a traditional metalworking industry, the government will have to play a large role in the maintenance and repair of pumps and other machinery. For the same reasons communal action is particularly important in East Pakistan; it will be necessary to rely on an expanded Works Programme and other forms of local joint initiative to carry out a large number of small local works for irrigation, drainage, and flood protection, which neither the private farmer nor the Water and Power Development Authority is well equipped to handle.

In short, in East Pakistan stronger indirect incentives will be required than in West Pakistan, and the government will have to play a larger role by direct intervention to develop both agriculture and industry.

AN INDIRECT CONTROL SYSTEM — CONSEQUENCES

As a result of the steps discussed, it would be possible gradually to abolish nearly all direct controls over private investment and imports which remained in 1965, and to rely instead on a comprehensive system of indirect taxes plus some direct government investment and management.* Imports in general would be restricted by the import surcharge, not by government-issued import licenses; domestic production would be encouraged by infant-industry import duties and export subsidies to broad categories of industries, not by quantitative restrictions on competing imports and specific subsidies to some exports; investment would be channeled into socially desired activities and areas by the differential excise taxes on broad groups of consumer goods, not by direct licensing of investment; guaranteed price levels for agricultural commodities and subsidized inputs would be used to obtain a desirable cropping pattern and a greater use of inputs, without a need for price control, rationing, or compulsory procurement; restrictions on consumption, and the attractiveness of investment, would encourage savings; and consumption would be discouraged by high taxes, not direct controls. As in the past, government plans would provide information and guidance.

Since this kind of indirect control system would be a logical extension of developments in Pakistan in the 1960's, one can draw on experience as a guide to its consequences. First, the government's administrative burden would decrease. Nearly all consumer goods, except necessities such as food, already bore some taxes in 1965, and greater reliance on indirect measures normally would involve only a change in tax rates, not new taxes. (Of course, even if a particular commodity bears three or four taxes for as many reasons, these could be amalgamated into a single, composite tax for collection purposes.) Officials administering

* Since 1964–65, the government of Pakistan has further increased the use of indirect taxes and subsidies. The export bonus scheme is more reliable. Indirect taxes were raised by roughly one-third in the 1966–67 budget, as compared to 1964–65 collections, with much of the increase on consumer goods and especially semiluxury and luxury goods.

the remaining direct controls could largely be diverted to other activities. The problem of corruption would be further reduced.

Second, there would be a further increase in competition. Entry in industry and the import trade would be essentially free. Anyone who was confident that he could make a profit after paying appropriate taxes could import or produce anything he wanted. The advantage possessed by the large established enterprise — because it is more acceptable and better able to influence government officials issuing permission to import or invest — would disappear. The result of more competition should be downward pressure on prices, pressure for efficiency, and decreased concentration of wealth.

Another major consequence of using commodity taxes, rather than direct controls, would be higher revenues and a tax system which is more equitable and progressive. If luxury goods and semiluxuries bear sufficient taxes to limit import or domestic production to the quantities previously allowed under direct control, the tax yield would be high. Taxes would be paid primarily by the upper-income groups, who would find it much more difficult to evade commodity taxes than they do income and profit taxes. Windfall profit would sharply decline as taxes eliminate high profits per unit earned on the import or production of some consumer goods. The reduction in some profits need not be serious for investment, since weaker profit incentives are adequate for well established industrialists. Also, businessmen would find weakened incentives offset to some extent by reduced administrative hurdles and less need for bribes. The somewhat lower private savings, due to lower profit rates, could be offset by higher government savings out of increased government revenues.

Fourth, the government, relieved of the need to administer many detailed direct controls, could concentrate on

government investment and management for the infrastructure and some industry; tax and subsidy programs;
and, above all, the large program to guarantee prices and
provide services, supplies, and credit to agriculture.

A final significant advantage of an indirect system would
be its flexibility. Industrialists could change the composition of outputs and inputs in response to consumer demand, international prices, or changes in technology;
businessmen could vary the composition of imports and
exports in response to changes in demand or supply;
farmers could change their cropping patterns. The government would have a great deal of flexibility as well.
Since taxes would be imposed on broad categories of goods
and collected from a limited number of units, it would be
administratively simple to change them. For instance, if
the import surcharge turned out to be inadequate or excessive, the whole surcharge could be adjusted. Similarly,
if investment in one group of industries greatly exceeds or
falls short of planned targets, the excise tax — or the tax
on competing imports — could be changed for the group
as a whole. Initially, a relatively large number of categories with different tax rates would give the government
a considerable measure of control, at some administrative
cost. As the country becomes wealthier, and shortages become less acute, while flexibility becomes more important,
categories could be amalgamated gradually. For instance,
it might be desirable to start with 4 or 5 tax rates on cotton
textiles, several dozen rates of infant-industry protection
for all of industry, and substantial differences in taxes between East and West Pakistan. Over the next 10 to 20
years, it would be possible to reduce the categories substantially and to eliminate the differential between the
two Provinces. The system also could be varied as different objectives change in importance. For instance, if
greater equality is desired, even at the cost of less growth,

excise taxes on nonnecessities could be raised sharply, reducing the consumption of upper income groups, but also reducing their profits, savings, and investment incentives. If investment in East Pakistan needs to be speeded up, the differential in taxes between the Provinces could be increased.

THE EFFECTIVENESS OF THE PROPOSED SYSTEM — CAPITALISM OR SOCIALISM

One cannot point to convincing evidence that a complete system of indirect measures, substituting for all major direct controls, would work without difficulty. Undoubtedly it would not. There are risks attached to carrying such a shift to its logical conclusion. Economists are notoriously unreliable as predictors of human behavior, in large part because human behavior is notoriously difficult to predict. With direct measures the government retains a great deal of control over private actions, and the danger of inaccurate predictions is much less. However, the steps so far taken to shift to indirect controls have been successful, and further steps would be warranted if the assumptions on which an indirect control system has to be based are accepted.

One of its basic assumptions is that Pakistani businessmen — and especially industrialists — respond to prices and profits in the same fashion as those in more developed countries; that greed, desire for power, for income, for social approval, personal satisfaction, and for the outward measures of success motivates them as it does their counterparts elsewhere. A good deal of evidence has been provided that industrialists in Pakistan respond to differences in profit possibilities, and that they do so quite rapidly. This is why the manipulation of relative prices can be used to affect what industrialists will produce (or what traders will import). This assumption also underlies the contention that industrialists, when exposed to competitive pressure and freed from direct controls, will improve the economic efficiency of their enterprises.

The second basic assumption is that, of the various motives which animate Pakistani businessmen, the desire for increased consumption is by no means of overriding importance. Therefore businessmen can be induced to save and invest productively if consumption continues to be made costly and is generally discouraged, while investment in some industries is made attractive. Evidence has been provided that savings out of industrial income are high and that industrial investment continues at a high rate despite sharp restrictions on consumption and declining profits. Accordingly, some further reduction in profits is possible as industrial investment becomes more routinized, as more consumer goods become available, and as the composition of available consumer goods reflects consumer preference.

The third basic assumption is that Pakistan has a government machinery capable of devising and implementing a system of indirect controls and carrying out a substantial program of direct investment. It is assumed that it could not simultaneously administer an effective, widespread system of direct controls. Again, some evidence has been provided both on the capacity and limits of the government machinery.

The final basic assumption is that a rapid increase in agricultural production can be obtained by substantial reliance on price incentives, accompanied by substantial, direct government intervention. The evidence is good that peasants behave to a considerable extent as economic men. Price incentives can be effective in inducing shifts in cropping patterns and in increasing the use of some agricultural inputs. There is also evidence, and it is gradu-

ally becoming quite persuasive, that an adequate government program (added to price and other incentives) can
change an essentially stagnant to a developing agriculture.
Such a program would include government organization
of cooperative efforts and the provision of goods and services which small, scattered agricultural units cannot provide for themselves.

Because the evidence seems to justify these assumptions, the proposed indirect control system seems a good
gamble. It would further concentrate government effort
where such an effort is required, by reducing it where it
is superfluous. Resources would be diverted to investment
from consumption — and especially from consumption by
the wealthier citizens — by government manipulation of
the price system. At the same time, decentralized private
ownership and management in agriculture, industry, and
distribution would improve the economic efficiency of the
system. To the extent that the indirect system would be
successful, it meets the objectives assumed as important
to Pakistan — a high rate of growth and a degree of equity
in the distribution of its economic costs and benefits.

The resulting system could be called socialism. It advocates substantial government planning and intervention in
the economy. The basic decisions on the functioning of the
economy would not result from the interaction of many
individual decisions, but from the political process. Government intervention would take place in order to achieve
two social objectives, which have become the essential
socialist objectives. The system could equally well be
called capitalism. Most of the means of production would
be privately owned. The individual firm would generally
be in private hands, with production, investment, and individual price decisions privately taken. Ownership and
decisions would be decentralized. The determinant of
most individual decisions would be private profit.

The proposed system assumes that, at present, economic policy in Pakistan cannot be based on socialism's attempt to use the machinery of the state to achieve "from each according to his ability, to each according to his needs," nor on capitalism's premise that it is possible to achieve social well-being as the by-product and result of the pursuit of self-interest by each economic unit. Rather, it attempts to use the machinery of government to harness self-interest to social goals.

Pakistan has been moving successfully toward an indirect control system for more than five years. Unlike some countries, especially in Asia and Africa, it has reduced its reliance on direct government controls, and on government ownership and management. Unlike other countries, particularly in Latin America of the 1950's, it has not let decisions be guided largely by market-determined prices. It has been suggested that in the second half of the 1960's Pakistan might move further toward a system of indirect measures to influence prices, with a minimum of government ownership and management in industry and commerce. Even for Pakistan, this does not mean that the proposed system would have been equally appropriate in the past, or that it will be in the future. During the early period of Pakistan's industrial development, a greater measure of direct government investment was necessary because there were not enough competent, private entrepreneurs with adequate capital. In the long run, industrial ownership and management may become as divorced in Pakistan as they are in the United States; the rate of change in the economy will slow down, so that decentralization of decisions may be less important; the ability of the government to administer the program it wants to carry out will increase; with affluence the tremendous drive of private entrepreneurs may flag, and their consumption levels increase; agriculture will become more commercialized and respond more readily to purely price incentives; small industry, relatively insensitive to market incentives, will decline in importance; the country will be much wealthier and better able to ignore the effect of policies on economic efficiency. In short, Pakistan will become a developed economy. The difference in efficiency between the government and private enterprise in industrial ownership and management will decrease with development. Ideological or equity considerations may be more important in deciding government's role. As the controlled engine of growth, self-interest or greed may be less necessary and less acceptable. Government intervention in agriculture and infrastructure development may be less important. For all these reasons, the government may then play a more active role in industrial investment and management, while reducing the scope of its indirect control system.

The economic performance of Pakistan in the last few years has been primarily the result of good economic management — sensible policies and plans. Most important has been Pakistan's pragmatic approach to the role of government and private enterprise. The efficiency of the economic system will need to be increased in the immediate future if Pakistan's goals — modest in absolute terms, but nevertheless difficult to achieve — are to be reached.

Pakistan needs to develop an economic system that takes advantage of the efficient functioning of the individual economic unit under private ownership and management, without sacrificing its social goals of growth and equity. A price system manipulated by the government, with individual owners making investment and production decisions, may be the best way to achieve both efficiency and social goals.

STATISTICAL APPENDIX

STATISTICAL APPENDIX

IT MAY seem gratuitous to state once again that much of the data which follow are not very accurate. Some uncertainty about the reliability of economic data is universal, but the problem is particularly severe in countries where a large proportion of output does not pass through the monetary sector and where only limited resources can be allocated to data gathering. On the whole, though, Pakistan's statistics are more reliable than those of a majority of underdeveloped countries. The gross movements indicated in the data are pretty certain to have taken place — if the domestic product is shown to have increased 10 percent it is quite possible that the increase was 8 or 12 percent, but the margin of error is unlikely to be greater.

In the last few years a great deal of statistical work has been done in Pakistan. Odd bits of data were searched out, compared, and manipulated. One result has been greater knowledge of economic events. Another was frequent changes in data, including basic indices. These changes have been regarded by some critics as indicative of haphazard work, uncertainty, and lack of competence; changes should be taken as the outward sign of constant attempts at improvement.

There follows yet another set of data, yet another attempt to shuffle the same basic set of sparse information. In a few cases the data may represent another step forward; in most cases they in turn will soon be outdated. Sources and methods are given in great detail so others can improve on and update the data presented, if they wish, without having to guess how the figures were derived.

References are given in the Bibliography. Most of the data in this Appendix, and in the body of the book, are presented in crores of rupees because this is a convenient magnitude for Pakistan. One crore is ten million; one crore of rupees, quite logically, is ten million rupees. Since August 1955 one rupee has been equal to $0.21; therefore one crore of rupees is roughly equal to $2 million. In all tables, totals may not add due to rounding. The sample survey ("Survey") which provided data on manufacturing is described in (*141*). The Statistical Appendix owes much to the herculean efforts of Stephen Guisinger.

Contents of Statistical Appendix

1. Gross Domestic Product

THE DATA used in this book to describe overall changes in the economy are "synthetic" gross domestic product estimates. To reduce random fluctuations due to weather, trend figures are used for major crops. Crop production figures are therefore supposed to show typical, rather than actual, value added.

Pakistan's National Accounts are usually estimated at factor cost. One good reason for this approach is that estimates at market prices involve the difficult task of allocating taxes and subsidies to particular sectors. Yet the rapid expansion of large-scale manufacturing is not adequately represented by estimates at factor cost. As industrial output increased, the government took an increasing share in the form of indirect taxes. The physical increase in the output of manufacturing then is not reflected in a factor-cost estimate at constant prices. National Accounts at factor costs therefore understate the structural change in the Pakistan economy and, to a lesser extent, the overall growth rate. Consequently, in this book the contribution of manufacturing has been estimated at market prices by including indirect excise and sales taxes paid by industry in that sector's value added. A similar argument applies, though less forcefully, to the export duties levied on agriculture and the subsidies on agricultural inputs, and these too have been added to (or substracted from) value added by agriculture. Unfortunately, it is not possible to allocate the remaining indirect taxes (and subsidies) to individual sectors. Most of the remaining taxes are collected on imports, and to allocate them to sectors would involve conceptual difficulties and computational nightmares. They have therefore been left unallocated in Tables 1, 5a, and 5b, and lumped under Other in tables limited to three sectors (agriculture, manufacturing, and other). This procedure is not very elegant and is bound to be incorrect to some extent but can be justified because there is no feasible alternative, and an allocation of the appropriate part of indirect taxes to agriculture or manufacturing would not significantly affect the results. The greatest change would be in the level of the value added in manufacturing and it would change the level by less than 10 percent.

TABLE 1. GROSS DOMESTIC PRODUCT IN CONSTANT
1959–60 PRICES.

Sector	1949–50	1954–55	1959–60	1964–65
	(crores of rupees)			
Agriculture (factor cost)	1,432	1,523	1,632	2,011
Major crops	817	859	950	1,147
Minor crops	245	250	218	277
Fishing	87	98	111	187
Forestry	7	9	11	20
Livestock	276	307	342	380
Indirect taxes on Agriculture	7	15	13	5
Subsidies to Agriculture	0	−2	−6	−16
Agriculture (market prices)	1,439	1,536	1,639	2,000
Manufacturing (market prices)	30	110	192	382
Other (factor cost)	950	1,127	1,316	1,819
Small-scale manufacturing	109	122	137	156
Mining and quarrying	3	5	7	13
Construction	24	42	65	192
Electricity, gas, water, and sanitary services	3	5	11	28
Transportation, storage, and communications	124	159	186	242
Wholesale and retail trade	286	326	367	511
Banking and insurance	8	11	22	36
Ownership of dwellings	139	156	177	202
Public administration and defense	106	124	133	184
Services	148	177	211	254
Indirect taxes on Other	77	90	88	191
Subsidies to Other	0	0	−1	−14
Other (market prices)	1,027	1,217	1,403	1,996
Gross domestic product at market prices	2,496	2,863	3,234	4,378
	(millions)			
Population	78.9	88.3	98.9	112.5
	(rupees)			
Per capita GDP	316	324	327	389

NOTES TO TABLE 1

See Tables 5 for sources and methods of calculation.

Comparison with other estimates

The GDP data in Table 1 differ from data used by the Planning Commission and other agencies of the Pakistan Government in a number of important respects: Table 1 is at market prices; most other GDP estimates are at factor cost. Table 1 uses trend values for major crops; most other estimates use actual values for the particular year. Table 1 derives figures for the large-scale manufacturing sector from the Survey; data for this sector are usually derived from the Census of Manufacturing Industry. The Census-derived estimates for value added are generally lower, and generally show a lower growth rate, than Survey data. For a comparison, see (*141*). Livestock data are from (*45; 46*).

2. Consumption, Saving, Investment

ESTIMATES of consumption, saving, and investment, have a wide margin of error. Investment estimates are in large part derived by multiplying estimated imports and production of capital goods by standard coefficients. The coefficients are far from accurate, and small changes in their magnitude produce large changes in investment estimates. Using plausible alternative assumptions, one can obtain a 20 or 30 percent increase or decrease in investment estimates.

The estimate of foreign resources is more accurate, but even here there are differences between figures based on payments and those based on arrivals and shipments. In addition, data on defense imports are not available and there are serious problems of valuation. Whether U.S. surplus commodities are valued at world market prices, or U.S. prices, or Pakistan prices, for instance, makes a good deal of difference to foreign resource estimates. Loans and grants tied to particular suppliers often involve prices that differ by up to 30 percent from competitive bids.

Saving estimates—total investment minus foreign resources—can compound the uncertainty and errors of both of the above estimates, and therefore have a particularly high margin of error.

TABLE 2A. CONSUMPTION, SAVING, INVESTMENT, AND GROSS DOMESTIC PRODUCT IN CURRENT PRICES.

Category	1949–50	1954–55	1959–60	1964–65
	(crores of rupees)			
1. Gross domestic product	2,029	2,170	3,234	4,684
2. Import surplus	35	9	104	315
3. Total resources	2,064	2,179	3,338	4,999
4. Monetized investment	76	162	350	812
Public	24	59	150	380
Private	52	103	200	432
5. Consumption (line 3 minus line 4)	1,988	2,017	2,988	4,187
6. Monetized saving (line 4 minus line 2)	41	153	246	497
	(rupees)			
7. Per capita				
Resources	262	247	338	444
Investment (monetized)	10	18	35	73
Consumption	253	229	302	371
	(percent)			
8. As percent of total resources				
Investment (monetized)	3.7	7.4	10.5	16.2
Saving (monetized)	2.0	7.0	7.4	9.9
9. As percent of GDP				
Investment (monetized)	3.7	7.5	10.8	17.3
Saving (monetized)	2.0	7.1	7.6	10.6

TABLE 2B. CONSUMPTION, SAVING, INVESTMENT, AND GROSS DOMESTIC PRODUCT IN CONSTANT 1959–60 PRICES.

Category	1949–50	1954–55	1959–60	1964–65
	(crores of rupees)			
1. Gross domestic product	2,496	2,863	3,234	4,378
2. Import surplus	69	17	104	325
3. Total	2,565	2,880	3,338	4,703
4. Monetized investment	100	203	350	745
Public	32	74	150	349
Private	68	129	200	396
5. Consumption (line 3 minus line 4)	2,465	2,677	2,988	3,958
6. Monetized Saving (line 4 minus line 2)	31	186	246	420
	(rupees)			
7. Per capita				
Resources	325	326	338	418
Investment (monetized)	13	23	35	67
Consumption	312	303	302	351
	(percent)			
8. As percent of total resources				
Investment (monetized)	3.9	7.0	10.5	15.8
Saving (monetized)	1.2	6.5	7.4	8.9
9. As percent of GDP				
Investment (monetized)	4.0	7.1	10.8	17.0
Saving (monetized)	1.2	6.5	7.6	9.6

NOTES TO TABLE 2A

Line 1. Gross domestic product in constant 1959–60 prices is from Appendix Table 1, line 24. To convert GDP at constant prices into GDP at current prices, the implicit GDP deflator (9f, pp. 232–235) was employed for the years 1949–50 and 1954–55. For 1964–65, an implicit deflator was calculated (151, pp. 169–170). It was 107.0.

2. Import surplus figures are taken from Appendix Table 4, Financing items.

4. Public investment comes from Table 3a, Total public investment. (Excludes loans to private enterprise.) Private investment comes from Table 3a, Total private investment.

7. The estimate for population appears in Appendix Table 1, line 11.

NOTES TO TABLE 2B

1. GDP from Table 1, line 24.

2. Import surplus is from Appendix Table 4, converted to constant

prices by splicing together at 1959–60 two "unit value of imports" indices. The first series, (29c, p. 1481), runs from 1949–50 to 1963–64 with 1948–49 equal to 100. This series was converted to 1959–60 = 100 and joined with the second series, (151, p. 172).

Year	1949–50	1954–55	1959–60	1964–65
Index	0.51	0.51	1.00	0.97

4. The current-price values of Table 2a were changed to constant prices by using the price index in the last row, following.

Component	1949–50	1954–55	1959–60	1964–65
a. Machinery	44	59	100	100
b. Iron, steel, and cement	90	83	100	117.1
c. Manufactures	93	89	100	107.1
d. Wages	74	89	100	111
e. $\dfrac{a + b + c + d}{4}$	76	80	100	109

Sources:

Machinery: For 1949–50 through 1959–60, see (141; p. 488). For 1964–65, the index for machinery in (174) is 103.3, on a base 1957–59 = 100; converting to a 1959–60 base gives 1964–65 as 99.9.

Iron, steel, and cement: For 1949–50 through 1959–60, see (141; p. 473). For 1964–65, (29f) gives: (1959–60 = 100) *East:* cement 149.0, (p. 500); metal products 133.20, (p. 498); average (weighted 1:1) 141.1. *West:* cement 115.06, (p. 511); metals 99.98, (p. 507); average (weighted 1:1) 107.5. Weighting East: West, 1:2.5 (see 141, p. 488), the index for 1964–65 is 117.1.

Manufactures: For 1949–50 through 1959–60, (see 141, p. 488). For 1964–65, (29f, p. 485) gives the wholesale price index for manufactures as 107.1.

Wages: The index of wages was constructed by converting a series of annual earnings of textile workers (27, p. 67) into an index with 1959–60 = 100. There are no data available on wages for 1964–65. One assumption, and this is strictly conjecture, is that the cost of living index (29f, p. 543) gives a good approximation of the change in wages over this period. Converted to a 1959–60 base, the index for 1964–65 is 111.2.

The choice of the weighting scheme is discussed in (141, pp. 471–472). The wage index is arbitrarily weighted 1:3 with the other columns to obtain the final investment price index in the last row.

TABLE 2C. MONETIZED AND NONMONETIZED INVESTMENT
IN CURRENT PRICES.

Investment	1949–50	1954–55	1959–60	1964–65
	(crores of rupees)			
1. Nonmonetized	19	32	48	58
2. Monetized	76	162	350	812
3. Total	95	194	398	870
	(percent)			
4. Row 3 as percent of GDP	4.7	9.0	12.3	18.6
5. Row 3 as percent of total resources	4.6	8.9	11.9	17.4
6. Monetized and nonmonetized saving as percent of GDP	3.0	8.6	9.1	11.9

Sources:

1. 1949–50: 25 percent of monetized investment for 1949–50 (see below). 1954–55: 20 percent of monetized investment for 1954–55 (see below). 1959–60 and 1964–65: Private communication reporting revision of estimates of nonmonetized investment in (175). They are as follows:

	1959–60	1960–61	1961–62	1962–63	1963–64	1964–65
Nonmonetized	48	53	58	56	58	58
Nonmonetized as percent of fixed monetized investment	15.7	12.3	10.8	8.8	7.8	7.0

Nonmonetized is a declining percentage of fixed monetized investment. A somewhat arbitrary extrapolation of this trend backward gives 25 percent for 1954–55 and 20 percent for 1949–50, more or less. Obviously, these estimates of nonmonetized investment have an extremely high margin of error, and are included primarily in order to give a basis for comparison with other countries.

Comparison with other estimates

Difference with other data may be because:

Tables 2a and 2b are limited to investment; some other estimates are for "development." (For a definition of noninvestment development expenditures, see the various five-year plans.)

Tables 2a and 2b class as "public" the investments made by semi-independent government corporations, which derive most of their funds from the government (e.g., PIDC, PIA); some other estimates class these as "private."

GDP is "synthetic," using trends, not actuals, for major crops; other estimates use actuals for crops, and differ in other respects as well (see Notes to Table 1).

It has been assumed that current domestic savings is investment minus the imbalance on current account. This imbalance or "import surplus" is financed by foreign loans, foreign grants, foreign private investment, drawing down of foreign exchange reserves, and changes in short term foreign balances. Other estimates leave out the last three items and naturally obtain different domestic saving estimates.

3. Investment by Sectors

IT IS obviously useful to have some breakup of investment; it is equally obvious that it will be quite rough. Definitions are to a large degree arbitrary (for example, a pipeline appears under Industry, fuels, and mining, although it might better be called Transportation) and data are often inadequate for decent estimates. Still, by looking at broad trends in the data, one can get some indication of the development strategy that was followed. Some estimates in Table 3 are incorrect; for example, there was private investment in education—but there simply are no data for this item.

TABLE 3A. GROSS MONETARY INVESTMENT BY ECONOMIC
SECTORS AND YEARS
(CRORES OF RUPEES, CURRENT PRICES).

Sector	1949–50		1954–55		1959–60		1964–65	
	Public	Private	Public	Private	Public	Private	Public	Private
Agriculture	1.8	1.5	2.9	2.5	11.8	7.0	20.5	15.0
Irrigation	7.2	0.5	15.1	1.0	43.8	2.5	50.4	8.5
Power	2.3	–	5.0	–	13.8	–	28.8	–
Industry, fuels, and mining	1.0	20.0	10.5	66.5	20.0	104.5	51.2	224.5
Transport and communications	(7.3)	(4.0)	(14.4)	(2.5)	(45.3)	(8.5)	(99.5)	(46.0)
Railways	4.7	–	7.6	–	25.3	–	37.2	–
Roads and road transport	1.2	3.5	2.2	2.0	9.2	8.0	36.1	37.0
Post, telephone, and telegraph	0.5	–	2.5	–	4.7	–	13.4	–
Other (aviation, ports, broadcasting, shipping)	0.9	0.5	2.1	0.5	6.1	0.5	12.8	9.0
Housing and urban development	5.5	14.5	8.7	20.5	15.6	47.0	37.7	84.5
Education, health, and other	0.7	–	3.3	–	5.5	–	29.4	–
Traders' stocks	–	11.0	–	10.0	–	30.0	–	53.0
Indus Basin	–	–	–	–	–	–	91.0	–
Subtotal	25.8	51.5	59.9	103.0	155.8	199.5	408.5	431.5
Net of public loans to private enterprise	24.3	51.5	58.9	103.0	149.5	199.5	380.4	431.5
Grand Total	75.8		161.9		349.0		811.9	

TABLE 3B. PERCENTAGE BREAKDOWN OF GROSS MONETARY INVESTMENT BY ECONOMIC SECTORS AND YEARS.

Sector	1949–50		1954–55		1959–60		1964–65	
	Public	Private	Public	Private	Public	Private	Public	Private
Agriculture	4	3	3	2	5	4	4	3
Irrigation	29	1	25	1	28	1	13	2
Power	10	–	8	–	9	–	8	–
Indus Basin	–	–	–	–	–	–	24	–
Industry, fuels, and mining	4	39	18	64	12	52	8	52
Transport and communications	(31)	(8)	(25)	(3)	(30)	(5)	(26)	(11)
Railways	20	–	13	–	17	–	10	–
Roads and road transportation	4	7	4	2	6	4	9	9
Post, telephone, and telegraph	2	–	4	–	3	–	4	–
Other (aviation, ports, broadcasting, shipping)	4	1	4	1	4	1	3	2
Housing and urban development	22	28	14	20	10	24	9	20
Education, health, and other	–	–	6	–	4	–	8	–
Traders' stocks	–	21	–	10	–	15	–	12
Total	100	100	100	100	100	100	100	100

Note: Figures do not add up because of rounding. Percentages for public investment are net of loans to private enterprise and individuals.

NOTES TO TABLES 3A AND 3B

PUBLIC INVESTMENT

A good breakdown of public investment by sector is found in (67, pp. 16, 55, 58). In many cases the subhead title provided sufficient information for the classification in Table 3. Where the description was too general (for example, civil works), it was necessary to consult budget documents for particular years. In several cases, especially in the earlier years, the budget documents were not sufficiently precise; sometimes other sources were used, sometimes allocations were sheer guesswork.

Some public expenditures are for loans to private individuals (for example, loans to cultivators) or firms (for example, loans via PICIC). Although these items are government expenditures in the first instance, the actual investment is in private hands and is shown as private investment in the summary table. To avoid confusion, these loans are shown by sector in separate columns. These items are followed by a (PE)—for private enterprise—in the accompanying notes.

TABLE 3C. PUBLIC INVESTMENT, 1949–50.

Sector	Center	West	East	Loans to private enter- prise[a]	Total
Agriculture	0.5	0.3	–	1.0	1.8
Irrigation	0.1	7.1	–	–	7.2
Power	–	2.3	–	–	2.3
Industry	1.0	–	–	–	1.0
Transport and communications					
Railways	4.7	–	–	–	4.7
Roads	–	–	1.2	–	1.2
Post, telephone, and telegraph	0.5	–	–	–	0.5
Other	0.9	–	–	–	0.9
Housing and urban development	2.2	2.5	0.8	–	5.5
Education, health, and other	0.2	–	–	0.5	0.7
Total	10.1	12.2	2.0	1.5	25.8

[a] Items under this heading are loans by the Central and Provincial governments to private enterprises and individuals.

TABLE 3D. PUBLIC INVESTMENT, 1954–55.

Sector	Center	West	East	Loans to private enter-prise[a]	Total
Agriculture	0.2	1.6	1.1	1.0	2.9
Irrigation	0.1	13.1	1.9	–	15.1
Power	–	4.1	0.9	–	5.0
Industry	9.8	0.7	–	–	10.5
Transport and communications					
Railways	7.6	–	–	–	7.6
Roads	0.3	2.1	−0.2	–	2.2
Post, telephone, and telegraph	2.5	–	–	–	2.5
Other	2.1	–	–	–	2.1
Housing and urban development	6.0	1.6	1.1	–	8.7
Education, health, and other	0.7	2.3	0.3	–	3.3
Total	29.3	25.5	4.1	1.0	59.9

[a] Items under this heading are loans by the Central and Provincial governments to private enterprises and individuals.

TABLE 3E. PUBLIC INVESTMENT, 1959–60.

Sector	Center	West	East	Loans to private enter-prise[a]	Total
Agriculture	5.2	1.1	1.2	4.3	11.8
Irrigation	3.0	27.3	13.5	–	43.8
Power	4.1	7.4	2.3	–	13.8
Industry	18.2	−0.6	0.4	2.0	20.0
Transport and communications					
Railways	25.3	–	–	–	25.3
Roads	2.0	4.2	3.0	–	9.2
Post, telephone, and telegraph	4.7	–	–	–	4.7
Other	5.8	–	0.3	–	6.1
Housing and urban development	9.4	3.7	2.5	–	15.6
Education, health, and other	1.5	3.5	0.5	–	5.5
Total	79.2	46.6	23.7	6.3	155.8

[a] Items under this heading are loans by the Central and Provincial governments to private enterprises and individuals.

TABLE 3F. PUBLIC INVESTMENT, 1964–65.

Sector	Center	West	WPWP[a]	East	EPWP[b]	Loans to private enterprise[c]	Total
Agriculture	1.5	9.7	0.6	1.7	1.9	5.1	20.5
Irrigation	–	28.9	0.6	19.4	1.5	–	50.4
Power	4.7	13.3	–	10.8	–	–	28.8
Indus Basin (from Table 7)	–	91.0	–	–	–	–	91.0
Industry	6.2	8.0	–	16.4	–	20.6	51.2
Transport and communications							
Railways	–	22.2	–	15.0	–	–	37.2
Roads	1.0	5.8	4.2	9.0	16.1	–	36.1
Post, telephone, and telegraph	13.4	–	–	–	–	–	13.4
Other	10.5	–	–	2.3	–	–	12.8
Housing and urban development	14.0	8.4	1.3	11.6	–	2.4	37.7
Education, health, and other	5.0	12.6	4.4	5.7	1.7	–	29.4
Total	56.3	199.9	11.1	91.9	21.2	28.1	408.5

[a] West Pakistan Works Programme.

[b] East Pakistan Works Programme.

[c] Items under this heading are loans by the Central and Provincial governments to private enterprises and individuals.

The categories in Tables 3 are identified in these notes by the first word only. For example, Education, health, and other is referred to as Education.

Data for this section are taken from (67). In most cases the description of an item corresponded to the classification in Tables 3a through 3f. The classification of items in (67) which was not obvious is explained below:

NOTES TO TABLE 3C

Center. Loans to semi-independent bodies is a payment to the Refugee Rehabilitation Finance Corporation (68, pp. 15, 80); of Rs. 1.5 crores, Rs. 0.5 crore is not considered investment (a subsidy for current expenses); 0.5 is allocated to Housing; and 0.5 to Education (PE). Civil works allocated to Housing (68, p. 112). Of Rs. 2.7 crores Rs. 1

crore is deducted because it is transferred to the Sind Government, presumably for current expenses. Railways includes Rs. 0.7 crore expenditure on the Chittagong Port (*66*, p. 201), which appears under Transport–Other.

West. Rs. 2.0 crores under Civil works and Other provincial works was arbitrarily allocated to: Roads — 0.7; Housing — 0.7; Education — 0.6. Loans and advances by Provincial Government — Rs. 1 crore — is arbitrarily allocated one half to municipalities (Housing) and one half to cultivators (Agriculture) (PE) on the basis of Explanatory Memoranda for later budgets.

East. Civil Works Rs. 1.8 crores — Rs. 1.2 crores allocated to Communications and Rs. 0.6 crore to Housing (*58*, p. 101). Loans by province are primarily loans to municipalities and cultivators and are allocated Rs. 0.5 crore to Agriculture (PE) and Rs. 0.2 crore to Housing (*58*, p. 120).

NOTES TO TABLE 3D

Center. Civil works is largely for refugee housing (*75*, p. 62); Rs. 2.6 crores is therefore allocated to Housing. Rs. 0.2 crore to Roads (*73*, p. 374). Other heads includes broadcasting equipment and/or printing presses. Rs. 0.4 crore is allocated to Transport–Other (*75*, p. 55). Direct expenditures from reserve funds — Rs. 0.7 crore — is arbitrarily allocated to Education 0.4 and Roads 0.3. Loans to semi-independent bodies (*68*, p. 73) — Rs. 3.4 crores — is allocated to Housing because it is a payment to the Karachi Joint Water Board (*69*, p. 67). Chittagong Port expenditure is 12 percent of Railways (*68*, p. 56), therefore 12 percent of 8.6, or Rs. 1 crore, was transferred from Railways to Transport–Other.

East. Civil Works is negative because of transfers among departments (Suspense Accounts), (*58*, pp. 105, 118). No attempt was made to allocate these reductions, and lump-sum deductions were made under Transport–Other (Rs. 0.2 crore), Housing (Rs. 0.1 crore), and Education (Rs. 0.1 crore). Loans to Municipalities, Port Funds, etc. — Rs. 2 crores — have been allocated Rs. 1 crore to Agriculture (PE) and Rs. 1 crore to Housing (*59*, pp. 120–121).

West. (N.B. All items below for 1954–55 are allocated on the basis of expenditures of the Government of the Punjab). Loans to municipalities — Rs. 2.9 crores — (*86*, p. 210), were allocated as follows:

Thal Development — total:	2.8
Agriculture	1.5
Industry	0.5
Roads	0.2
Power	0.2
Housing	0.2
Education	0.2
Housing	0.1

Civil Works — 3.5 — (*86*, pp. 184–191). In 1954–55 the Punjab spent almost Rs. 1 crore for Civil Works, which was distributed Rs. 0.4 crore to Roads and Rs. 0.6 crore to Education and Health. The Rs. 3.5 crores for West Pakistan were allocated in the same proportion. Miscellaneous investment — Rs. 0.5 crore — (*86*, p. 209), was allocated to Roads.

NOTES TO TABLE 3E

Center. Civil works — Rs. 4 crores — is allocated to Housing except for 10 percent to Education (*78*, p. 107). Direct expenditure — Rs. 0.7 crore — is allocated to Roads (*76*, p. 89). Miscellaneous investment — Rs. 3 crores — is allocated Rs. 2 crores for oil and gas prospecting (Industry), and Rs. 1 crore for Roads (*76*, p. 88). Other works — Rs. 0.7 crores — and Other heads — Rs. 0.7 crores — seem to be for Agriculture (0.7) and Education (0.7) (*78*, p. 88). Loans to local funds in (*76*, p. 89), is allocated as follows:

Karachi Development Authority	5.3 Housing
Foreign Project Assistance	1.4 Power; 0.7 Irrigation
Karachi Road Co.	0.3 Roads
Pakistan Industrial Finance Corp.	1.5 Industry (PE)
Karachi Municipal Corp.	0.4 Housing
Cultivators	0.4 Agriculture (PE)
Others	0.4 Education
	9.7

Rs. 0.3 crore spent on Chittagong Port is deducted from Railways and added to Other transport (*77*, p. 125).

East. Civil Works (*59*, p. 139) is Rs. 3.8 crores — of this, Rs. 0.8 crore is allocated to Roads, Rs. 3 crores to Roads. Of 0.8 for buildings, 0.4 is arbitrarily allocated to Housing and 0.4 to Education. Loans to municipalities, etc. — Rs. 18 crores — (*59*, p. 157) is allocated to: Agriculture: 1.6 (1.4 to (PE)); Industry: 0.5 (PE); Irrigation: 13.5; Housing: 0.3; Transport–Other: 0.3; Power: 1.7. WAPDA (Power and Irrigation) total and allocations were obtained from a private communication based on government records.

West. Civil Works — Rs. 10.3 crores — (*83*, p. 123). This item is divided between: Housing: 3.0; Education: 3.3; Roads: 4.0. Industrial Development. This item is negative because Receipts and recoveries exceed expenditure (*87*, p. 128). Miscellaneous investment (*87*, p. 246–9) — Rs. 0.4 crores — is allocated: 0.2 Roads; 0.2 Other. Loans and advances — Rs. 18.9 crores — (*83*, p. 165):

Cultivators	2.5 Agriculture (PE)
Thal Development	1.0 Agriculture
WAPDA	7.4 Power
	8.1 Irrigation

WAPDA is allocated between Power and Irrigation on the basis of their shares in the 1962–63 budget (*83*, Vol. II, p. 299).

NOTES TO TABLE 3F

Center. Irrigation — Rs. 25.30 crores — this item is excluded entirely as it represents the contribution of the Pakistan Government to the Indus Basin (72, p. 544). The full investment in the Indus Basin works is shown separately. Civil Works — Rs. 3.9 crores — this sum is allocated 2.0 to Housing and 1.9 to Education (72, pp. 436–457). Miscellaneous government investments — Rs. 3.7 crores — (72, p. 550). The total is allocated to Industry (nuclear energy and oil investment). Other works — Rs. 5.6 crores — (72, pp. 428, 484, 550). This is Rs. 5.8 crores in (72, p. 15) and Rs. 5.3 crores in (67, p. 17). The sum of individual items in (72, pp. 428, 484, 550) is Rs. 5.6 crores and is allocated to Agriculture 1.5; Education 3.1; and Roads 1.0. Other direct outlays, mainly shown under other heads, total Rs. 3.1 crores.

Items	Allocated to	Amount	Reference in (74)
Rehabilitation of refugees	Housing (PE)	0.2	p. 458
Ports	Transport and communications — Other	0.2	p. 484
Printing	Transport and communications — Other	0.4	p. 538
Broadcasting	Transport and communications — Other	0.9	p. 553
Television	Transport and communications — Other	1.4	p. 557

Loans to semi-independent bodies, etc. — Rs. 2.8 crores — appears in (67, p. 17). In 1964–65 this category seems to exclude loans of Rs. 25.7 crores from foreign sources to the private sector via semi-independent intermediaries — for example, PICIC (67, p. 17) and (72, p. 17 and p. 509). The allocation of Rs. 2.84 crores was made on the basis of the 1964–65 Revised estimates (70, p. 343):

Azard Government	0.6	Excluded; probably not investment
House Building Finance Corp.	2.2	Housing (PE)

Foreign loans, shown in (72, p. 508), but seemingly not reported in (67), were allocated as follows:

Items	Amount	Allocated to:
Karachi Development	0.1	Housing
Industrial Development Bank	12.4	Industry (PE)
PICIC	7.7	Industry (PE)
Karachi Port Trust	0.7	Transport–Other
Karachi Electric Supply	3.6	Power
National Shipping	1.2	Transport–Other
	25.7	

East. Civil Works — Rs. 17.1 crores — (*61*, p. 179) was allocated to:

Buildings	8.3	For breakdown, see (*61*, pp. 187–216).
Housing	3.6	
Education	4.7	
Roads	8.4	
Transport–Other	0.4	

Schemes of state trading were omitted for reasons described in Appenix Table 7, item 11. Provincial miscellaneous investments — Rs. 0.4 crore — allocated to Transport–Other (*61*, p. 184). Railroads (*67*, p. 55) shows no expenditures on railroads because this item now appears only in the railway budgets. An estimate of the 1964–65 investment of Rs. 15 crores is found in (*62; 63*).

Loans and advances — Rs. 55.6 crores — (*61*, p. 10). The "actuals" (expenditures) for each loan recipient (for example, Khulna Development Authority) are given in (*61*, pp. 229–241). But there is no breakdown of actual expenditure by sector (for example, how much WAPDA spent on water and how much on power). This breakdown was estimated from a private communication based on government records.

Items in (*18c*)	Amount in (*18c*)	Allocation	Table 3f classification
WAPDA	30.2		
		19.4	Water
		10.8	Power
IWTA	1.5		Transport–Other
DIT	2.5		Housing
CDA	1.4		
		0.4	Industry
		0.6	Housing
		0.4	Roads
KDA	0.4		
		0.2	Roads
		0.1	Industry
		0.1	Housing
FIDC	0.8		
		0.4	Agriculture
		0.4	Industry
EPIDC	13.1		Industry
WASA	1.4		Housing
EPSIC	0.5		Industry (PE)
Cooperatives	0.8		
		0.4	Industry
		0.4	Agriculture
Cultivators	3.0		Agriculture (PE)
Total	55.6		

West. Civil works — Rs. 19.2 crores (*85*, pp. 145–198) was allocated to: Housing 3.8; Education 9.4; Agriculture 1.4; Roads 4.6. Railways —

Rs. 22.2 crores — is not included in the budget and is estimated from (87). Loans and advances — Rs. 41.3 crores — is allocated (on basis of private communication) to:

Item in (85)	Amount	Allocation	Table 3f classification	Remarks
Thal Development	0.3			
		0.2	Agriculture	
		0.1	Housing	(arbitrary)
WAPDA	27.7	12.1	Power	
		15.0	Irrigation	
		0.6	Housing	
Lahore Improvement Trust	0.3		Housing	
Agric. Devel. Corp.	5.6		Agriculture	
Agriculture	0.2		Agriculture	
WPIDC	0.3		Industry	
Cooperatives	0.4			
		0.2	Agriculture	(arbitrary)
		0.2	Industry	
Road transport	1.2		Roads	
Loans to municipalities	1.0		Housing	
Cultivators	2.1		Agriculture (PE)	
Karachi Development Authority	1.8		Housing	
Others	0.1		Housing	
Others	0.3		Education	
	41.3			

Works Programme

West. Total — Rs. 11.1 crores (private communication). Distributed to sectors on the basis of the percentages given in (151, p. 162). See separate column in 1964–65 table.

East. Total — Rs. 21.2 crores. Estimated as follows:

Total for Pakistan (72, p. 7) — Rs.	32.3 crores
Minus expenditure in West (above)	−11.1
	21.2 crores for East

The distribution of expenditures to sectors is on the basis of (64, pp. 15–16).

PRIVATE INVESTMENT

There is little direct information on private investment. Fragmentary evidence on inputs, on surveys of housing and industry, and so on, must be fitted into a consistent pattern, the missing pieces either inferred or left blank. A useful tool is the identity between the total investment by sectors (for example, industry) and the total investment by investment categories (for example, construction, machinery). In Table 3h the sectors and categories are arrayed in matrix form. In some cases, column totals (categories) can be estimated. In other cases, it is easier to estimate row totals (sectors). Then, if all but one of the elements of the column (or row) are known, the missing item can be calculated as a residual.

TABLE 3G. PRIVATE INVESTMENT.

Sector	1949–50	1954–55	1959–60	1964–65
1. Agriculture	1.5	2.5	6.9	14.9
2. Irrigation	0.5	1.0	2.5	8.3
3. Large-scale industry	18.0	64.0	102.0	224.4
4. Small-scale industry	2.2	2.4	2.5	3.5
5. Road transport[a]	3.4	2.2	7.8	33.2
6. Ships	0.3	0.4	0.7	8.7
7. Housing	14.6	20.5	47.1	84.6
8. Traders' stocks	11.0	10.0	30.0	53.0
9. Total	51.5	103.0	199.5	430.6

[a] Excludes investment in motor vehicles made by large-scale industry.

TABLE 3H. PRIVATE INVESTMENT, 1949–50.

	A Construction	B Machinery excluding transport	C Transport equipment	D Changes in working capital	E
Sector					Total
1. Agriculture	1.0	0.5	—[a]	—[a]	1.5
2. Irrigation	0.2	0.3	—[a]	—[a]	0.5
3. Large-scale industry	3.0	7.7	0.3	7.0	18.0
4. Small-scale industry	1.3	0.9	—[b]	—[b]	2.2
5. Road transport	—[a]	—[a]	3.4	—[a]	3.4
6. Shipping	—[a]	—[a]	0.3	—[a]	0.3
7. Housing	14.6	—[a]	—[a]	—[a]	14.6
8. Changes in commercial trader's stocks	—[a]	—[a]	—[a]	11.0	11.0
9. Total	20.1	9.4	4.0	18.0	51.5

[a] Not applicable.
[b] Negligible.

NOTES TO TABLE 3H

A. *Construction*

1A and 2A are guesses based on subsequent years.

3A. The Survey shows that investment in construction by large-scale manufacturing is 15 percent of total investment; 15 percent of Rs. 18 crores (3E) is Rs. 3.0 crores.

4A is from Table 31.

7A is 9A minus sum of 1-4A.

9A. It was arbitrarily assumed that the value of domestically produced cement is a constant share of total private expenditure on construction. An average taken over 1951–52 to 1953–54 shows this to be 18 percent (*149*, p. 19). Domestic production of cement in 1949–50 is taken as the average of 1949 and 1950: 418,000 tons (*10*, p. 187). The price of cement (including sales tax) is assumed to be 102 rupees per ton (*149*, p. 21, figure for 1951). The value of domestically produced cement is therefore Rs. 4.26 crores. On the above assumption that cement is 18 percent of the private construction, there were Rs. 23.5 crores of private investment in construction.

B. *Machinery* (excluding Transport equipment)

1B and 2B are guesses based on subsequent years.

3B. The Survey shows that 45 percent of total investment in large-scale manufacturing is in machinery; 45 percent of Rs. 18 crores (3E) is Rs. 8 crores.

4B is from Table 31.

9B is the sum of items 1B-4B.

C. *Transport equipment*

5C. Transport equipment is estimated from total domestic supply (imports plus domestic production).

IMPORTS: No breakdown of 1949–50 vehicle imports seem to be available. The earliest breakdown is for 1951–52 (*106*, p. 143), and includes only the value of all vehicles used for investment purpose according to a very broad definition. The figure for "investment" vehicle imports in (*106*) had to be reduced to correspond to the definition used in this book. In 1951–52, "investment goods" were estimated at Rs. 2.95 crores at CIF prices (*106*) or 30 percent of total vehicle imports of Rs. 9.3 crores (*10*, p. 272). The low share of investment goods is partly explained by the exclusion of (a) all railway equipment and (b) semi-finished vehicles (for example, bus chassis — Rs. 1.5 crores in 1951–52). Railways are publicly owned, but imported railway equipment seems to be included in "vehicles" under Private Accounts. Semi-finished vehicles are imports of domestic industry and show up under domestic production.

Applying the above 30 percent estimate to total 1949–50 vehicle imports of Rs. 5.8 crores (*10*, p. 272) gives Rs. 1.7 crores of investment imports at CIF prices. To this, tariffs and transport markups must be added. An unweighted average of these costs is 75 percent of CIF prices. (See notes to 1959–60 transport equipment estimates below.) Adding this amount to Rs. 1.7 crores gives Rs. 3 crores total.

DOMESTIC: No detailed data exist on domestic production for 1949–50. As a guess, if 1951–52 imports of bus chassis were Rs. 1.5 crores, 1949–50 imports could have been Rs. 1.0 crores; adding tariffs of 40 percent and value added and domestic markup of 20 percent (a guess), yields Rs. 1.7 crores.

TOTAL: Total investment in vehicles, then, appears to be Rs. 4.7 crores. Some of this represents government investment. Assuming that 78 percent of motor vehicles are privately owned (175), one can correct for public investment: $0.78 \times 4.7 = 3.7$. Some investment in motor vehicles has already been included under large-scale industry. According to the Survey, vehicles are about 1.5 percent of total capital at cost. 1.5 percent of Rs. 18 crores is Rs. 0.3 crore; therefore nonindustrial private investment in transport equipment is Rs. 3.4 crores.

6C is from private communication.

D. *Working capital*

3D. Survey shows 40 percent of total investment (3E) to be changes in working capital.

8D. Stocks of domestically produced goods held by traders are assumed to be one third of total annual sales (145). Sales figures, taken from the Survey, show Rs. 114.6 crores for 1948–49 and Rs. 148.6 crores for 1949–50. Because sales increased by Rs. 34 crores during the period and stocks are one third of sales, investment in stocks is Rs. 11 crores. Stocks of imported goods were considered to be negligible in 1949–50.

9D is the sum of 3D and 3E.

E. *Total investment by sector*

3E. (141, p. 474).

TABLE 3I. PRIVATE INVESTMENT, 1954–55.

Sector	A Construction	B Machinery excluding transport	C Transport equipment	D Changes in working capital	E Total
1. Agriculture	0.5	2.0	—a	—a	2.5
2. Irrigation	0.5	0.5	—a	—a	1.0
3. Large-scale industry	9.6	27.9	1.0	25.5	64.0
4. Small-scale industry	1.4	1.0	—b	—b	2.4
5. Road transport	—a	—a	2.2	—a	2.2
6. Shipping	—a	—a	0.4	—a	0.4
7. Housing	20.5	—a	—a	—a	20.5
8. Changes in commercial traders' stocks	—a	—a	—a	10.0	10.0
9. Total	32.5	31.4	3.6	35.5	103.0

a Not applicable.
b Negligible.

NOTES TO TABLE 3I

A. *Construction*

1A and 2A are guesses based on subsequent years.

3A. The Survey shows that investment in machinery is 15 percent of total investment in large-scale manufacturing (3E).

4A. See Table 31.

7A is 9A less items 1A-4A.

9A was obtained from (33, p. 19).

B. *Machinery* (excluding transport equipment)

1B. Domestic production of agricultural machinery was Rs. 1 crore in 1957 (17, p. 11). Adding 10 percent transportation gives Rs. 1.1 crores. Assuming that, as in 1959–60, imports of agricultural machinery at landed cost are about 50 percent higher than domestic production, total investment in agricultural machinery for 1957 can be estimated at Rs. 2.8 crores. For 1954–55, investment was probably lower, and Rs. 2.0 crores is a rough estimate.

2B. Information is extremely sparse and only a gross approximation is possible. For 1957, domestic production of pumps and compressors was Rs. 0.32 crore (17, p. 11). Assuming that most pumps were used for irrigation and adding imported pumps, plus transportation and installation costs, one can guess total private investment in irrigation machinery at Rs. 0.5 crore.

3B is 43 percent of (3E); same procedure as in 1949–50.

4B. See Table 31.

9B is the sum of items 1-4B.

C. *Transport equipment*

3C. The Survey shows that transport equipment was 1.5 percent of assets in large-scale industry, therefore 3C is 1.5 percent of 3E.

5C is 9C less (3C + 6C).

6C is private communication.

9C. *Imports:* The procedure used is identical with that in the notes for 1949–50. Thirty percent of Rs. 4.5 crores (*10*, p. 272) is Rs. 1.35 crores. Adding tariffs and markup gives Rs. 2.4 crores.

Domestic: In 1954, domestic production of "mechanically propelled vehicles" was Rs. 1.24 crores (*26*, p. 13). The growth rate implied by the data is roughly 40 percent per annum (*17*, p. 13). Thus, for 1954–55, the value can be estimated as Rs. 1.5 crores (1.24 × 1.20). Adding sales taxes of 10 percent yields a total of Rs. 1.7 crores.

Total transport equipment for investment purposes is Rs. 4.1 crores. Deducting the public share (see 1949–50) leaves total private expenditures at Rs. 3.2 crores for transport equipment excluding ships.

D. *Working capital*

3D is 40 percent of 3E. See same item for 1949–50.

8D. For procedure see under 1949–50. Increase in sales (from Survey) was Rs. 33.3 crore; therefore the change in stocks was Rs. 10 crores.

E. *Total investment*

3E. (*141*, p. 474).

TABLE 3J. PRIVATE INVESTMENT, 1959–60.

Sector	A Construc- tion	B Machinery excluding transport	C Transport equipment	D Changes in working capital	E Total
1. Agriculture	1.5	5.4	—a	—a	6.9
2. Irrigation	1.9	0.6	—a	—a	2.5
3. Large-scale industry	15.0	41.0	2.0	44.0	102.0
4. Small-scale industry	1.5	1.0	—b	—b	2.5
5. Road transport	—a	—a	7.8	—a	7.8
6. Shipping	—a	—a	0.7	—a	0.7
7. Housing	47.1	—a	—a	—a	47.1
8. Changes in commercial traders' stocks	—a	—a	—a	30.0	30.0
9. Total	67.0	48.0	10.5	74.0	199.5

a Not applicable.
b Negligible.

TABLE 3K. PRIVATE INVESTMENT, 1964–65.

Sector	A Construc- tion	B Machinery excluding transport	C Transport equipment	D Working capital	E Total
1. Agriculture	2.5	12.4	—a	—a	14.9
2. Irrigation	5.9	2.4	—a	—a	8.3
3. Large-scale industry	33.0	90.7	3.7	97.0	224.4
4. Small-scale industry	2.0	1.5	—b	—b	3.5
5. Road transport	—a	—a	33.2	—a	33.2
6. Shipping	—a	—a	8.7	—a	8.7
7. Housing	84.6	—a	—a	—a	84.6
8. Changes in commercial traders' stocks	—a	—a	—a	53.0	53.0
9. Total	128.0	107.0	45.6	150.0	430.6

a Not applicable.
b Negligible.

NOTES TO TABLE 3J AND 3K

A. *Construction*

1A and 2A are calculated in the following manner:

Item	1959–60	1964–65	Sources
i. Number of tubewells installed	1,352	6,600	(*41*, p. 11), 1964–65 assumed same as 1963–64.
ii. Cost per tubewell	Rs. 10,000	Rs. 10,000	(*41*, p. 11).
iii. Total cost of tubewells (crores)	1.4	6.6	i × ii
iv. Construction cost of tubewells (2/3 of iii)	0.9	4.4	Based on cost estimates in private communication.
v. Other monetized (non-tubewell) construction in irrigation	1.0	1.5	(*175*) assuming 10 percent of irrigation construction is monetized. Data in (*175*) is for 1962–63, and it is assumed to be slightly less for 1959–60, slightly more for 1964–65.
vi. Total irrigation construction (2A)	1.9	5.9	ii + v
vii. Agricultural construction (1A)	1.5	2.5	(*175*) for 1962–63. It is assumed to be less for 1959–60 and more for 1964–65.

3A. The Survey shows that investment in construction by large-scale manufacturing is 17.6 percent of investment in machinery (3B), transport equipment (3C), and working capital (3D).

4A is from Table 3l.

7A equals 9A minus sum of 1A-4A.

9A. Data on total construction for 1959–60 and 1964–65 is from (*145*). There is no indication of the private sector's share. This was calculated from data in the same memorandum. (*145*) gives the deliveries of cement to public authorities in West Pakistan for the years 1960–61 through 1964–65. By multiplying the quantity of cement by its price (*145*), the total value of cement used in the public sector was calculated. The ratios of total value of cement used to total value of construction, inferred from data in (*145*), (5 percent for 1959–60 and 7 percent for 1964–65) were used to estimate total public construction. Having estimated public construction and obtained total construction from (*145*), the percentage of public in total construction was calculated — 65 percent for 1959–60 and 72 percent for 1964–65.

Similar calculations for East Pakistan were not possible because deliveries of cement to the public sector were not available. However, estimates of ownership of buildings by the public and private sectors

were available for 1962–63 (*175*). Private individuals appeared to own
30 percent of total buildings (including rural and urban dwellings, barns,
schools, offices, and factories), and it was assumed that 30 percent of
construction in 1959–60 and 1964–65 was also undertaken by the private
sector.

Applying these percentages to the provincial construction estimates
contained in (*145*), total private construction was estimated.

B. *Machinery*

1B and 2B:

	Crores of rupees		
Item	1959–60	1964–65	Sources
i. Irrigation (pumps, etc., for tubewells	0.5	2.2	1/3 of iii in 1A + 2A above.
Adjustment plus 10 percent for transportation	0.6	2.4	
ii. Imports for agriculture at landed cost	3.8	8.6	1959–60 — (*20, 21, 22*, pp. 74, 77, 92) 1964–65 — (*29h*, p. 2000)
iii. Domestic production for agriculture	1.1	2.7	1964–65 — 1959–60 value multiplied by an index (2.44) for Machinery except electric (*28*).
	——	——	
Total agricultural machinery	4.9	11.3	ii + iii
Adjustment plus 10 percent for transportation	5.4	12.4	

3B is 9B minus items 1B, 2B and 4B.

4B. See Table 31.

9B. Data on imports and domestic production for 1959–60 and 1964–
65 was taken from (*145*). Again it was necessary to divide total expenditure on machinery between the private and public sectors. Few
data are available. It was assumed that the distribution of ownership of
stocks of machinery in 1962–63 (*175*) is a good indication of the distribution of purchases by the public and private sectors for the two
years. The share of the private sector was: West, 61.5 percent and East,
56 percent.

C. *Transport equipment*

3C. The Survey shows that 1.7 percent of investment by large-scale
industry in items 3A + 3B + 3D is equal to investment in transport
equipment (assumed slightly higher for 1959–60).

5C. Domestic Production: For 1959–60 this was Rs. 8.6 crores for
motor transport and Rs. 0.7 crores for water transport (*18*). According
to (*18*), motor cars represent one fourth of all domestically produced

transport equipment, and half of them are assumed to be consumer goods. One eighth of Rs. 8.6 crores is Rs. 1.0 crores. Subtracting this from Rs. 8.6 crores leaves Rs. 7.6 crores of domestic production of motor vehicles for investment.

For 1964–65 an index (28) for transport equipment (equal to 3.89) was applied to the 1959–60 data to obtain the following values for 1964–65:

$$7.6 \times 3.89 = \text{Rs. } 29.6 \text{ crores — motor vehicles}$$
$$0.7 \times 3.89 = \text{Rs. } \underline{2.8} \text{ crores — water transport}$$
$$32.4$$

These values are in 1959–60 prices. The adjustment for 1964–65 prices would involve negligible changes.

5C. Imported equipment: (*20; 21; 22, and 29h*)

	a	b	c	d	e	f
			Tariff	Trans-		
	CIF	CIF	as	portation	Total	Total
	value	value	percent	as percent	value	value
Type	1959–60	1964–65	of a, b	of a, b	1959–60	1964–65
One half motor cars	1.4	3.9	1.60	1.21	2.7	7.6
Trucks	—ᵃ	4.8	1.38	1.21	–	8.0
Busses	0.8	0.2	1.38	1.21	1.3	0.3
One half motorcycles	0.1	0.9	1.38	1.21	0.2	1.5
Vehicles n.s.	0.5	0.2	1.38	1.21	0.8	0.3
					5.0	17.7

ᵃ Possibly included under vehicles n.s.

6C. Ships: Except for ships imported for scrapping, three quarters of recorded ship imports were arbitrarily assumed to be private investment. (The remaining one quarter would be railway ferries and other vessels purchased by the government.) Imports were zero in 1959–60 and Rs. 5.9 crores in 1964–65.

Total investment in transport.

Type of investment	1959–60	1964–65
a. Motor vehicles		
Domestic	7.6	29.6
Imported	5.0	17.7
	12.6	47.3
b. Share of private investment (inferred from *175*)	0.78	0.78
c. Private motor vehicles	9.8	36.9
d. Ships	0.7	8.7
e. Total private investment in transportation	10.5	45.6

9C is the sum of items in column.

D. *Working capital*

3D. The ratio of the stock of working capital to the stock of machinery at cost was calculated from the Survey. (The figure for 1958 is 1.07). It was assumed that this average ratio also held true for incremental changes. Expenditures on machinery by large-scale industry were multiplied by 1.07 to obtain the change in working capital. Thus for 1959–60: $41 \times 1.07 = 44$; and for 1964–65, $91 \times 1.07 = 97$.

8D. These are taken from (*145*). Changes in stocks were assumed to be one third of changes in total sales for domestically produced goods and half of changes in total sales of imported consumer goods. It was assumed that changes in traders' stocks of raw materials and investment goods were negligible.

TABLE 3L. INVESTMENT IN SMALL-SCALE INDUSTRY.

Item	1948–49 to 1949–50	1953–54 to 1954–55	1958–59 to 1959–60	1963–64 to 1964–65
a. Change in value added (in crores) at constant 1959–60 prices (*29f*, pp. 418–19)	2.5	2.7	3.1	4.0
b. Total investment (a multiplied by capital output ratio 0.87)	2.2	2.4	2.7	3.5
c. Investment in machinery (b multiplied by 0.43, the share of machinery in investment, calculated from the Survey)	0.9	1.0	1.2	1.5
d. Investment in construction (b minus c)	1.3	1.4	1.5	2.0

Note: Investment in small-scale industry for all years was calculated from data in a survey of East Pakistan small-scale industries which (*37*) shows the total depreciated stock of capital and total value added in 1961. The capital stock at cost was estimated by multiplying depreciated capital stock by the ratio between capital at cost and depreciated capital for firms in the "small" category of the Survey (N.B. Firms in this "small" category are larger than those in "small-scale" industry). The estimated capital at cost was then divided by value added to obtain a capital–output ratio (equal to 0.87). Assuming that the marginal cost is equal to the average cost and that East Pakistan data apply for West Pakistan as well, the capital–output ratio was then multiplied by the change in value added by small-scale industry for all years.

Comparison with other estimates

Differences may be because:

Table 3 is limited to investment and classifies government corporations as "public."

Table 3 excludes nonmonetary investment and investment in stocks (working capital) by agriculture and government. It includes all fixed investment, plus industrial working capital and traders' stocks. Other estimates include all working capital and nonmonetary investment.

Table 3 uses "actual" government investment expenditures as shown in budgets; some other estimates use "revised estimates" or "budget estimates."

Table 3 includes in public gross investment the expenditures for the Indus Basin Replacement Works and the Works Programme; the former are often excluded in other estimates because they are considered political rather than development expenses, whereas the latter are sometimes excluded as having a special character.

4. Balance of Payments

Data on the balance of payments are among the most reliable, in Pakistan as elsewhere. However, comparisons over time are complicated by sharp changes in international prices and devaluation in 1955. In addition the breakdown of imports involves some arbitrary assumptions.

TABLE 4A. BALANCE OF PAYMENTS (CURRENT PRICES, CRORES OF RUPEES).

Category	1949–50	1951–52	1954–55	1959–60	1964–65
A. Exports of goods and services					
1. Raw materials	87	212	114	125	160
2. Manufactures	–	2	4	53	80
3. Invisibles	8	23	14	34	62
Total	95	237	132	210	302
B. Imports of goods and services					
4. Consumer goods (CO)	45	98	22	41	60
5. Raw materials for consumer goods (RCO)	18	44	13	25	61
6. U.S. surplus commodities — PL 480 (mostly food)	–	–	–	38	81
7. Defense	12	19	16	20	20
8. Capital goods (CA)	17	45	47	94	222
9. Raw materials for capital goods (RCA)	11	24	11	43	55
10. Invisibles	27	51	32	53	118
Total	130	281	141	314	617
C. Financing items					
11. Grants and loans	–	–	17	115	314
12. Private investment	–	2	2	9	8
13. Loan repayments	–	–	–1	–4	–14
14. Changes in reserve (– is increase)	70	47	–7	–13	28
15. Short term changes, errors and omissions	–35	–7	–2	–3	–21
Total	35	44	9	104	315
16. Technical assistance	–	1	2	5	10

TABLE 4B. BALANCE OF PAYMENTS
(CURRENT PRICES, MILLIONS OF U.S. DOLLARS).

Category	1949– 50	1951– 52	1954– 55	1959– 60	1964– 65
A. Exports of goods and services					
1. Raw materials	263	641	345	257	335
2. Manufactures	–	6	12	110	167
3. Invisibles	24	70	42	71	130
Total	287	716	339	439	632
B. Imports of goods and services					
4. Consumer Goods (CO)	136	290	67	84	125
5. Raw materials for consumer goods (RCO)	54	133	339	52	128
6. U.S. surplus commodities — PL 480 (mostly food)	–	–	–	79	169
7. Defense	36	57	48	42	42
8. Capital goods (CA)	51	136	142	199	464
9. Raw materials for capital goods (RCA)	33	73	33	90	115
10. Invisibles	82	154	97	111	247
Total	393	849	426	657	1291
C. Financing items					
11. Grants and loans	–	–	51	241	657
12. Private investment	–	6	6	19	17
13. Loan repayments	–	–	−3	−8	−29
14. Changes in reserves (− is increase)	212	142	−21	27	59
15. Short term changes, errors and omissions	−106	−15	−6	−6	−44
Total	106	133	27	218	659
16. Technical assistance	–	3	6	10	21

Note: Figures do not always add up because of rounding. The following exchange rates were used to convert rupees to United States dollars: for 1949–50, 1951–52 and 1954–55 — one rupee = 30.225 cents; for 1959–60 to 1964–65 — one rupee = 20.9162 cents.

NOTES TO TABLES 4A AND 4B

A. *Exports of goods and services*

Lines 1 and 2. Total exports: 1949–50 to 1954–55 (*166*, p. 2); 1959–60 (*167*, p. 5); 1964–65 (*168*, p. 3).

Allocation of total exports to raw materials or manufactures are as follows: 1949–50 — (*6*, negligible); 1951–52 to 1959–60 — (*27*, p. 163); 1964–65 — (*29d*, pp. 2017–2039).

3. Same sources as (1) and (2) for respective years.

B. *Imports of goods and services* (Data are poor, especially for government accounts.)

Government expenditure, 1949–50 to 1954–55

Expenditure included government payments of all kinds, from the purchase of goods for government use to expenses of embassies. A breakdown is almost a pure guess.

Government expenditures.

Item	1949–50	1951–52	1954–55	Classification
a. Sugar	5	13	2	Consumer goods
b. Coal	6	8	4	Raw material for capital goods
c. Defense	12	19	16	Defense
d. Services	6	6	7	Invisibles
e. Current supplies	2	3	4	Consumer goods
f. Investment	3	11	15	Capital goods
g. Total	34	60	48	

Sources:

g. Total government expenditure: (*166*, p. 195).

a. and b. Sugar, coal: 1951–52 and 1954–55, (*118*). 1949–50 were guessed from figures for 1951–52 and 1954–55.

c. Defense: one fourth of total budgeted defense expenditure. Pure guess.

d. Services: in 1959–60 these were Rs. 9 crores (*170*) and were extrapolated backwards.

e. and f. The residual of g minus (a + b + c + d), allocated largely arbitrarily. Obviously, there may be a large margin of error.

Unfortunately, it is not possible to derive government development imports from its development program because the government bought some investment goods from commercial importers and domestic processors and because, until June 1953, some government imports were recorded under "private."

Classification: Coal is wholly classified as a raw material for capital goods production by the Planning Commission and will be so classified here also, although this seems somewhat doubtful.

Private merchandise imports for 1949–50 to 1954–55

These imports also have to be broken down rather arbitrarily because only broad classifications are available. For 1949–50 almost no detail could be found. The first step, therefore, was to classify 1951–52 and 1954–55 imports, using the Planning Commission's classification system. Explanations follow table.

PRIVATE MERCHANDISE IMPORTS 1949–50 TO 1954–55.

Sector	1951–52				1954–55			
	CO	RCO	RCA	CA	CO	RCO	RCA	CA
1. Food, drink	13.5	–	–	–	3.0	–	–	–
2. Tobacco	–	5.5	–	–	–	0.5	–	–
3. Cotton	–	0.5	–	–	–	–	–	–
4. Nonmetallic minerals	–	–	1.5	–	–	–	1.0	–
5. Oils	3.0	4.5	6.0	–	2.0	4.0	5.5	–
6. Paper-making materials	–	–	–	–	–	0.5	–	–
7. Rubber	–	0.5	–	–	–	0.5	–	–
8. Seeds	–	2.0	–	–	–	0.5	–	–
9. Tallow	–	0.5	–	–	–	–	–	–
10. Wool	–	0.5	–	–	–	1.0	–	–
11. Wood	–	1.0	1.0	–	–	0.5	0.5	–
12. Miscellaneous raw material	–	2.0	1.0	–	–	0.5	–	–
13. Apparel	1.0	–	–	–	0.5	–	–	–
14. Arms	0.5	–	–	–	–	–	–	–
15. Chemicals, drugs	3.5	3.0	–	–	2.5	2.5	–	–
16. Cutlery, implements	3.5	–	–	–	1.5	–	–	–
17. Dyes and colors	–	3.0	–	–	–	2.0	–	–
18. Electric goods	1.0	–	–	2.0	0.5	–	–	1.5
19. Glass and earthenware	0.5	–	–	1.0	–	–	–	0.5
20. Hides	–	0.5	–	–	–	–	–	–
21. Machinery	–	–	–	17.5	–	–	–	32.0
22. Iron and steel	–	–	4.5	12.0	–	–	2.0	5.0
23. Nonferrous metals	–	–	0.5	1.0	–	–	–	1.0
24. Paper	3.0	1.5	–	–	1.5	0.5	–	–
25. Rubber manufactures	–	–	1.5	–	–	–	1.0	–
26. Vehicles	3.5	1.5	1.5	4.5	1.5	–	–	3.0
27. Cotton yarn and manufactures	45.5	19.0	–	–	5.0	2.0	–	–
28. Jute manufactures	2.0	–	–	–	–	–	–	–
29. Silk yarn and manufactures	0.5	–	–	–	–	–	–	–
30. Wool yarn and manufactures	2.5	–	–	–	0.5	–	–	–
31. Other yarns and textiles	3.0	4.0	–	–	1.0	1.5	–	–
32. Miscellaneous	5.0	–	0.5	–	3.0	0.5	–	–
Total	91.5	48.5	18.0	38.0	22.5	17.0	10.0	43.0
Grand total	196.0				92.5			

Source: (27, p. 161).

CO = Consumer goods; RCO = Raw materials for consumer goods; RCA = Raw materials for capital goods; CA = Capital goods.

For items whose classification is not self-explanatory, the following allocations were made, based on 1955 data when more detail was available than in earlier years. (Numbers refer to lines in previous table.)

5. Of Rs. 12.5 crores for oil imports in 1955, the following allocation was plausible:

Oils	CO	RCO	RCA
Kerosene	2.4		
One half motor spirit		3.8	
Vegetable oil		0.2	
Synthetic oil		0.3	
		———	
		4.3	
Other oils (incl. half motor spirit)			5.8

In 1951–52 there were Rs. 13.4 crores of oil imports, and in 1954–55 the total was Rs. 11.5 crores. 1954–55 was allocated to subcategories on the same basis as in 1955, whereas a somewhat higher proportion CO was assumed in 1951–52.

12. No details: Arbitrary.

15. In 1955 total chemicals and drugs were Rs. 5.9 crores, of which drugs and medicines were Rs. 3.3 crores, allocated to CO. The rest is sodium compounds and chemicals n.s., probably for the textile and soap industries. Rs. 2.6 crores were allocated to RCO.

16. In 1955 — Rs. 1.5 crores. Of this, Rs. 0.1 crore was builders' hardware; the remainder was almost all consumers goods.

18. In 1955 — Rs. 2.5 crores. Of this, Rs. 1.7 crores was CA (wires mostly), and Rs. 0.5 crore was CO (wireless parts, bulbs, etc.)

19. In 1955 — Rs. 0.8 crore, of which Rs. 0.4 crore was bottles, earthenware, and tableware (CO).

22. In 1955 — Rs. 10.0 crores, of which Rs. 2.8 crores was ingots, bars and pig iron (RCA). Tinplate was Rs. 1.3 crores, but it and everything else in the group (except Rs. 2.8 crores to RCA above) seems to have been defined as CA by the Planning Commission, although tinplate is probably largely for kerosene tins and seems more logically to belong in RCO.

23. In 1955 about 20 percent were nonworked, nonferrous metals, RCA, rather than CA.

24. In 1955 — Rs. 4.5 crores. Halt of the cars (Rs. 0.8 crore) and all vehicle parts (Rs. 0.8 crore) are classified as CO. Therefore, total CO equalled Rs. 1.6 crores. The remaining Rs. 2.9 crores is CA, which includes all buses, trucks, aircraft and cycles.

For 1951–52, total imports equalled Rs. 9.5 crores. Of this amount, 30 percent or Rs. 3.0 crores, goes directly to CA (see notes to Private Investment, 1949–50 — transportation). An arbitrary allocation of Rs. 1.5 crores to CA was made for railway rolling stock and other public investment in transport equipment. Total CA equals Rs. 4.5 crores. (*106*, p. 143) shows Rs. 1.5 crores of "buses without chassis" that is RCA. The remainder, Rs. 3.5 crores, is allocated to CO.

27. 1955 — Yarn, etc., (RCA) Rs. 1.2 crores; Cloth, etc., (CO) Rs. 2.8 crores.

31. 1955 — Art silk goods, etc., (CO) Rs. 1.4 crores; Yarn, Fents, (RCO) Rs. 2.0 crores.

32. 1955 — Rs. 3.5 crores, of this Rs. 3.0 crores was probably CO, Rs. 0.3 crore was RCO and Rs. 0.2 crore was RCA.

In general, the classification follows that adopted by the Planning Commission (modified ECAFE classification), with the exception of vehicles.

The Central Statistical Office (CSO) provides detailed data on merchandise imports based on customs information. Data from the State Bank is less detailed, but total State Bank figures, based on actual payments, are more accurate. The breakdown given above, which was derived from CSO data, therefore, needs to be reconciled with totals from the State Bank (in crores of rupees).

	1949–50[a]	1951–52	1954–55
State Bank total	75	176	68
CSO totals	n.a.	196	92.5
CSO as percent State Bank	n.a.	111	136
Classification based on CSO data adjusted to State Bank total			
Consumer goods (CO)	37	82	16
Materials for consumer goods (RCO)	18	44	13
Materials for capital goods (RCA)	5	16	7
Capital goods (CA)	15	34	32
Total	75	176	68

[a] Estimate for 1949–50 is based on 1951 proportions, but on assumption that CO was a somewhat larger proportion than in 1951–52.

Summary of imports of goods and services for 1949–50, 1951–52, 1954–55

Goods and Services	1949–50	1951–52	1954–55
CO — private	38	82	16
Sugar	5	13	2
Government current supplies	2	3	4
Consumer goods — total:	45	98	22
Materials for consumer goods — RCO	13	44	13
RCA — private	5	16	7
Coal	6	3	4
Material for capital goods — total:	11	24	11
CA — private	14	34	32
Government investment	3	11	15
Capital goods — total:	17	45	47
Defense	12	19	16
Invisibles — private[a]	21	45	25
government	6	6	7
Invisibles — total:	27	51	32

[a] Items 2–5, 7, and 9 from (*169*, pp. 2, 4, 7).

Imports of goods and services, 1959–60 and 1964–65

Commodity imports have already been classified in Planning Commission documents. However, as noted above, the classification of vehicles in these documents differs from the classification used here. In addition, the Planning Commission total for commodity imports differs from the total imports which could be financed, if available foreign exchange and other uses of foreign exchange were correctly estimated ("commodity imports" is regarded as the residual estimate). The adjustment, to embrace a different classification of vehicles and to conform to total financing, is shown below. The original data are from (*156*, Table II, p. 23) for 1959–60 and (*172*) for 1964–65. Estimates of financing available are from section C below.

Classification of commodity imports, 1959–60 and 1964–65 (crores of rupees).

	Original data		Adjustment for vehicles		Adjustment for financing	
	1959–60	1964–65	1959–60	1964–65	1959–60	1964–65
CO	40.2	59	+1.7	+4	41	60
RCO	25.6	64			25	61
RCA	43.9	57			43	55
CA	98.9	238	−1.7	−4	94	222
Total	208.6	418			203	398

U.S. Surplus commodities. For 1959–60, (5, Table 10.3); for 1964–65; (*172*, p. 3) but increased by Rs. 7 crores to conform to data provided by U.S. AID Mission.

Defense. The guess for 1959–60 is that, as a result of military aid starting in 1955, defense imports came down from 25 to 20 percent of the defense budget — Rs. 20 crores. For 1964–65 it was assumed that increased defense aid compensated for the slight increase in the defense budget.

Invisibles. For 1959–60, (*170*). For 1964–65, this includes all items of transport, insurance, investment income, plus a small amount of "government not included elsewhere," which probably is embassy and conference costs (*171*).

C. *Financing items (and reconciliation of data)*

Sources for lines 11–15 in Tables 4a and b

Lines 11 and 12. 1949–50 to 1954-55 (*169*, pp. 2, 4, 7). 1959–60, line 11 (5, Table 8.1) and (2). 1959–60, line 12 (*156*), figures for 1960–61 and 1961–62 used. 1964–65 (*172*, p. 3).

Line 13. 1959–60 (*170*). 1964–65 (*172*).

Line 14. (*166; 167; 168; 170;* and *172*).

Line 15. 1949–50 to 1954–55 (169) items 13 (iii) to 13 (ix), but excluding changes in reserves. One crore of rupees was added or subtracted, where necessary, to balance accounts and compensate for rounding. 1959–60 (170). 1964–65 (172). Short term changes, errors, and omissions were increased to Rs. 21 crores to conform to State Bank data and correct for computational error in source.

Line 16. 1951–52 and 1954–55 — guess. 1959–60 (5, Table 8.1) and (6) 1964–65 (172).

Reconciliation to 1959–60 payments data

As mentioned earlier, balance of payments data are more reliable but less detailed than trade data. Payments data indicate that Rs. 314 crores were earned (Rs. 210 crores from earnings and Rs. 104 crores from Financing items, see Table 4a and sources above). On the assumption that payment for invisibles, defense, and surplus agriculture imports have been correctly estimated (Rs. 111 crores), an adjustment needs to be made in other commodity imports to bring them in line with estimated total available financing. Whereas financing equals Rs. 203 crores, other commodity imports, classified from commodity data, was Rs. 209 crores, or 103 percent of the financing available. It therefore needs to be reduced accordingly.

Reconciliation to 1964–65 payments data

Earnings plus financing items total Rs. 617 crores (Table 4a). Subtracting invisibles, defense and surplus agricultural imports, Rs. 398 crores remain for other commodity imports. Because (172) showed commodity imports of Rs. 418 crores, each category of such imports has to be reduced proportionately to bring the total to Rs. 398 crores.

Comparison with other estimates — balance of payments

Other estimates for earnings and payments are sometimes based on balance of payments data and sometimes on customs data; for loans and grants they are sometimes based on budgets, sometimes on receipts, and sometimes on donor's data. Tables 4 use a combination of these sources, in an attempt to obtain the most reliable data.

Tables 4 use data from donors to estimate foreign loans and grants. These reflect disbursements by donors at their prices. (U.S. surplus commodities are charged at prices set by the U.S. government, which are usually below U.S. government costs). Other estimates sometimes use arrival data, which may differ in timing and pricing.

Tables 4 include shipping costs and insurance under invisibles. Other estimates sometimes allocate them to particular commodity groups.

Tables 4 show defense as a separate item, guessed on the basis of budgeted defense figures; most other estimates ignore defense. Other estimates, by adjusting commodity data and breakup to balance of payments data, in effect act as though defense imports (not included in commodity import data) have the same composition (in terms of consumer goods, capital goods, etc.) as nondefense commodity imports.

5. Regional Data

All the caveats on unreliability of data need to be re-emphasized, first, because disaggregation naturally increases chances for error in particular items (especially for Survey data); second, because less material is available on regional outputs and arbitrary assumptions are more important; third, because regional growth is a very sensitive political issue.

These data are *not* reliable. By some plausible changes in assumptions, East Pakistan's domestic product can be shown to have grown more *or* less rapidly than West Pakistan's in the 1959–60 to 1964–65 period. Much more work needs to be done on these data, and only very broad and definite trends in the following tables should be taken into account.

The Regional Tables, like Table 1, are "synthetic" in using trend data for major crops and in using marked prices, with a partly arbitrary allocation of indirect taxes and subsidies.

TABLE 5A. REGIONAL GROSS DOMESTIC PRODUCT AT CONSTANT 1959–60 PRICES.

Category	1949–50 East	1949–50 West	1954–55 East	1954–55 West	1959–60 East	1959–60 West	1964–65 East	1964–65 West
	(crores of rupees)							
1. Agriculture								
Major crops	517	300	536	323	601	349	699	448
Minor crops	163	82	164	86	129	89	171	106
Fishing	82	5	92	6	104	7	175	12
Forestry	4	3	5	4	8	3	14	6
Livestock	77	199	83	224	89	253	95	285
Total	843	589	880	643	931	701	1,154	857
2. Indirect taxes on agriculture	7	0	8	7	10	3	4	1
3. Subsidies to agriculture	0	0	−1	−1	−3	−3	−7	−9
4. Agriculture (market prices)	850	589	887	649	938	701	1,151	849
5. Manufacturing (market prices)	12	18	31	79	50	142	80	302
6. Other (factor cost)	425	525	488	639	548	768	722	1,097
7. Indirect taxes on Other	26	51	26	64	19	69	56	135
8. Subsidies to Other	0	0	0	0	0	−1	−10	−4
9. Other (market prices)	451	576	514	703	567	836	768	1,228
10. Gross domestic product at market prices	1,313	1,183	1,432	1,431	1,555	1,679	1,999	2,379
	(millions)							
11. Population	43.1	35.8	48.1	40.2	53.9	45.0	61.2	51.3
	(rupees)							
12. Per capita GDP	305	330	298	356	288	373	327	464

TABLE 5B. REGIONAL PER CAPITA GDP IN 1959–60
MARKET PRICES (IN RUPEES).

	1949–50		1954–55		1959–60		1964–65	
Category	East	West	East	West	East	West	East	West
4. Agriculture	197	165	184	161	174	156	188	165
5. Manufacturing	3	5	6	20	9	32	13	59
9. Other	104	161	106	173	105	185	124	240
Total	304	330	297	354	288	372	326	464

NOTES TO TABLES 5A AND 5B

1. *Agriculture*

Major crops: Linear trends were calculated for each major crop, and appropriate trend values were used. (See Table 6 for the gross value of major crops). From this, value added was calculated on the basis of data on agricultural inputs (*43*, p. 53; *44*, p. 41). For 1964–65 the value added/gross value added ratio in agriculture was 91.5. Information in (*43*) and (*44*) concerning trends in various inputs over time (in the number of tubewells and quantities of fertilizer used) was used to calculate the value added/gross value added ratios for the three earlier years. These ratios are:

	1949–50	1954–55	1959–60	1964–65
East	0.940	0.914	0.939	0.936
West	0.914	0.914	0.906	0.885

Minor crops: 1949–50 — 1959–60 came from worksheets of (*28*), 1964–65 total from (*29i*, p. 2057); allocation on the basis of 1963–64 breakup is from worksheets of (*110*).

Fishing and Forestry: 1959–60 is from worksheets of (*110*). 1949–50, 1959–60, and 1964–65 totals are from (*29i*, p. 2057). For 1949–50 and 1954–55, they are regionally allocated on basis of 1959–60 shares and 1964–65 is on the basis of 1963–64 shares in worksheets of (*110*).

Livestock: This was calculated from (*45; 46*).

2. *Indirect Taxes on Agriculture*. See line Ib of Table 5c (below). Current prices were converted to constant prices using index of line VII in Table 5c.

3. *Subsidies to Agriculture*. See Lines IIb and IIc of Table 5c. Conversion to constant prices as above.

5. *Manufacturing*. 1949–50, 1954–55 is from (*141*, p. 481). 1959–60 was estimated by comparing the share of East Pakistan implied in (*55*, p. 2) with all-Pakistan totals (*155*, p. 2). This division is consistent with (*110*). This share was then applied to total value added (*141*, p. 467). The data for 1964–65 are rough estimates, based on previous years.

6. *Other*. For 1949–50 through 1959–60, the shares of value added in Other for each province were taken from (*110*). The exception is Banking and insurance which was divided, in (*110*), one half to West and one half to East. In Table 5a West has been allocated 75 percent and East 25 percent (see *161*).

7. *Indirect Taxes on Other*. These are derived from Lines Ia, Ie, If, Ig and Ih of Table 5c; plus line Ic and line Id, sales and excise taxes not paid by Large-scale manufacturing, minus line V (converted according to the price index).

8. *Subsidies to Other*. These come from lines IIa, IId and IIe in Table 5c (converted by the price index).

11. *Population*. Except for 1954–55, this was obtained by dividing aggregate GNP by per capita GNP (*155*, p. 11). The share of provincial population in total population for 1949–50 and 1959–60 are very close together (less than 0.2 percent difference). An average of these shares was taken to obtain the total population figures for 1954–55.

Comparison with other estimates

Like Table 1, Tables 5 use crop trends rather than crop actuals; livestock data from (*45; 46*), not national accounts; industry data from (*141*), not national accounts; market prices rather than factor costs.

In addition: Tables 5 allocate all of the domestic product to a province; other estimates sometimes leave part unallocated. Because crops in East Pakistan were particularly poor in 1958–59 and shot up sharply in 1963–64, estimates using these two years will show a very high growth rate for East Pakistan.

TABLE 5C. INDIRECT TAXES AND SUBSIDIES BY REGION (CURRENT PRICES, CRORES OF RUPEES).

Category	1949–50			1954–55			1959–60			1964–65		
	East	West	Total	East	West	Total	East	West	Total	East	West	Total
I. Indirect Taxes												
a. Import duties	11.5	26.7	38.2	10.6	26.1	36.7	10.1	39.2	49.3	36.1	73.4	109.5
b. Export duties	7.0	0	7.0	7.0	5.5	12.5	10.0	2.5	12.5	4.5	0.5	5.0
c. Sales taxes	5.3	7.8	13.1	4.2	14.8	19.0	7.3	24.2	31.5	19.2	55.3	74.5
i: on imports	2.4	5.7	8.1	3.2	8.5	12.0	5.5	15.2	20.7	16.0	43.9	59.9
ii: on domestic product	2.9	2.1	5.0	1.0	6.3	7.0	1.8	9.0	10.8	3.2	11.4	14.6
d. Excise duties	2.2	3.0	5.2	2.9	14.1	17.0	8.4	24.8	33.2	18.2	65.8	84.0
e. Cement surcharge	–	–	–	–	–	–	–	–	–	–	1.3	1.3
f. Petroleum products surcharge	–	–	–	–	–	–	0.2	0.7	0.9	1.3	7.9	9.2
g. Miscellaneous central indirect taxes	1.0	3.0	4.0	2.0	4.7	6.7	–	–	–	1.3	2.8	4.1
h. Provincial indirect taxes	6.6	7.7	14.3	6.3	6.6	12.9	0.9	2.2	3.1	1.5	4.5	6.0
II. Subsidies												
a. Wheat	–	–	–	–	–	–	–	–	–	9.4	3.0	12.4
b. Fertilizer	–	–	–	1.0	1.0	2.0	1.8	2.2	4.0	4.2	7.4	11.6
c. Plant protection	–	–	–	–	–	–	0.8	0.8	1.6	2.6	2.6	5.2
d. Pakistan International Airlines	–	–	–	–	–	–	0.4	0.5	0.9	1.1	0.9	2.0
e. Cement subsidy	–	–	–	–	–	–	–	–	–	1.3	–	1.3
III. Total Indirect Taxes	33.6	48.2	81.8	33.0	71.8	104.8	36.9	93.6	130.5	82.1	211.5	293.6
IV. Total Subsidies	–	–	–	1.0	1.0	2.0	3.0	3.5	6.5	18.6	13.9	32.5
V. Indirect taxes on large-scale manufacturing	1.0	1.5	2.5	3.5	9.0	12.5	8.0	22.5	30.5	18.0	67.0	85.0
VI. Total indirect taxes net of taxes paid by large-scale manufacturing	32.6	46.7	79.3	29.5	62.8	92.3	28.9	71.1	100.0	64.1	144.5	208.6
VII. Price index	0.99	0.91	0.93	0.88	0.90	0.89	1.00	1.00	1.00	1.07	1.07	1.07

NOTES TO TABLE 5C

Sources:

1949–50

Ia. Total from (*67*, pp. 10–11, 44–45, 48–49). Provincial share based on imports (*29c*)

Ib. (*68*, pp. 38, 168)

Ic. Total from (*67*, pp. 10–11, 44–45, 48–49). Regional breakup from (*154*), assuming 1949–50 is equal to 1950–51 and 1951–52. Division between imports and domestic goods is on basis of (*146*), for 1959–60.

Id. Total from (*67*, pp. 10–11, 44–45, 48–49), regional breakup from (*148*) assuming 1949–50 is equal to 1950–51, 1951–52.

Ig. Arbitrary allocations based on (*67*, p. 18).

Ih. Allocated from (*67*, pp. 44–45, 48–49).

1954–55

Ia, Ic, Id. Totals from (*115*), Appendix. Provincial breakup for Ic and Id from (*154*), Ia breakup based on share of imports (*29c*). For Ic breakup between imports and domestic goods see 1949–50 above.

Ib. (*115*) breakup on basis of crops: for example, jute — East Pakistan; cotton — West Pakistan.

Ig, Ih. (*67*, pp. 44–45, 48–49). (Breakup of Ig between provinces is arbitrary.)

IIb. (*43; 44*).

1959–60 and 1964–65

Ia, Ic to Ih, IIa to IIe. (*148*)

Ib. 1959–60 (*115*, p. 526); 1964–65 (*71*, p. 28)

V. Line 9 of Table 5d

VII. (*141*, p. 486). It was arbitrarily assumed that the index for 1949–50 equals the index for 1951–52. The index has been extended to 1964–65 using the wholesale price index from (*29f*, pp. 486–7).

TABLE 5D. CALCULATION OF SALES AND EXCISE TAXES PAID BY LARGE-SCALE MANUFACTURING.

Item	1949–50	1954–55	1959–60	1964–65
	(crores of rupees)			
1. Value-added in small-scale manufacturing (factor cost)	106	108	137	166
2. Value added in large-scale manufacturing (market prices)	28	98	192	409
	(percent)			
3. Share of large-scale in total manufacturing	0.21	0.48	0.58	0.71
	(crores of rupees)			
4. Total excise duties	5.2	17	33.2	84.0
5. Total excise duties paid by large-scale manufacturing	1.1	8.2	19.3	59.6
6. Sales taxes collected on domestic production	6.0	9.3	19.5	35.5
7. Sales taxes paid by large-scale manufacturing	1.3	4.5	11.3	25.2
8. Total sales and excise taxes paid by large-scale manufacturing	2.4	12.7	30.6	84.8

Item	E	W	E	W	E	W	E	W
9. Regional breakdown of large-scale taxes (E: East, W: West)	1	1.5	3.5	9.0	8	22.5	18.0	67.0

Sources:

1. (*29*, pp. 2052–3).
2. Line 2, Table 5a but at current prices; see (*141*).
3. 2 ÷ (1 + 2).
4. 1949–50 (*67*, pp. 10–11, 44–45, 48–49).
    1954–55 and 1959–60 (*115*).
5. 3 × 4.
6. 1949–50 (*67*, pp. 10–11, 44–45, 48–49). 1954–55 and 1959–60 (*115*). 1964–65 — Total sales tax from (*146*), breakdown between imports and domestic product according to 1962–63 ratios of (*115*).
7. 3 × 6.
8. 5 + 7.
9. Breakdown on basis of shares in line 5 of Table 5a.

Note: The rate of excise duty and sales tax is likely to be higher for large- than for small-scale manufacturing because the latter benefits from a number of exemptions. This difference has been incorporated in the above table by implication because large-scale is taken at market prices and small-scale at factor costs. The data are consistent with those generated by the Survey, which shows Rs. 30 crores as the excise and sales tax collected from large-scale manufacturing in 1958.

6. Crop Production

To eliminate the random effects of weather, trends were calculated for each major crop and the trend values used to derive "synthetic" production and value figures.

TABLE 6A. TREND VALUES OF CROP PRODUCTION IN WEST PAKISTAN

Crop	1949–50		1954–55		1959–60		1964–65	
	Production[a]	Value[b]	Production[a]	Value[b]	Production[a]	Value[b]	Production[a]	Value[b]
Wheat	3,497	143.4	3,364	137.9	3,654	149.8	4,403	180.5
Rice	764	41.6	833	45.4	920.3	50	1,355.0	73.8
Other foodgrains	1,215	42.5	1,215	42.5	1,152	40.3	1,245	43.6
Gram	569	22.2	604	23.5	624	24.3	624	24.3
Rape, mustard, and sesamum	171	11.5	200	13.4	241	16.1	241	16.1
Cotton	1,245	29.4	1,595	37.6	1,605	37.9	2,293	54.1
Tobacco	54	5.6	102	10.5	128	13.2	179	18.4
Sugar cane	6,366	31.8	8,476	42.4	10,700	53.5	18,800	94.0
Total		328.0		353.2		385.1		504.8

[a] Production in thousands of tons except for tobacco, which is in millions of pounds, and cotton, which is in thousands of bales.

[b] Value in crores of rupees, constant 1959–60 prices.

TABLE 6B. TREND VALUES OF CROP PRODUCTION IN EAST PAKISTAN.

Crop	1949–50		1954–55		1959–60		1964–65	
	Production[a]	Value[b]	Production[a]	Value[b]	Production[a]	Value[b]	Production[a]	Value[b]
Rice	7,270	428.9	7,501	442.5	8,690	512.7	10,310	608.3
Other foodgrains	39	1.6	39	1.6	66	2.3	66	2.3
Gram	48.7	2.2	48.7	2.2	34	1.6	34	1.6
Sugar cane	3,365	15.1	3,745	16.9	3,560	16.0	6,052	27.2
Rape, mustard, and sesamum	119	10.6	119	10.6	123	11.0	123	11.0
Jute	5,434	70.6	5,527	71.9	5,750	74.8	5,750	74.8
Tea	38.4	11.5	49.4	14.8	53	15.9	53	15.9
Tobacco	99.2	9.6	99.2	9.6	56	5.4	56	5.4
Total		550.1		570.1		639.7		746.5

[a] Production in thousands of tons, except tea and tobacco which are in thousands of pounds.
[b] Value in crores of rupees, constant 1959–60 prices.

NOTES TO TABLES 6A AND B

Production data for all years is reproduced in Tables 6c and 6d, and constant price data is in Table 6e.

The data for each crop were broken into two sub-periods — 1947–48 to 1957–58, and 1959–60 to 1964–65 — on the assumption that new policies introduced in 1958–59 by the new government would begin to have an effect in 1959–60. Straight lines were then fitted to the data for each sub-period. Where there was no trend, a simple average over the sub-period was computed. This averaging was appropriate in the first period for: East — Other foodgrains, Gram, Rape, and Mustard; West — Other foodgrains; and in the second period for: East — Other foodgrains, Gram, Rape, Mustard, Jute, Tea, Tobacco; West — Gram, Rape, and Mustard.

Trend values for rice in East Pakistan for the period 1959–60 to 1964–65 were taken from (42; pp. 40 and 44). Trend values are therefore values read off the fitted lines, or averages as the case may warrant, and the production figures appearing in the table correspond to the trend values for the appropriate years. Prices for each of the crops are from Table 6c. Prices are per ton unless otherwise specified. Cotton prices have been recalculated per thousand bales.

TABLE 6C. PRODUCTION OF MAJOR CROPS IN WEST PAKISTAN.

Crop	1947–48	1948–49	1949–50	1950–51	1951–52	1952–53	1953–54	1954–55	1955–56	1956–57	1957–58	1958–59	1959–60	1960–61	1961–62	1962–63	1963–64	1964–65
	(in thousand tons)																	
Rice (cleaned)	682	735	792	852	719	819	906	826	828	832	862	976	979	1,014	1,109	1,078	1,173	1,361
Wheat	3,301	3,974	3,862	3,930	2,961	2,367	3,587	3,136	3,377	3,581	3,508	3,845	3,847	3,754	3,963	4,104	4,084	4,378
Bajra	296	394	370	386	265	267	461	348	340	363	274	309	324	301	364	416	356	439
Jowar	202	242	237	244	205	220	288	220	249	255	183	212	229	217	244	247	234	288
Maize	353	373	401	381	377	346	402	426	450	462	440	481	478	432	480	481	518	520
Barley	111	175	146	129	99	92	127	105	126	114	157	158	137	118	114	122	109	116.3
Gram	465	754	599	744	422	316	561	593	688	681	653	568	598	600	613	671	600	661
Sugar cane	5,712	6,818	7,711	5,482	5,355	7,220	8,909	8,758	8,070	8,806	11,116	12,292	10,494	11,457	14,130	18,148	15,886	18,373
Rape and Mustard	172	185	142	196	197	125	163	216	220	222	229	268	235	211	202	253	208	212
Sesamum	8	5	6	8	7	6	6	6	6	6	6	6	8	7	11	8	8	8
	(in thousand bales)																	
Cotton	1,106	964	1,239	1,406	1,397	1,784	1,425	1,583	1,678	1,711	1,708	1,587	1,639	1,692	1,823	2,060	2,354	2,124
	(in million lbs.)																	
Tobacco	31.3	39.7	55.6	66.3	78.3	57.4	84.0	162.6	107.6	102.8	124.8	128.4	137.2	132.4	153.0	160.0	166.0	182.0

Source: (153).

TABLE 6D. PRODUCTION OF MAJOR CROPS IN EAST PAKISTAN.

Crop	1947–48	1948–49	1949–50	1950–51	1951–52	1952–53	1953–54	1954–55	1955–56	1956–57	1957–58	1958–59	1959–60	1960–61	1961–62	1962–63	1963–64	1964–65
									(in thousand tons)									
Rice (cleaned)	6,736	7,673	7,377	7,343	7,084	7,335	8,245	7,589	6,384	8,185	7,598	6,921	8,482	9,519	9,466	8,730	10,456	10,442
Wheat	20	19	23	20	23	24	24	26	22	23	23	22	29	33	39	44	34	29
Bajra	–	–	–	–	–	–	–	–	–	–	–	–	–	–	–	–	–	–
Jowar	–	–	–	–	–	–	–	–	–	–	–	–	–	–	–	1	–	–
Maize	2	2	3	3	2	3	3	2	3	2	2	1	2	7	7	5	4	3
Barley	15	16	17	15	16	16	16	17	17	16	12	14	12	17	18	21	13	–
Gram	51	50	52	47	52	53	54	63	44	35	35	38	29	36	37	34	33	34
Sugar cane	3,270	3,411	3,097	3,335	3,425	3,675	3,967	3,696	3,975	3,911	3,765	3,834	3,611	3,955	4,418	4,749	5,362	6,231
Rape and mustard	78	83	86	89	100	103	100	105	104	93	67	105	83	97	103	104	89	95
Sesamum	28	24	21	27	28	30	30	30	31	27	21	28	26	24	26	25	26	25
									(in thousand bales)									
Jute	6,842	5,479	3,333	6,007	6,331	6,823	3,610	4,662	5,592	5,514	6,200	6,000	5,554	5,626	6,969	6,300	6,000	5,441
Cotton	14	18	16	18	18	17	17	17	15	14	14	18	18	19	17	16	16	15
									(in million lbs.)									
Tea	28.1	34.2	38.9	37.9	47.1	51.3	52.0	54.0	52.6	54.7	44.5	53.5	57.0	42.0	58.8	52.0	55.0	63
Tobacco	99.9	101.8	98.1	96.1	100.6	109.7	110.4	118.3	89.8	89.4	77.5	93.2	60.9	56.2	70.0	64.0	62.0	63.0

Source: (*153*).

TABLE 6E. PRICES OF MAJOR CROPS IN 1959–60.

Crop	West	East
Wheat	410	–
Rice	545	590
Other foodgrains	350	350
Gram	390	460
Rape	670	900
Cotton	236	–
Tobacco	1.03 per lb.	0.97 per lb.
Sugar cane	50	45
Jute	–	130
Tea	–	3 per lb.

Source: (*42*, pp. 26 and 32).

Comparison with other estimates

Tables 6 are estimates of value of output; some other estimates are of value added. Trends for individual crops were calculated in Table 6 and then summed; the sum of the trends may differ from the trend of sums estimated elsewhere.

7. Government Accounts

TABLE 7. CENTRAL AND PROVINCIAL GOVERNMENT
ACCOUNTS (CURRENT PRICES, CRORES OF RUPEES).

Category	1949–50	1954–55	1959–60	1964–65
A. Revenues				
1. Customs duties	46	46	56	108
2. Excise and sales taxes	22	36	68	152
3. Income and profits taxes	12	23	36	63
4. Agricultural taxes	16	18	33	35
5. Other taxes	6	11	17	46
Total taxes	102	134	210	404
6. Other revenues — Center	16	24	46	49
7. Other revenues — Provinces	9	19	25	52
Total other revenues	25	43	71	101
Total revenues	127	177	281	505
B. Expenditures — current				
8. Administration	61	97	150	289
9. Defense	77	75	112	134
10. Debt service	4	13	25	43
11. State trading (see note)	–	–	–	–
Total budgeted	142	185	287	466
12. Accretions to reserve funds	−3	−12	−14	2
Net current expenditures	139	173	273	468
13. Gross public saving (A minus B)	−12	+4	+8	+37
C. Public investment — gross				
14. Budgeted investment	26	60	156	285
15. Works Programme	–	–	–	32
16. Indus Basin Works	–	–	–	91
Total	26	60	156	408
D. Estimated financing				
17. Required (C minus 13)	38	56	148	371
18. Foreign loans and grants	–	4	81	248
19. Borrowing from public	3	7	13	21
20. Sales of assets and recoveries of loans	4	11	14	53
21. Estimated borrowing from banks or drawing on cash balances (residual)	31	34	40	49

NOTES TO TABLE 7

Note: C = Central Government; E = East Pakistan; W = West Pakistan.
Lines 1 to 3. C (*67*, pp. 10, 11) plus E (*67*, pp. 44–45) plus W (*67*, pp. 48–49).

4. Same as 1–3 above. It is the sum of Land revenue, plus Irrigation, Navigation, etc., plus Agricultural income taxes. The latter is shown under Taxes on income other than corporation tax in (*67*) and was estimated from (*88*, p. 2); (*60*, p. 1). There is no entry for C. Note that Irrigation is net of direct expenditures.

5. Same as 1–3 above. Residual under *Principal Heads of Revenue* in accounts after subtracting items 1–4 above.

6. Same as 1–3 above. Interest is net of receipts from the Provinces (transfer item), estimated from (*79*, p. 11) for 1964–65 and from (*145*) for earlier years.

Central government — other revenues:

Source	1949–50	1954–55	1959–60	1964–65
Railways	2	6	13	–
P T & T	–	1	3	6
Civil administration	1	2	4	14
Currency and mint	1	2	4	6
Defense	5	4	10	10
Other heads	0.5	1	1	1
Interest (excludes provinces)	5	5	7	3
Miscellaneous	1	2	4	8
Extraordinary (except aid)	0.5	1	–	–
	16	24	46	48

7. (*67*, pp. 44–45, 48–49). Total Other heads of revenue less: Irrigation — accounted for in line 4. Grants in aid from Center — transfer item. Extraordinary receipts — these are principally sales of land and represent dissaving rather than revenue.

8. (*67*, pp. 10–11, 46–47, 50–51).

	1949–50			1954–55			1959–60			1964–65		
	Center	East	West	Center	East	West	Center	East	West	Center	East	West
Administration	17	18	28	37	25	39	55	36	63	77	76	132
Debt service	3	–	2	9	3	4	21	2	2	40	23	21

Administration is the same as total Expenditure met from revenue in government accounts less: Debt services — separate item. Defense services — separate item. Civil works and Central Road Fund. This is a payment to a reserve fund and not a current expenditure. Subsidies on imported wheat — a transfer item. This presumably represents the difference between U.S. and world prices. For 1964–65 this item is Rs. 12 crores; see (70, p. 83). Contributions and miscellaneous adjustments between the Central and Provincial Governments — a transfer item. Constabulary in Frontier regions — a defense item.

9. For 1964–65 and 1959–60, see (68, pp. 10, 11, 16, 17) Defense Services. To this must be added expenses for Constabulary found in the budget allocation for Frontier regions (76, p. 120; 77, p. 85). For 1954–55 and 1949–50, see (32, p. 13), Defense expenditure. For Constabulary in 1954–55, see (71, p. 179). For 1949–50 Constabulary is just a guess at Rs. 2 crores.

10. Debt service is from line 8, minus interest paid by Provinces to Center (a transfer item, also excluded from line 6 above).

	1949–50	1954–55	1959–60	1964–65
Debt service	5	16	25	84
Interest to Center	−1	−3	–	−39
Net debt service	4	13	25	45

11. This item is not treated as a current expense for any one year because it reflects mainly changes in stocks.

12. These accretions seem to be amounts charged to Revenue expenditures but transferred to various reserve funds (for example, to the Civil works and Central Road Fund), mostly for investment (for example, roads and petroleum exploration). To the extent that this is the case, they are not current expenditures and are therefore subtracted from total current expenditures. However, where there are Direct expenditures from reserve funds (66) under Non-development expenditure, these sums should be subtracted to get net accretions. The net accretions, if positive, are entered as negative items which correctly raises Public savings by the amount of the net accretions. This process is correct only if these reserve funds are indeed spent on public investment items. A breakdown of the ultimate use of the reserve funds does not seem to be available.

13. Public savings is here defined as total revenues minus net current expenditures, for central and provincial governments only. Note that a substantial part of revenues came from depreciation funds, and that much of the investment in railways, etc., compensates for depreciation, so net public savings would be much smaller or negative.

14. From Table 3. This includes direct expenditures and loans and advances of the Center, East, and West governments. Note that loans and advances going to private enterprise are included, whereas in Table

3 they were treated as private enterprise investment. Excluded is the part of the Indus Basin Replacement Works, which is financed through the Budget (72, p. 544). This amount, Rs. 25.3 crores for 1964–65, is included in line 16.

 15. See Table 3, Notes for 1964–65.

 16. Private communication to the author.

 17. Public investment minus public savings.

 18. From (67, pp. 14–15) item Total external resources (includes Foreign grants transferred to reserve account) for all years except 1964–65, which is:

a. Total external resources	Rs. 175 crores	(67, p. 15)
b. Foreign loans to semi-independent bodies	10	(67, p. 8)
c. Indus Basin Works	63	
Total foreign loans and grants	Rs. 248 crores	

 c. is total expenditure on Indus Basin (Rs. 91 crores — see line 16 above) minus Expenditure against foreign loans (Rs. 26 crores) which are already included in capital budget (72, p. 544) and minus Rs. 2 crores of nonreimbursable expenditures (private communication).

Total Foreign loans and grants in the above will differ from the similar heading in Table 4, primarily because of different recording methods. For example, the budget figure includes expenditure from counterpart funds, whereas Table 4 would record the funds when they originally accrued.

 19. Borrowing from the public is composed of unfunded debt and, for 1964–65, the net receipts of Prize Bonds. (67, pp. 14–15, 52–53, 56–57).

	1949–50			1954–55			1959–60			1964–65		
	Center	East	West	Center	East	West	Center	East	West	Center	East	West
Unfunded:	2.8	–	–	6.6	0.3	0.3	11.4	0.4	1.1	17.8	1.1	2.5

 20. This covers, for the central government, Recoveries of loans and advances — semi-independent bodies and other debtors (67, p. 15) plus Other capital receipts, and for both Provincial Governments Recoveries of loans and advances — municipalities, etc., and government servants (67, p. 53 (E), p. 57 (W). For West Pakistan it also covers Extraordinary receipts (67, p. 49).

Part or all of the last item represents sales of assets (land). This is clearly the case for the Extraordinary receipts of the West Pakistan Government. Other capital receipts of the Central government includes primarily sales of PIDC assets, and perhaps some land in Karachi.

		1949–50	1954–55	1959–60	1964–65
Recoveries	Center	1.3	1.0	4.7	7.6
	East	0.3	1.8	0.7	3.7
	West	0.6	0.8	1.6	5.9
	Subtotal	2.2	3.6	7.0	17.2
Other capital	Center	0.3	3.3	0.4	4.3
Extraordinary	West	1.7	4.3	6.4	31.2
	Subtotal	2.0	7.6	6.8	35.5
	Total	4.2	11.2	13.8	52.7

Recoveries of loans and advances need not be deducted from public investment since they simply reflect repayment of previous loans. The correct procedure is to treat them as a financing item for new investment.

Because sales of factories, etc. by the government should be called public disinvestment (and private investment), they should in principle be subtracted from government investment. But given that such private purchases are not included in private investment (see introductory notes to Private Investment, Appendix Table 3), the deduction is not made.

21. Residual item. Not equal to Permanent and floating debt plus Cash balance utilization shown in budgets, because (a) actual annual figures for state trading were not taken; (b) transfers to State Bank, offset by borrowings from State Bank were not included; (c) foreign loans were not included here but in a separate item; (d) transfers between central and provincial governments were excluded; (e) deposits and remittances were left out. Deposits and remittances do not quite net out over the years since there are somewhat greater accruals than withdrawals. However, in any one year they can be a plus or minus item and they are therefore difficult to show on a selected year basis. The small net accrual under this head may just balance the small net losses on State Trading in earlier years.

Comparison with other estimates

In Table 7 public savings were defined as the difference between government revenues and current expenditures; other estimates sometimes define public savings as equal to domestic financing of the government development (or investment) program. Under the latter definition, public saving includes funds borrowed from the public and the banking system (and may even include funds derived from the sale of U.S. surplus commodities), and is therefore much larger than under the definition used in Table 7.

Public investment includes the Works Programme and Indus Basin Works in Table 7, since both are clearly gross investment. Some other estimates exclude one or both of these expenditures.

Development expenditures that are not investment (e.g., operating expenses of some new development projects) are shown as current expenditures on Administration. Some estimates show them as Development.

Table 7 excludes intergovernmental transactions and state trading transactions. Some estimates include both.

Table 7 does not cover governments other than the Central and Provincial governments; it does, however, include loans by these governments to government corporations (PIA, PIDC, Port Trusts, Improvement Trusts). Some estimates include local bodies, others exclude some or all government corporations.

BIBLIOGRAPHY

BIBLIOGRAPHY

Abdul Aziz Anwar see Anwar, Abdul Aziz

1 Adamjee, Ashraf, "The Jute Industry in Pakistan," unpub. honors thesis (Cambridge, Mass.: Harvard College, 1964).

2 Adelman, Morris A., "Monopoly and Concentration: Comparisons in Time and Space," *Rivista Internazionale di Scienze Economiche e Commerciali*, Vol. XII, No. 8 (August 1965), pp. 725–748.

3 Agency for International Development, "Long-Range Assistance Strategy," mimeo (Karachi, Pakistan: U.S. Government, 1963).

4 Agency for International Development, "The Present State of Pakistan Agriculture," mimeo (Karachi, 1963?).

5 Agency for International Development, "Statistical Fact Book, Selected Economic and Social Data on Pakistan," mimeo (Karachi: USAID Planning Advisory Staff, May 1965).

6 Agency for International Development, "Supporting Documentation, V, Statistical Appendix," mimeo (Karachi: USAID, August 10, 1964).

7 Ahmed, Muneer, *The Civil Servant in Pakistan* (Oxford: Oxford University Press, 1964).

8 Ahmed, Mushtaq, *Government and Politics in Pakistan*, 2nd ed. (Karachi: Pakistan Publishing House, 1963).

9 Akhter, Farkunda, "Characteristics of the Members of the Comilla Cooperatives," *Survey and Research Bulletin*, No. 10 (Comilla: Pakistan Academy for Rural Development, November 1964).

10 Andrus, J. R. and A. F. Mohammed, *The Economy of Pakistan* (Stanford: Stanford University, 1958).

Anisur Rahman see Rahman, Anisur

11 Anisuzzaman, Mohammad, *The Circle Officer, A Study of his Role* (Dacca: National Institute of Public Administration, No. 2, 1963).

12 Anwar, Abdul Aziz, *A Socio-Economic Survey of Industrial*

   Labor in Selected Centers (Lahore: Board of Economic
   Inquiry, Punjab, 1959).

13 Ayub, M. CSP, *Public Industrial Enterprises in Pakistan*
   (Karachi: PIDC, 1960).
   Azizur Rahman Khan see Khan, Azizur Rahman

14 Basic Democracies and Local Government Department, *Performance Report on Rural Works Programme 1964/65*
   (Dacca: Government of East Pakistan, January 1966).

15 Bruton, H. J., and Swadesh R. Bose, *The Pakistan Export Bonus Scheme*, Economics of Development, Monograph
   II (Karachi: Institute of Development Economics, April
   1963).

16 Central Statistical Office, *Bulletins* (Karachi: Government of
   Pakistan, May 1964 and March 1966).

17 Central Statistical Office, *Census of Manufacturing Industries,*
   1957 (Karachi: Government of Pakistan, 1960).

18 Central Statistical Office, *Census of Manufacturing Industries,*
   1959/60 (Karachi: Government of Pakistan, 1962).

19 Central Statistical Office, *Census of Manufacturing Industries,*
   1959/60 *Bulletin* (Karachi: Government of Pakistan,
   1965).

20 Central Statistical Office, *Foreign Trade Statistics of Pakistan,*
   July–Sept. 1959 (Karachi: Government of Pakistan, 1960).

21 Central Statistical Office, *Foreign Trade Statistics of Pakistan,*
   October–December 1959 (Karachi: Government of Pakistan, 1960).

22 Central Statistical Office, *Foreign Trade Statistics of Pakistan,*
   January–June 1960 (Karachi: Government of Pakistan,
   1961).

23 Central Statistical Office, *National Family Expenditure Survey, 1955–56: Urban Centers* (Karachi: Government of
   Pakistan, undated).

24 Central Statistical Office, *National Sample Survey, Second
   Round* (Karachi: Government of Pakistan, 1960).

25 Central Statistical Office, *National Sample Survey, Third
   Round,* 1961 (Karachi: Government of Pakistan, 1963).

26 Central Statistical Office, *Pakistan Statistical Yearbook, 1957*
   (Karachi: Manager of Publication, 1959).

27 Central Statistical Office, *Pakistan Statistical Yearbook, 1963*
   (Karachi: Manager of Publication, 1964).

28 Central Statistical Office, *Revised CSO Index of Industrial*

Production, 1964–65, mimeo (Karachi: Government of Pakistan, no date).

29 Central Statistical Office, *Statistical Bulletins* ᵃ(September 1960; ᵇApril 1965; ᶜJune 1965; ᵈAugust 1965; ᵉOctober 1965; ᶠMarch 1966; ᵍMay 1966; ʰSeptember 1966; ⁱDecember 1966).

30 Central Statistical Office, *Wholesale Price Study for Pakistan* (Karachi: Government of Pakistan, 1963).

31 Chaudhuri, M. A., *The Civil Service in Pakistan* (Lahore: National Institute of Public Administration, No. 1, 1963).

32 Clark, Ralph, "The Economic Determinants of Jute Production," *FAO Monthly Bulletin of Agricultural Economics and Statistics,* Vol. VI, No. 9 (September 1955).

33 Department of Interior, Panel on Waterlogging and Salinity in West Pakistan, *Report on Land and Water Development in the Indus Plain* (Washington: U.S. Government Printing Office, 1964). Referred to as the Revelle Report.

34 Department of Investment Promotion and Supplies, *Review of the Progress of Implementation of the Revised Investment Schedule* (Karachi: Government of Pakistan, July 1964).

35 Department of Investment Promotion and Supplies, *Revised Industrial Investment Schedule* (Karachi: Government of Pakistan, 1963).

36 East Pakistan Industrial Development Corporation, *EPIDC: Progress Report 1964–65* (Dacca: EPIDC, 1965).

37 East Pakistan Small Industries Corporation, *Survey of Small Industries in East Pakistan* (Dacca: Government of East Pakistan, June 15, 1964).

38 Falcon, Walter P., "Farmer Response to Price in an Underdeveloped Area: A Case Study of West Pakistan," unpub. diss. (Cambridge: Harvard University, 1962).

39 Falcon, Walter P., "Farmer Response to Price in a Subsistence Economy," *American Economic Review,* Vol. LIV, No. 3 (May 1964).

40 Falcon, Walter P., "Farmers and Economic Rationality in Pakistan" (tentative title), to be published in G. F. Papanek, ed., *Government Policy and Private Enterprise in Pakistan* (tentative title).

41 Falcon, Walter P., and Carl H. Gotsch, "Agricultural Development in Pakistan: lessons from the Second-Plan Period,"

Bellagio Conference, Development Advisory Service, mimeo (Cambridge: Harvard University, June 1966).

42   Falcon, Walter P., and Carl H. Gotsch, "Agricultural Development in Pakistan: Past Progress and Future Prospects," draft (Cambridge: Harvard University, January 1966).

43   Falcon, Walter P., and Carl H. Gotsch, "Agriculture in West Pakistan: An Analysis of Past Progress and Future Prospects," mimeo (Karachi: Planning Commission, December 1964).

44   Falcon, Walter P., and Carl H. Gotsch, "An Analysis of East Pakistan Agriculture during the Second and Third Plan Periods," mimeo (Karachi: Planning Commission, March 1965).

45   Falcon, Walter P., and Carl H. Gotsch, "Livestock Growth in West Pakistan," mimeo (Karachi: Harvard University, Development Advisory Service, Pakistan Advisory Group, May 25, 1965).

46   Falcon, Walter P., and Carl H. Gotsch, "Livestock in East Pakistan," mimeo (Karachi: Harvard University, Development Advisory Service, Pakistan Advisory Group, May 21, 1965).

47   Falcon, Walter P., and Carl H. Gotsch, "A Note on the Foodgrain Situation in East Pakistan," unpub. report (Karachi: Harvard Advisory Group, 1964).

48   Ferguson, Ben R., "A Report of the Operation of a New Extension System for East Pakistan," mimeo (Karachi: U.S. Agency for International Development, July 1963).

49   Food and Agriculture Organization, "The Competitive Position of Jute Manufactures in Western Europe and the Far East," *FAO Monthly Bulletin of Agricultural Economics and Statistics*, Vol. II, No. 3 (March 1962).

50   Galbraith, John K., *Economic Development* (Cambridge, Mass.: Harvard University Press, 1964).

51   Geiger, Theodore, and Winifred Armstrong, *The Development of African Private Enterprise*, National Planning Association, Pamphlet No. 120 (Washington, D.C.: National Planning Association, March 1964).

52   Ghouse, Agha M., ed., *Economic Planning and Development in Pakistan* (Karachi: Trade and Industry Publication Ltd., 1961).

Ghulam Mohammad, see Mohammad, Ghulam

53 Gilbert, Richard, "The Works Programme in East Pakistan," *International Labor Review,* Vol. LXXXIX, No. 3 (March 1964).

54 Gladieux, Bernard L., *Reorientation of Pakistan Government for National Development,* Planning Commission pamphlet CDN-1 (Karachi: Government of Pakistan, May 1955).

55 Goodnow, Henry, *The Civil Servant in Pakistan: Bureaucracy in a New Nation* (New Haven: Yale University Press, 1964).

56 Government of East Pakistan, *Details of Demands for Grants (Developmental), 1965/66* (Dacca: East Pakistan Government Press, 1965).

57 Government of East Pakistan, *Economic Survey of East Pakistan, 1964/65* (Dacca: East Pakistan Government Press, 1965).

58 Government of East Pakistan, *Explanatory Memorandum on the Budget of the Government of East Pakistan, 1955/56* (Dacca: East Pakistan Government Press, 1955).

59 Government of East Pakistan, *Explanatory Memorandum on the Budget of the Government of East Pakistan, 1960/61* (Dacca: East Pakistan Government Press, 1960).

60 Government of East Pakistan, *Explanatory Memorandum on the Budget of the Government of East Pakistan, 1965/66* (Dacca: East Pakistan Government Press, 1965).

61 Government of East Pakistan, *Explanatory Memorandum on the Budget of the Government of East Pakistan, 1966/67* (Dacca: East Pakistan Government Press, 1966).

62 Government of East Pakistan, *Pakistan Eastern Railways Budget 1964/65* (Dacca: East Pakistan Government Press, 1964).

63 Government of East Pakistan, *Pakistan Eastern Railways Budget 1965/66* (Dacca: East Pakistan Government Press, 1965).

64 Government of East Pakistan, *Performance Report on Rural Works Programme, 1964/65* (Dacca: Government of East Pakistan, January 1966).

65 Government of Pakistan, *The Budget 1960/61, Economic Survey and Statistics* (Karachi: Government of Pakistan, 1960).

66 Government of Pakistan, *Budget in Brief, 1965/66* (Karachi: Department of Films and Publications, 1965).

67   Government of Pakistan, *Budget in Brief, 1966/67* (Karachi: Department of Films and Publications, 1966).

68   Government of Pakistan, Ministry of Finance, *Budget of the Government of Pakistan, 1947/48 to 1951/52* (Karachi: Manager of Publications, 1954).

69   Government of Pakistan, Ministry of Finance, *Budget of the Government of Pakistan, 1951/52* (Karachi: Manager of Publications, 1954).

70   Government of Pakistan, Ministry of Finance, *Budget of the Government of Pakistan, 1955/56* (Karachi: Manager of Publications, 1955).

71   Government of Pakistan, Ministry of Finance, *Budget of the Government of Pakistan, 1965/66* (Karachi: Manager of Publications, 1965).

72   Government of Pakistan, Ministry of Finance, *Budget of the Government of Pakistan, 1966/67* (Karachi: Manager of Publications, 1966).

73   Government of Pakistan, *Demands for Grants, 1954/55* (Karachi: Government of Pakistan Press, 1954).

74   Government of Pakistan, *Explanatory Memorandum for the Budget of the Government of Pakistan, 1954/55* (Karachi: The Manager, Government of Pakistan Press, 1954).

75   Government of Pakistan, *Explanatory Memorandum for the Budget of the Government of Pakistan, 1955/56* (Karachi: The Manager, Government of Pakistan Press, 1955).

76   Government of Pakistan, *Explanatory Memorandum for the Budget of the Government of Pakistan, 1959/60* (Karachi: The Manager, Government of Pakistan Press, 1959).

77   Government of Pakistan, *Explanatory Memorandum for the Budget of the Government of Pakistan, 1960/61* (Karachi: The Manager, Government of Pakistan Press, 1960).

78   Government of Pakistan, *Explanatory Memorandum for the Budget of the Government of Pakistan, 1964/65* (Karachi: The Manager, Government of Pakistan Press, 1964).

79   Government of Pakistan, *Explanatory Memorandum for the Budget of the Government of Pakistan, 1965/66* (Karachi: The Manager, Government of Pakistan Press, 1965).

80   Government of Pakistan, *Report of the Food and Agriculture Commission* (Karachi: Government of Pakistan, 1960).

81   Government of Pakistan, *Review of the Progress of the Revised Industrial Investment Schedule during March 1963–*

October 1964 (Karachi: Government of Pakistan, 1964).

82 Government of Pakistan, *The West Pakistan Civil List* (Karachi: Government of West Pakistan, January 1, 1959).

83 Government of West Pakistan, *Details of Demands and Appropriations, 1960/61* (Lahore: Government Printing, 1965).

84 Government of West Pakistan, *Details of Demands and Appropriations, 1962/63* (Lahore: Government Printing, 1965).

85 Government of West Pakistan, *Details of Demands for Grants, 1965/66* (Lahore: Government Printing, 1965).

86 Government of West Pakistan, *Explanatory Memorandum of the Budget of the Government of West Pakistan, 1955/56* (Lahore: Superintendent, Government Printing, 1955).

87 Government of West Pakistan, *Explanatory Memorandum of the Budget of the Government of West Pakistan, 1960/61* (Lahore: Superintendent, Government Printing, 1960).

88 Government of West Pakistan, *Explanatory Memorandum of the Budget of the Government of West Pakistan, 1965/66* (Lahore: Superintendent, Government Printing, 1965).

89 Habibullah, M., *Some Aspects of Rural Capital Formation in East Pakistan* (Dacca: University of Dacca, 1963).

90 Hagen, Everett E., *On the Theory of Social Change* (Homewood, Ill.: Dorsey Press, 1962).

91 Haq, Mahbub ul, "Planning Machinery in Pakistan" (Karachi: Government of Pakistan Press, November 3, 1965).

92 Haq, Mahbub ul, "Rationale of Government Controls and Policies in Pakistan," *Pakistan Economic Journal,* Vol. XIII, No. 1 (March 1963).

93 Haq, Mahbub ul, and Khadija Khanam, *Deficit Financing in Pakistan, 1951–1960,* Economics of Development, Monograph 3 (Karachi: Institute of Development Economics, February 1961).

94 Hendry, J. B., and U Hpu, *East Pakistan Agriculture During the Third Five Year Plan,* mimeo (East Pakistan Planning Department, July 1964).

95 Higgins, Benjamin, *Economic Development* (New York: W. W. Norton, 1959).

96 Hirschman, Albert O., *Strategy of Economic Development* (New Haven: Yale University Press, 1958).

97 Hoselitz, Bert F., *Sociological Aspects of Economic Growth* (Glencoe, Ill.: Free Press, 1960).

98 Huq, A., and Peter Babcox, "Patterns of Resistance to the Continued Growth and Programme Evolution of Village Cooperative Societies in Comilla–Kotwali Thana," *Journal of the Pakistan Academy for Rural Development*, Vol. IV, No. 2 (October 1963).

Huq, Mahbub ul see Haq, Mahbub ul

99 Hussain, Syed Mushtaq, "A Note on Farmer Response to Price in East Pakistan," *Pakistan Development Review*, Vol. IV, No. 1 (Spring 1964).

100 Inayatullah, ed., *Bureaucracy and Development in Pakistan* (Peshawar: Pakistan Academy for Rural Development, 1963).

101 Industrial Development Bank of Pakistan, *Annual Report, 1962* (Karachi: Government of Pakistan Press, 1962).

102 Industrial Development Bank of Pakistan, *The First 11 Months* (Karachi: Government of Pakistan Press, 1961).

103 Industrial Development Bank of Pakistan, *The First 23 Months* (Karachi: Government of Pakistan Press, 1962).

104 Institute of Development Economics, *A Measure of Inflation in Pakistan*, Economics of Development, Monograph 4 (Karachi: Institute of Development Economics, March 1961).

105 International Labor Organizations, *Report to the Government of Pakistan on Productivity in the Textile Industry* (Karachi: Manager of Publications, 1959).

106 Islam, Nurul, *A Short-Term Model of the Pakistan Economy* (Oxford: Oxford University Press, 1965).

107 Khan, Azizur Rahman, "Import Substitution, Export Expansion and Consumption Liberalization," *Pakistan Development Review*, Vol. III, No. 2 (Summer 1963).

108 Khan, Mohammed Irshad, "A Note on Consumption Patterns in the Rural Areas of East Pakistan," *Pakistan Development Review*, Vol. II, No. 3 (Autumn 1963).

109 Khan, Mohammad Irshad, "The Development of Institutional Agricultural Credit in Pakistan," *Pakistan Development Review*, Vol. III, No. 1 (Spring 1963).

110 Khan, Taufiq, and Asbjørn Bergan, "A Study of Regional Products," *Pakistan Development Review*, Vol. VI, No. 2 (Summer 1966).

111 Krishna, R., "Farm Supply Response in Indo-Pakistan: A

Case Study of the Punjab Region," *Economic Journal,* Vol. LXXIII, No. 291 (September 1963).

112 Lewis, Stephen R., Jr., "Domestic Resources and Fiscal Policy in Pakistan: Second and Third Plans," *Pakistan Development Review,* Vol. V, No. 3 (Autumn 1965).

113 Lewis, Stephen R., Jr., and Mohammad Irshad Khan, "Estimates of Noncorporate Private Savings in Pakistan: 1949–1962," *Pakistan Development Review,* Vol. IV, No. 1 (Spring 1964).

114 Lewis, Stephen R., Jr., and Ronald Soligo, "Growth and Structural Change in Pakistan's Manufacturing Industry, 1954–1964," *Pakistan Development Review,* Vol. V, No. 1 (Spring 1965).

115 Lewis, Stephen R., Jr., and Sarfraz K. Qureshi, "The Structure of Revenues from Indirect Taxes in Pakistan," *Pakistan Development Review,* Vol. IV, No. 3 (Autumn 1964).

116 Lewis, Stephen R., Jr., and Syed Mushtaq Hussain, "Relative Price Changes and Industrialization in Pakistan: 1951–1964," *Pakistan Development Review,* Vol. VI, No. 3 (Autumn 1966).

117 Little, Arthur D., Inc., "The Metalworking Industry in Pakistan," report to the Planning Commission of Pakistan (Cambridge, Mass.: Arthur D. Little, 1961).

Mahbub ul Haq see Haq, Mahbub ul

118 Mallon, Richard, "Economic Development and Foreign Trade of Pakistan," unpub. diss. (Cambridge, Mass.: Harvard University, 1963).

Mati Lal Pal see Pal, Mati Lal

119 McClelland, David, *The Achieving Society* (Princeton: Van Nostrand, 1961).

120 Mears, Leon, and U Hpu, "The Role of Fertilizer in Increasing the Growth Rate of Production of Major Crops in East Pakistan during the Third Plan," mimeo (Dacca: Harvard Advisory Group, December 1964).

121 Millikan, Max, and W. W. Rostow, *A Proposal: Key to an Effective Foreign Policy* (New York: Harper, 1957).

122 Ministry of Commerce, *Report of the Jute Enquiry Commission* (Karachi: Government of Pakistan, 1961).

123 Ministry of Finance, Economic Affairs Division, *Report of the Prices Commission* (Karachi: Government of Pakistan, June 1960).

124   Ministry of Industries, *Implementation of Industrial Investment Schedule* (Karachi: Government of Pakistan, August 1961).

125   Ministry of Industries, *Report of the Textile Enquiry Commission* (Karachi: Government of Pakistan, March 1960).

126   Mohammad, Ghulam, "Private Tubewell Development and Cropping Problems in West Pakistan," *Pakistan Development Review*, Vol. V, No. 1 (Spring 1965).

127   Mohammad, Ghulam, "Some Strategic Problems in Agricultural Development in Pakistan," *Pakistan Development Review*, Vol IV, No. 2 (Summer 1964).

128   Motheral, Joe R., "The Effect of Government Policy and Programs on Agricultural Production in Pakistan," mimeo (Cambridge, Mass.: Center for International Affairs, Harvard University, December 1960).

Muneer Ahmed see Ahmed, Muneer

Mushtaq Ahmed see Ahmed, Mushtaq

129   National Income Commission, *Interim Report of the National Income Commission* (Karachi: Central Statistical Office, September 1964).

Nurul Islam see Islam, Nurul

130   Office of the Chief of Engineers, *Transportation Survey of East Pakistan* (Washington, D.C.: Department of the Army, 1962), Vol. I.

131   Office of the Chief of Engineers, *Transportation Survey of West Pakistan* (Washington, D.C.: Department of the Army, 1962), Vols. I and II.

132   Pakistan Academy for Rural Development, *An Evaluation of the Rural Public Works Programme, East Pakistan 1962–1963* (Comilla: Pakistan Academy for Rural Development, 1963).

133   Pakistan Academy for Rural Development, *An Evaluation of the Rural Works Programme, 1963–1964* (Comilla: Pakistan Academy for Rural Development, 1965).

134   Pakistan Academy for Village Development, Comilla: *A New Rural Co-operative System for Comilla Thana,* Pakistan Academy for Village Development (Comilla: East Pakistan, 1962). *The Comilla Rural Administrator Experiment, History and Annual Report, 1962–63, Pakistan Academy* for Rural Development (Comilla: East Pakistan, 1963). *The Comilla District Development Project,* Pakistan Academy for Rural Development (1964). *The Comilla Pilot Project in Irrigation and Rural Electrification*, Pakistan Academy for Rural Development (Comilla: East Pakistan, 1964). *Fifth Annual Report, June 1963–May 1964*, Pakistan Academy for Rural Development (1964).

135 Pakistan Industrial Credit and Investment Corporation, *PICIC at Work* (Karachi: PICIC, March 1962 and June 1963).

136 Pakistan Industrial Credit and Investment Corporation, *Sixth Annual Report* (Karachi: PICIC, 1963).

137 Pakistan Industrial Development Corporation, *Annual Report, 1956–57* (Karachi: Pakistan Industrial Development Corporation, 1958).

138 Pakistan Western Railways, *Yearbook of Information* (Lahore: Pakistan Western Railways, 1961, 1962).

139 Pal, Mati Lal, "The Determinants of the Domestic Prices of Imports," *Pakistan Development Review*, Vol. IV, No. 4 (Winter 1964).

140 Pal, Mati Lal, "Domestic Price of Imports in Pakistan," *Pakistan Development Review*, Vol. V, No. 4 (Winter 1965).

141 Papanek, Gustav F., "Industrial Production and Investment in Pakistan," *Pakistan Development Review*, Vol. IV, No. 3 (Autumn 1964).

142 Papanek, Gustav F., "The Location of Economic Policy Decisions in Pakistan," *Public Policy* (Cambridge: Harvard Graduate School of Public Administration, 1959).

143 Papanek, Hanna, "The Business Communities in Industry" (tentative title), to be published in Gustav F. Papanek, ed., *Government Policy and Private Enterprise in Pakistan* (tentative title).

144 Papanek, Hanna, "Leadership and Social Change in the Khoja Ismaili Community," unpub. diss. (Cambridge, Mass.: Harvard University, 1962).

145 Parkinson, J. R., "An Alternative Estimate of Development Expenditure during the Second Plan," mimeo (Karachi: Harvard Advisory Group, August 22, 1966).

146 Planning Commission, *Budgetary Data of Central and Provincial Government*, mimeo (Karachi: Planning Commission, July 1960).

147 Planning Commission, "Central Indirect Taxes by Provinces," Memorandum from Wouter Tims (April 28, 1966).

148 Planning Commission, "An Estimate of Regional Indirect

Taxes and Subsidies, 1959/60–1964/65," Memorandum from Wouter Tims (April 28, 1966).

149 Planning Commission, *Estimates of Private Investment 1951/ 52 to 1958/59* mimeo (Karachi: Planning Commission, International Trade Section, September 1959).

150 Planning Commission, *Evaluation of the First Five-Year Plan,* draft (Karachi: Government of Pakistan, 1963?)

151 Planning Commission, *Evaluation of the Second Five-Year Plan* (Karachi: Government of Pakistan, May 1966).

152 Planning Commission, *Mid-Plan Review* (Karachi: Government of Pakistan, 1964).

153 Planning Commission, "Production of Principal Crops in Pakistan," mimeo (Karachi: Planning Commission, undated). Also typed extension for 1964–65 (May 10, 1965).

154 Planning Commission, "Regional Breakup of Collection of Central Taxes," Memorandum from U. Suleman to Javaid Azfar, October 16, 1963.

155 Planning Commission, *Third Five-Year Plan 1965–70* (Karachi: Planning Commission, May 1965).

156 Planning Commission. Economic Research Section, *A Revised Balance of Payments 1960/61–1962/63,* mimeo (Karachi: Planning Commission, April 1964).

157 Power, John H., "Industrialization in Pakistan: A Case of Frustrated Take-Off?" *Pakistan Development Review,* Vol. III, No. 2 (Summer 1963).

158 Rabbani, F. A., "Private Investment in 1956/57," mimeo (Karachi: 1958).

159 Rabbani, A. K. M. Ghulam, "Economic Determinants of Jute Production in India and Pakistan," *Pakistan Development Review,* Vol. V, No. 2 (Summer 1965).

160 Rahim, S. A., *Diffusion and Adoption of Agricultural Practices* (Comilla: Pakistan Academy for Rural Development, 1963).

161 Rahman, Anisur, "East–West Pakistan: A Problem in the Political Economy of Planning," to be published in Gustav F. Papanek, ed., *Government Policy and Private Enterprise in Pakistan* (tentative title).

162 Ranis, G., *Urban Consumer Expenditure and the Consumption Function,* Economics of Development, Monograph 6 (Karachi: Institute of Development Economics, August 1961).

163 Rashid, M., "Outline of a Proposed Strategy for Increased Agricultural Growth During the Third Five-Year Plan," mimeo (Dacca: East Pakistan Planning Department, November 21, 1964).

164 Smith, Wilfred Cantwell, *Modern Islam in India* (Lahore: Ripon Printing Press, 1947).

165 State Bank of Pakistan, *Annual Report, 1963–64* (Karachi: State Bank of Pakistan, 1964).

166 State Bank of Pakistan, *Report on Currency and Finance, 1949–50* (Karachi: Department of Research, State Bank of Pakistan, 1951).

167 State Bank of Pakistan, *Report on Currency and Finance, 1951–52* (Karachi: Department of Research, State Bank of Pakistan, 1953).

168 State Bank of Pakistan, *Report on Currency and Finance, 1954–55* (Karachi: Department of Research, State Bank of Pakistan, 1956).

169 State Bank of Pakistan, *Pakistan Balances of Payments, July 1948–June 1959* (Karachi: Department of Statistics, State Bank of Pakistan, 1960).

170 State Bank of Pakistan, *Bulletin, July 1959–June 1956* (Karachi: Department of Statistics, State Bank of Pakistan, Sept. 1960).

171 State Bank of Pakistan, *Bulletin, July 1964–June 1965* (Karachi: Department of Statistics, State Bank of Pakistan, Sept. 1965).

172 Stern, Joseph J., "Balance of Payments," mimeo (Karachi: Planning Commission, February 28, 1966).

Taufiq Khan see Khan, Taufiq

173 Thomas, Philip S., "Import Licensing and Import Liberalization in Pakistan," Report No. 38, mimeo (Karachi: Pakistan Institute of Development Economics, February 1966).

Tims, Wouter, see items 147 and 148.

174 U.S. Bureau of Labor Statistics, "Wholesale Prices and Price Indices, July 1964–June 1965" (Washington, D.C.: U.S. Bureau of Labor Statistics, 1966).

175 van den Elshout, Dr. J. R. L., "A (Revised) Estimate of the Gross Investment in Fixed Capital Assets in Pakistan, 1962–63," mimeo (Karachi, Harvard Advisory Group, December 18, 1964).

176   Waterston, Albert, *Planning in Pakistan* (Baltimore: Johns Hopkins, 1963).

177   Weeks, Richard V., *Pakistan: Birth and Growth of a Muslim Nation* (Princeton: Van Nostrand, 1964).

178   Wilcox, Clair, "Pakistan," in E. Hagen, ed., *Planning in Economic Development* (Homewood, Ill.: Irwin, 1963).

179   Wilson, John, "Technical Report — Agriculture," mimeo (Washington, D.C.: U.S. Agency for International Development, May 1964).

INDEX

Publications Written under the Auspices of the
Center for International Affairs
Harvard University

Created in 1958, the Center for International Affairs fosters advanced study of basic world problems by scholars from various disciplines and senior officials from many countries. The research at the Center focuses on economic and social development, the management of force in the modern world, and the evolving roles of Western Europe and the Communist bloc. The published results appear here in the order in which they have been issued. The research programs are supervised by Professors Robert R. Bowie (Director of the Center), Hollis B. Chenery, Samuel P. Huntington, Alex Inkeles, Henry A. Kissinger, Edward S. Mason, Thomas C. Schelling, and Raymond Vernon.

Books

The Soviet Bloc, by Zbigniew K. Brzezinski (jointly with the Russian Research Center), 1960. Harvard University Press.

The Necessity for Choice, by Henry A. Kissinger, 1961. Harper & Bros.

Strategy and Arms Control, by Thomas C. Schelling and Morton H. Halperin, 1961. Twentieth Century Fund.

Rift and Revolt in Hungary, by Ferenc A. Váli, 1961. Harvard University Press.

United States Manufacturing Investment in Brazil, by Lincoln Gordon and Engelbert L. Grommers, 1962. Harvard Business School.

The Economy of Cyprus, by A. J. Meyer, with Simos Vassiliou (jointly with the Center for Middle Eastern Studies), 1962. Harvard University Press.

Entrepreneurs of Lebanon, by Yusif A. Sayigh (jointly with the Center for Middle Eastern Studies), 1962. Harvard University Press.

Communist China 1955–1959: Policy Documents with Analysis, with a Foreword by Robert R. Bowie and John K. Fairbank (jointly with the East Asian Research Center), 1962. Harvard University Press.

In Search of France, by Stanley Hoffmann, Charles P. Kindleberger, Laurence Wylie, Jesse R. Pitts, Jean-Baptiste Duroselle, and François Goguel, 1963. Harvard University Press.

Somali Nationalism, by Saadia Touval, 1963. Harvard University Press.

The Dilemma of Mexico's Development, by Raymond Vernon, 1963. Harvard University Press.

Limited War in the Nuclear Age, by Morton H. Halperin, 1963. John Wiley & Sons.

The Arms Debate, by Robert A. Levine, 1963. Harvard University Press.

Africans on the Land, by Montague Yudelman, 1964. Harvard University Press.

Counterinsurgency Warfare, by David Galula, 1964. Frederick A. Praeger, Inc.

People and Policy in the Middle East, by Max Weston Thornburg, 1964. W. W. Norton & Co.

Shaping the Future, by Robert R. Bowie, 1964. Columbia University Press.

Foreign Aid and Foreign Policy, by Edward S. Mason (jointly with the Council on Foreign Relations) 1964. Harper & Row.

Public Policy and Private Enterprise in Mexico, by M. S. Wionczek, D. H. Shelton, C. P. Blair, and R. Izquierdo, ed. Raymond Vernon, 1964. Harvard University Press.

How Nations Negotiate, by Fred Charles Iklé, 1964. Harper & Row.

China and the Bomb, by Morton H. Halperin (jointly with the East Asian Research Center), 1965. Frederick A. Praeger, Inc.

Democracy in Germany, by Fritz Erler (Jodidi Lectures), 1965. Harvard University Press.

The Troubled Partnership, by Henry A. Kissinger (jointly with the Council on Foreign Relations), 1965. McGraw-Hill Book Co.

The Rise of Nationalism in Central Africa, by Robert I. Rotberg, 1965. Harvard University Press.

Communist China and Arms Control, by Morton H. Halperin and Dwight H. Perkins (jointly with the East Asian Research Center), 1965. Frederick A. Praeger, Inc.

Pan-Africanism and East African Integration, by Joseph S. Nye, Jr., 1965. Harvard University Press.

Problems of National Strategy, ed. Henry Kissinger, 1965. Frederick A. Praeger, Inc.

Deterrence before Hiroshima: The Airpower Background of Modern Strategy, by George H. Quester, 1966. John Wiley & Sons.

Containing the Arms Race, by Jeremy J. Stone, 1966. M.I.T. Press.

Germany and the Atlantic Alliance: The Interaction of Strategy and Politics, by James L. Richardson, 1966. Harvard University Press.

Arms and Influence, by Thomas C. Schelling, 1966. Yale University Press.

Political Change in a West African State, by Martin Kilson, 1966. Harvard University Press.

Planning without Facts: Lessons in Resource Allocation from Nigeria's Development, by Wolfgang F. Stolper, 1966. Harvard University Press.

Export Instability and Economic Development, by Alasdair I. MacBean, 1966. Harvard University Press.

Foreign Policy and Democratic Politics, by Kenneth N. Waltz (jointly with the Institute of War and Peace Studies, Columbia University), 1967. Little, Brown & Co.

Contemporary Military Strategy, by Morton H. Halperin, 1967. Little, Brown & Co.

Sino-Soviet Relations and Arms Control, ed. Morton H. Halperin (jointly with the East Asian Research Center), 1967. M.I.T. Press.

Africa and United States Policy, by Rupert Emerson, 1967. Prentice-Hall.

Europe's Postwar Growth, by Charles P. Kindleberger, 1967. Harvard University Press.

The Rise and Decline of the Cold War, by Paul Seabury, 1967. Basic Books.

Student Politics, ed. S. M. Lipset, 1967. Basic Books.

Strike a Blow and Die: A Narrative of Race Relations in Colonial Africa, by George Simeon Mwase, ed. Robert I. Rotberg, 1967. Harvard University Press.

Pakistan's Development: Social Goals and Private Incentives, by Gustav F. Papanek, 1967. Harvard University Press.

Occasional Papers, Published by the
Center for International Affairs

1. *A Plan for Planning: The Need for a Better Method of Assisting Underdeveloped Countries on Their Economic Policies,* by Gustav F. Papanek, 1961.

2. *The Flow of Resources from Rich to Poor*, by Alan D. Neale, 1961.
3. *Limited War: An Essay on the Development of the Theory and an Annotated Bibliography*, by Morton H. Halperin, 1962.
4. *Reflections on the Failure of the First West Indian Federation*, by Hugh W. Springer, 1962.
5. *On the Interaction of Opposing Forces under Possible Arms Agreements*, by Glenn A. Kent, 1963.
6. *Europe's Northern Cap and the Soviet Union*, by Nils Örvik, 1963.
7. *Civil Administration in the Punjab: An Analysis of a State Government in India*, by E. N. Mangat Rai, 1963.
8. *On the Appropriate Size of a Development Program*, by Edward S. Mason, 1964.
9. *Self-Determination Revisited in the Era of Decolonization*, by Rupert Emerson, 1964.
10. *The Planning and Execution of Economic Development in Southeast Asia*, by Clair Wilcox, 1965.
11. *Pan-Africanism in Action*, by Albert Tevoedjre, 1965.
12. *Is China Turning In?* by Morton H. Halperin, 1965.
13. *Economic Development in India and Pakistan*, by Edward S. Mason, 1966.
14. *The Role of the Military in Recent Turkish Politics*, by Ergun Özbudun, 1966.
15. *Economic Development and Individual Change: A Social-Psychologcial Study of the Comilla Experiment in Pakistan*, by Howard Schuman, 1967.